Artificial Intelligence
and Human Reason

Artificial Intelligence and Human Reason

A Teleological Critique

Joseph F. Rychlak

Columbia University Press
NEW YORK

Publication of this book was supported in part by a gift from the Internal Research Awards Program of Loyola University of Chicago.

Columbia University Press
New York   Oxford
Copyright © 1991 Columbia University Press
All rights reserved

Library of Congress Cataloging-in-Publication Data

Rychlak, Joseph F.
Artificial intelligence and human reason :
a teleological critique
Joseph F. Rychlak.
p.   cm.
Includes bibliographical references.   Includes index.
ISBN 0-231-07290-2
1. Artificial intelligence.   2. Teleology.
3. Reasoning.   4. Cognition.   I. Title.
[DNLM: 1. Artificial Intelligence.   2. Computer Simulation.
3. Cognition.   4. Mental Processes.   BF 311 R991a]
Q335.R93 1990   153—dc20   DNLM/DLC
for Library of Congress   90-2382   CIP

Casebound editions of Columbia University Press books are Smyth-sewn and printed on permanent and durable acid-free paper

Printed in the United States of America

c 10 9 8 7 6 5 4 3 2 1

To Mae Belle Smith,
And in memory of Luther L. Smith . . .

Contents

Introduction	ix
1. The Chinese Room and Its Implications	1
2. Predicational Explanation Across the Ages	15
3. The Many Faces of Cognitive Simulation	43
4. Language in Cognitive Representation	66
5. Learning as a Predicational Process	83
6. Agency in Artificial Intelligence	102
7. Predication in Animal Cognition	126
8. Predication in Human Perception and Brain Functioning	138
9. The Computer Analogue and Human Nature	161
References	179
Author Index	195
Subject Index	201

Introduction

Although I was not then aware of it, I actually began work on this book about seven years ago, when a colleague startled me one day. I had just told her something helpful, and she replied, "Thanks, I'll store that." I had, of course, been hearing about the cognitive revolution taking place in my speciality of psychology, and I knew that psychologists liked to use the prevailing technical lingo informally, as a kind of slang really. But for some reason I found this particular comment, made by a leading and widely cited psychologist, especially disturbing. The thought flashed "My God, does she really think she 'stores' thoughts like a computer?" I also pondered why I was so upset by this minor event. I decided that it was all due to the fact that I had for twenty years previous to this time been railing against the stimulus-response lingo that had dominated psychology, and now just when it seemed to be fading from the scene *this* had to happen. Psychologists had believed that we humans mechanically responded to stimuli yesterday, and now today they were apparently shifting to the view that we stored and retrieved information in an equally mechanical fashion. I had a sinking feeling of "Here we go again."

My colleague had as much right to think of herself as a computer-like information processor as I did to think of myself as a freely willing person. Right! Who can argue with this? I had written dozens of papers saying this one way or another and at least three books detailing why such alternative assumptions occur in all sciences. And yet, this kind of dispassionate scholarly understanding failed to take hold when this simple statement from a friend hit me, probably because I had also been arguing that more psychologists should make an effort to examine and help establish human agency rather than just accept a mechanistic thesis without question. With the decline of stimulus-response conditioning theorizing I had hopes for a better future. I was therefore angry and disappointed with my colleague. "Psychologists are among the most suggestible people in the world," I thought. "They grab onto anything having the sound of a mechanical process. They'll never learn. I'll never convince them."

Looking back, I think that I had not yet convinced myself—at least, not about the cognitive revolution and the theory of artificial intelligence on which it is based. Was this revolution what it was cracked up to be? Was it really taking care of the shortcomings of traditional, stimulus-response psychology? I was not totally naive about the nature of computer processing. Following graduation from high school I had spent three years in the (Army) Air Corps/Force working in the Statistical Control Section of the Air Training Command. This was in the late 1940s, and we did not have anything like the computers that exist today. But I obtained a good sense of what it meant to punch information (by way of holes) into cards, sort, collate, tabulate statistics and draw inferences from the data. Later, I purchased a kit enabling me to assemble the hardware of a crude plastic "computer" that worked with the use of rubber bands and manual manipulation. I puttered around with programming for a time. And for some years I have owned a computer and love it dearly (I am writing on it now). Through all of these experiences, at no time did I ever think of the computer as anything more than an instrumentality, a tool.

But now, my friend was doing a reverse simulation on me and emulating the computer. Well, I thought it was about time to "dig in" and and see if I could specify exactly what it is about the computer analogue that is lacking when it comes to accounting for human reason. Not all cognitive scientists are interested in accounting for human reason, of course. Many are simply interested in the applications of cognitive technology to various organizational problems, the relation of person to machine, and so forth. I do not want to demean such efforts. I do not even deny that there are aspects of the computer analogue that are relevant to human cognition. But, in my estimation, there are a couple of major differences between artificial intelligence and human reason that must be more widely appreciated.

If I were a reporter, I would probably be the investigative type rather than the "news of the day" type. There is always sensationalism in the fleeting stories of the latter activity, but for the longer lasting satisfaction of a complete and sometimes subtle story we require the investigative writer as well. I think it is relatively easy to write a superficial book "picking" on the computer as somehow inadequate to the description of human beings. We all know this already. What is different about the present effort is that I name the *specific* aspects of human reasoning that are missing in artificial intelligence and review the vast empirical evidence in support of these missing links.

It is only proper that I admit to one more personal motive that I have for writing a book like this at this time. My major scientific motivation is, of course, to present the most accurate, well-researched picture of human behavior that I can. Thirty years of study and empirical research have failed to shake my conviction that people are agential or intentional animals. I espouse a teleological or humanistic brand of psychology, and this does not mean I think that all people are marvelous, well-intentioned beings who "go wrong" only because they have been manipulated into doing so by a malevolent societal pressure of some sort. People can intend evil as well as good actions. They are influenced by factors in their social environment but they are not slaves to this environment.

One of the more harmful influences that I have seen being advanced for too long in psychology is the picture of the human being as a bundle of mechanical processes under the control of influences from outside its identity. I think that the time is ripe for an alternative view in psychology, one that puts responsibility and self-determination back into the conception of a person. This is not a political statement. It is simply a realistic appraisal of the current status of our society, in which values seem to have deteriorated to instrumentalities, mere "tags" placed on courses of action that are supposed to mean something but no longer carry the weight of duty, no longer engender the sting of guilt when transgressed.

So, I have to admit that I believe the nonteleological, mechanical image of the person that has been promulgated by the social and now the cognitive sciences of this century has failed to aid the self-understanding of what human behavior entails. We have totally lost the sense of human beings as evaluating creatures. Evaluations have become what we will be calling "mediators" in this volume, pumped in by influences from outside the person on the one hand, and carried forward to behavior by a process without intrinsic meaning on the other. One cannot accept this formulation of the human being and come away with a sense of confidence in the potentials of people to overcome their circumstances, to take responsibility, and to mend wrongdoings. The mechanical theories of psychology throughout the twentieth century have seemed to me to rob the person not only of agency but also of character. But then, I cannot see how one can have character without first having agency.

With this personal concern off my chest, I would now like to invite the reader to take a critical journey with me, as we study together the core differences between artificial intelligence and human reason. We begin with an interesting "thought experiment" that brings out the primary concepts we will be pursuing throughout the chapters to follow. We will then have a brief overview of historical themes before moving on to a careful look at the nature of simulation in computer modeling. We will then consider the role of language in human versus machine reasoning, as well as the nature of learning. We will explore the question of agency or "free will" in some detail. There will also be coverage of animal cognition, human perception, and human brain functioning before we return to a summing-up of our total critique. I hope the study we carry out will be both interesting and instructive. The one thing I can promise is that it will be specific and thorough on the question we are seeking to answer: "How well does the computer analogue, as reflected in artificial intelligence, capture or simulate what is going on in the reasoning of a human being?"

Artificial Intelligence
and Human Reason

1.
The Chinese Room and Its Implications

The philosopher John Searle (1980) has posed a marvelous thought experiment having important implications for the study of artificial intelligence and human reason. I will use it as a frame of reference to begin our study. Computers are notorious as simulators of human behaviors like the asking or answering of questions in an ongoing dialogue. This is made possible by the writing of a program that allows the machine to input information, collate it, and relate it to stored information, and then output something having relevance to what has been taken in. Well, suppose that such a program has been written for a computing machine to simulate the understanding of the Chinese language. A question put to this computer in Chinese would activate it to search its memory base and to produce appropriate answers to the question in Chinese. Indeed, the computer's answers can be said to be as accurately and appropriately given as the replies of a native Chinese person. Does this mean that we have captured in the computer process the way in which the human being processes his or her ideas? This is the issue that Searle raises.

To deal with this issue Searle, in effect, has us take the role of a quasi-homunculus, acting as a "little person" carrying out the machine processes ourselves in the way that the machine carries them out. We cannot climb into an actual computer, of course, but pretend that we are locked in a room where there are several baskets of little cards on which are printed Chinese figures. There are also two little windows through which such cards can be passed in and out of the room. We understand no Chinese but do understand English. A rule book is given to us, written in English, which specifies many rules of syntax for how to match up the Chinese figures. A rule might say something like "Take a squiggle-squiggle sign out of basket number one and put it next to a squoggle-squoggle sign from basket number two" (ibid.: 32). The figures would be printed as pictures in the rule book, of course, so they would easily be matched up in this fashion.

Now, suppose some other Chinese figures are passed into the room through one of the windows, and we are given further rules for passing back through the other window strings of figures that have been aligned to these input figures according to the syntax of the rule book. Although we are not cognizant of this fact, the input strings of figures are certain questions and the output strings of figures are answers to these questions. If our rule-book writers were clever enough to give us the proper instructions it would be possible for a person looking at our performance from outside the room to believe that we were actually answering "in Chinese" the questions being put to us. Yet, the truth is that we would have no inkling of what the Chinese figures mean nor would we be able to learn the Chinese language by following the "programmed" rules even if we worked at this task for the rest of our lives.

Searle's point is that the mechanical process of shuffling the figures about without meaningful understanding is precisely what the computer does. The rule book is like the software of the computer and the person's physical movements of taking the input and turning it into output is like the hardware. There are four implications to be drawn from Searle's thought experiment and they provide the organization of chapter 1.

Extraspective Versus Introspective Description

The first thing we notice about the Chinese room is that there are two quite different ways of describing what is going on there. We can situate ourselves outside the room, and look "at" what is taking place as cards go into one window and out the other, or we can step into the room and be looking "with" the person doing the card sorting. This is an immensely important distinction in how to frame, describe, and explain human behavior. I refer to this as the difference between an extraspective and an introspective theoretical perspective (Rychlak 1981a:27–34). An *extraspective* theoretical description is expressed in third-person terms, about "that" or "it" under observation and description "over there." One looks "at" the item or process and tries to account for it without necessarily taking the perspective or viewpoint of this item or process into consideration. In contrast, when we describe something from an *introspective* perspective we definitely want to take the item or process into consideration from its unique slant on what is taking place. Such accounts are expressed in the first-person because they refer to the "I" or "me" that is looking out onto experience rather than being pushed about by experience. It is common for extraspective theoretical descriptions to be called "objective" and introspective descriptions to be called "subjective" (for arguments against this equation of terms see chapter 2).

The extraspective versus introspective distinction has received empirical support in the work of Jones and Nisbett (1971), who studied both actors in situations and observers of these actors. The purpose of this study was to find out what the actors and observers felt were the relevant causes of the behavior carried out by the actors in these situations. The actors claimed that it was the logically relevant factors in the circumstances facing them that caused them to behave as they did, whereas the observers of these same actors were prone to attribute the cause of the latter's behavior to presumed habits or personality traits that directed the actor no matter what the logic of the situation dictated. In other words, the observers made no real effort to look at things from the point of view of an actor—unless they became actors themselves! That is, when the observer of an action was given a videotape of the actor's view of things, the circumstances confronting the actor were then given weight as a cause of the actor's behavior. And, vice versa, when actors took the perspective of observers they too tended to view extrapersonal factors as the primary causes of behavior in the situation.

Surely an observer of another person is capable of viewing things through the eyes of the person under observation. This is what any good psychoanalyst does—sees things through the conceptual eyes of the client. Even so, there does seem to be a requirement here for the person doing the observing to empathize with the person observed before the introspective account will eventuate. But how does one empathize with a machine process in which there is no introspective formulation of events to begin with? In Searle's example, our empathy rests with the person caught up within the process of shifting the Chinese figures about. As a result, even when we leave the room to look extraspectively at the exchange of inputs to outputs we are not much impressed with the supposed intelligence being reflected in the "information process." We know full well that the person introspectively taking the mechanical steps according to the rule book is engaged in a communication or conversation totally without personal intelligence about what is taking place.

Our introspective grasp of the process is quite at variance with the typical approach taken in artificial intelligence research, where we are supposed to accept a simulation of human reasoning exclusively on the basis of the extraspective perspective. This is well represented in the so-called "Turing test." In 1950, Alan Turing proposed what he then called an "imitation game" to test whether or not a machine could be said to "think" (Turing 1964). The game is played with a man *(A)* and a woman *(B)* located in one room, and an interrogator *(C)* located in another room. The object of the game is for *C* to determine which of the other two players is the man and which is the woman. Thus, *C* asks *A* and *B* various questions in making the determination about their respective sexes. For example, *C* might ask *A* "How long is your hair?" Presumably, a woman's hair would tend to be longer than a man's (especially in the 1940–1950s). However, if *A* were the man, *A* could tell lies to deceive *C*, claiming to have long hair, done in large curls, and continue doing so even though *B* complains with justification that *A* is using deceit and that she is really the woman. But then, from *C*'s perspective, *B* could be the man doing the lying. The essence of the Turing test is what might happen if a machine took the part of *A*. Could a program be written so that the interrogator would have no cognizance of the fact that *A* is a machine replying, misleading, and following through on questions just as the actual human being would?

The Turing test has been given a more liberal interpretation with time, so that this specific procedure is no longer followed. As Gardner says of any interaction with a machine today, "if an observer cannot distinguish the responses of a programmed machine from those of a human being, the machine is said to have passed the Turing test" (1985:17). But the essential point is that in passing this test, the machine—which can only be described in an extraspective fashion—gives us the illusion that an introspective process is underway. This is what convinces us that the machine really is thinking. There seems to be a "point of view" involved when there really is not! Searle's person, mechanically shifting symbols from inputs to outputs without meaningful understanding, is never in a position to express a point of view. Reasoning is a rule-defined fait accompli and not an intentional formulation of meanings.

Endel Tulving (1983) has raised a similar issue in his critique of the computer as a complete model for the depiction of human cognition. Tulving notes that human beings have "episodic" memories, by which he means the more introspectively conceived, highly personal events and interpretations of "life episodes" that play such a significant role in the human experience. Since computers never live according to the introspective perspective within which such life episodes are framed, it follows that there is a significant impasse between what human and machine cognition involves. In discussing this issue, Tulving reminds me of Searle. Thus, he notes that if we gave computers pseudo-episodic memories they would, in recalling such events, simply be "manipulating certain symbols according to certain rules, they would be talking only about words, rather than about original experiences organized temporally in their personal past and related to their sense of personal identity, or continuity in subjective time" (p. 53). In short, the computer in this instance would be conveying no more meaning than Searle's person moving Chinese symbols about in the solitary room.

Meaningful Information Versus Signals

Searle's primary motive in advancing his Chinese room example was not to distinguish between extraspective and introspective theoretical formulations. He was specifically interested in highlighting the question of semantics or meaning in the reasoning of human beings. How, he wants to know, can computer enthusiasts hope to account for the human experience if they do not place meaning at the center of their investigation? Claude Shannon, one of the "fathers" of information-processing theory, has made it clear that in a strictly engineering sense, information has nothing to do with the meanings of the message being communicated (Shannon and Weaver 1962:3, 99). The basic unit of "information" in a digital computer is the *bit*, short for binary digit. This refers to the amount of information required to select one electrical impulse or signal from two equally probable alternatives. A bit involves halving the total complex of information available in the sense of "either/or." Thus, if there were four equally probable alternatives open to a course of electrical signaling, it would require two bits of information to decide on a singular course of action. One bit would reduce the four alternatives to two, and another would select one of the two remaining possibilities.

If we think of information processing as halving electrical impulses in this fashion, it is possible to equate a decision such as "true-false" with the electronic switch that is either "on" *(true)* or "off" *(false)*. This was Shannon's (1938) insight. Subsequently, McCulloch and Pitts (1943) argued that the all-or-none firing properties of nerve cells could be construed in this binary fashion. An active or firing neuron was "on" and an inactive neuron was "off." McCulloch and Pitts perfected the neural network conception and tried to map the binary logic of the machine on the structure of the central nervous system. This line of theorizing was completely extraspective, of course. The basic engineering question dealt with the carrying of electrical impulses or signals and the reduction of redundancy in the system. But once it was realized that meanings could be assigned to these electrical signals, a new opportunity arose. Information in the sense of a hardware process of electrical impulses was extended to and combined with information of a more meaningful variety.

Searle reminds us that meaningful information has nothing to do with the strictly machine properties of a computer. Meaningful information is on the side of introspective understanding, something that is totally beyond the machine per se. For the person "in the machine," the Chinese figures are akin to the machine's electrical transmission of signals from input to output. The person understands the meaning of the English rule book. But there is no more meaningful information in the person's understanding of the squiggles and squoggles than there is in Shannon's electrical impulses of the machine process. Something is totally lost in the machine process that is central to the human cognitive process.

Logical Versus Mechanical Process

If meaning is fundamental to human reason, as Searle believes, then how are we to think of this reasoning process? Is there, for example, a logical process paralleling the mechanical process of electrical impulses triggering signal transmission in a network of neurons? The person in Searle's Chinese room is reasoning according to a rule book. Mechanical processes are said to follow "laws of nature." Are rules the same as laws? Laws strike us as the result of mechanical regularities whereas rules are more akin to guiding regularities. A law obtains when we have observed a reliable course of action, so that what takes place is not in any sense arbitrary or modifiable—as in the "law of gravity." Mechanisms are the very embodiment of lawful events. A rule, on the other hand, always bears a sense of the "as a rule" qualification. As Dreyfus has noted, rules suggest that they are valid over time so long as everything else remains equal (1979:56–57). But if conditions change the rules can be quickly changed to adapt to the new circumstance. This happens because in the final analysis rules are arbitrary. They are framed based on precedent meanings aimed at lending order to events. Coulter recognized this fact when he observed that "rule-ordered reasoning [is] itself dependent upon assumptions and judgments which fall outside the rules we learn to apply" (1983:67).

This falling outside of the specific ruling suggests that there is always a wider context of meaning within which rules are situated. Could it be that in speaking of rules we are involved in a logical rather than a mechanical process of some sort? Rules do imply that they are premised in some fashion, and premises always embody predications. Predication is concerned with the ordering of meanings and not with the ordering of motions. *Predication involves the cognitive act of affirming, denying, or qualifying broader patterns of meaning in relation to narrower or targeted patterns of meaning.* The ancient Greeks referred to this process as reasoning from universals "to" particulars. The Greek word *kategorein* means "to predicate," so in a true sense, when we seek to organize, categorize, and classify information we are predicating it in some fashion.

The person in the Chinese room has no predication for the figures he is matching, one to another. Computing machines employing programs "match" in this fashion (Winograd 1980:220). But matching is not predicating! In order to predicate, the person requires a wider context of meaning within which to situate the squiggles and squoggles acting as mere signs for the semantic information being sent inward. This context turns such signs into meaningful symbols. Thus, a predicational process is not simply mechanically conveying signs from input to output, but involves actually creating symbolical expressions by using a known meaning as the predicating context within which to situate another meaning, qualify its participation in the context, or remove it from this context entirely. The person in the room has no such capacity since the rule book does not define the Chinese figures. Note that once a broader meaning engulfs a narrower meaning, the extension from the *precedent* (wider) to the *targeted* (narrower) *meaning* is immediate. Once we align "A squiggle-squiggle means happiness" or "George is reliable" or "A human being is like a precious flower" we extend the meaning of the right-lying concepts to the left-lying concepts and *immediately* create a meaningful understanding. I refer to this immediacy as a *sequacious* extension of meaning, in the sense of logical necessity.

In referring to the precedent-sequacious extension of meaning I am presuming that a *logical process* occurs in human reason, one that is separate and distinct from the specific words being used in that process. The term "process" is used here as a discernible procedure or course of events. In this case, the events reflect a meaning extension from wider (broader) to narrower (targeted) extent (range, scope, etc.). The number of "steps" one wishes to elucidate in this process is arbitrary; the main point to grasp is that in a predicational process we always move from a wider to a narrower range of meaning.

The wider referent of the precedent is not simply the abstractness of a word's meaning, and the target is not simply a more concrete referent. The logical process of predication can be demonstrated by contrasting two sentence meanings using the same words in different positions. In the sentence "A person is like a tree" the meaning of "tree" is the predicate, acting as the wider referent within which to situate the concept of a "person." This sentence conveys a metaphorical allusion in which we would be thinking of the person as "rooted" in tradition, as possibly having a "hide" as wrinkled and thick as bark, as shedding hair like leaves in the autumn of life, and so forth. But in the sentence "A tree is like a person" we would grasp quite different understandings, to the effect that the limbs of a tree "reach out," that a tree can "bend" under the weight of environmental pressure, or that it can lose its "individuality" when swallowed up by the crowding woods. The meanings being conveyed in such statements are therefore not simply "in" the words but primarily "in" the process that winds them together in a certain way. And this "way" I am suggesting is through the logical process of predication, which immediately creates a meaningful understanding depending upon the patterned order resulting.

In contrast to the immediacy of the predicational process we can speak of a *mediational* process—once again, using the term "process" in the sense of a procedure or course of events. To mediate is to intervene or come between other active processes, bringing about some kind of action indirectly. The mediator is one who settles disputes between parties, each of whom has framed a predicated "position" on some issue. The conflicting parties are the direct or "immediate" parties to the dispute, acting on a first-hand basis. Immediacy signifies the instantaneous organization of experience that I suggest is fundamental to the predicational process. Mediacy signifies an interdependent (interactive, etc.) organization of experience. Time is required to effect a mediation.

It is possible, however, to think of what we might call a "mediation among conflicting predications" taking place, as when a negotiator attempts to settle a dispute between management and labor over a work contract. Possibly there is some common ground that the disputants have overlooked, and if it is made clear to them they may repredicate their position in light of this newly recognized context of meaning and avoid the necessity of a labor strike. But there is also a kind of mediation in events that does not address such assumptive understandings among disputants—including the internal disputes that take place among different attitudes within the same person (as in a Freudian conflict among id, ego, and superego). In this case, we are dealing with a "mediation among mechanical forces." A simple lever serves in such a mechanical, mediational capacity, whereby a downward pressure applied at one end results in a force of lift at the other end. The mediational influence varies depending on the placement of the lever on the fulcrum. Another form of mechanical mediation occurs when a thermostat in an automobile engine opens or closes depending upon the temperature of the coolant in the radiator, allowing for greater or lesser circulation of the coolant through the engine while it is running.

The meaning of "mediation" changes dramatically when we move from the negotiator between disputants to the mechanical processes of levers and thermostats. In the present volume the term mediation will be employed *only* in this latter, mechanical sense so as to contrast it with predication. *Mediation* in this mechanical sense occurs when *something that is taken in or input comes indirectly to play a role in a process that was not initially a part of this process*. The process under description in mediation is conceived, not as the immediate creator of what is to be active within it, but rather as the conveyor of that which it takes in "as given" and proceeds thereafter on the basis of. The items under processing are always "mediate," since they are never aligned or framed immediately by the process per se but are merely employed by this process instrumentally. Time's passage is essential to the mediational process whereas it is irrelevant to the predicational process (where "order" is primary).

We see the mediational aspect of the Chinese room in the fact that the person "takes in" the squiggles and squoggles "whole hog," that is, as shaped externally and sent inward—like placing well-formed teacups in a cupboard. The process then moves along and is influenced by these patterns according to the prearranged dictates of the rule book. As a result, an influence takes place on the process that was not itself created by the process. The mediational process acts as a conduit for the externally derived influencers. Strictly speaking, of course, there *are* predications going on in the head of the person who is reading the rule book. The English words, which draw their meaning from a wider realm of meaningfulness known as their "definition," assist the person to conduct the quasi-mechanical task. But strictly in the sense of moving input squiggles to output squoggles there is nothing but raw mediation taking place.

Is there not a series of new arrangements made possible through the ongoing experience of the mediating mechanism that can approximate predications like "George is reliable"? After the mechanism has taken in a number of concepts like "George" and "reliable," as well as the connecting links such as "is," through sheer association over time the mediational process can surely combine such free-standing word units into a sentence like "George is reliable." This alignment of concepts would presumably occur, not through an extension of the wider semantic range known as "reliability" to the targeted identity of "George" (in which case we would have a predication occurring), but strictly on the basis of the frequency of past life inputs that have repeatedly imprinted what reliability signifies and why it can, therefore, be associated to a dependable companion by the name of George. A mediational process would not, strictly on its own account, draw the implication that George was reliable because he works with Patrick, and their mutual boss happened to comment yesterday on Patrick's *lack* of reliability. A predicating organism, on the other hand, reasoning from a wider range of possibilities, might readily draw the implication that since the boss specifically chose to comment on Patrick's unreliability, it follows (sequaciously) that he or she had dismissed similar tendencies in George's behavior. This takes us to the final lesson drawn from Searle's Chinese room example.

Opposition Versus Apposition

The suggestion that people can reason from what "was said" to what "was not said" and draw thereby an implication that may or may not be true highlights another characteristic of the Chinese room. Nothing like such oppositional reasoning is to be found there. Everything that takes place in relation to the matching of the figures is intrinsically unipolar. Each Chinese figure is a totality, a unit, a building block that is added to other building blocks to make a string of some sort. There is no pattern between the figures tying them together as a context of intrinsic meaning. That is, the figures do not delimit and enter into the meanings of other figures "by definition." If a series of three Chinese figures were to mean "good," "bad," and "day," there is no basis on which to suggest that two of these meanings were intrinsically tied together. Thus, a string like "good-bad" would be no different than a string like "good-day" or "bad-day."

This singularity of meaning is true in the "working" of the input-output process being mediated by the motions of the person in the room (who has no grasp of the meanings in the first place). But would this be true of an actual Chinese person who was using these figures as signifiers of meaning? The latter individual would doubtless sense an implicit tie between the meanings of "good" and "bad" that would not obtain between "good" and "day." The good-bad meanings do in fact delimit each other, they enter *intrinsically* into each other's meaning. In a sense, they define each other. Human reason seems fraught with such oppositionally related word meanings, as in left-right, up-down, tall-short, early-late, and so forth. Indeed, it is doubtful that a person can know the meaning of only one of these bipolar pairings and *not* the other.

We might even surmise that one of the major reasons why predication proceeds from a wider to a narrower range of meaning in precedent-sequacious fashion is that the precedent context is *always* that of an oppositionality. To return to our example of "George is reliable," is it not the case that in coming to this conclusion we have considered the "unreliable" end of the reliable-unreliable bipolarity and decided to place our acquaintance closer to one meaning than the other? A case could therefore be made that it is due to the oppositionality of meanings in experience that the person is forced to "take a position" at one end of the bipolarity, the other end, or at some point in between. Human beings do not simply string meanings together. They frame them in wide-ranging oppositional contexts acting as predicating backgrounds against which understanding is fashioned. For empirical evidence in support of this suggestion see Lamiell (1987).

Whether we accept this line of argument or not, it is clear that computer reason is lacking in a fundamental oppositionality. There is a reason for this. The binary logic (bits, etc.) of the machine that was discussed above is underwritten by a certain mathematical approach to the processing of information. I refer here to Boolean algebra. The fundamental emphasis in Boolean algebra is on what is termed a "universe class" and a "null class," which can be represented by the numbers *1* and *0* respectively (Boole 1854/1958; Reese 1980:64). The complement of each class is everything that is not that class, so that in the case of *1* this would be *1-x;* and *1−x=0*. In effect, Boole took disjunction to mean "either-or, but not both" so that the sum-total of events x and y would be $x+y$ excluding those cases that would be *both* x and y. It is this strictly either-or characterization of classes that underwrites the binary calculations of the digital computer. If we think of meaningful classes as always divisible into one or the other and never "both" as possibilities, then it is possible to equate a decision such as "true-false" with the electronic switch that is either "on" (true) or "off" (false).

The computer cannot predicate because it has no wider background of "both" meanings (x and y) from which it proceeds in the reasoning process. As we have seen, the computing process is strictly that of matching one item to another. The computer knows, so to speak, what "is" the case but never has an inkling of what "is not" the case. This is both the source of its vaunted power as "intelligent" processor and also its notorious reputation as a literal, rigid, "wooden" reasoner. Things have to match up "perfectly" or the calculating process will not proceed. The computer is not going to "presume" anything. Here is where Searle's Chinese room analogue begins to lose relevance, because the truth is that the person in the room would sometimes mismatch the figures. Machines never do this because their electrical process is "hardwired" in a way compatible with Boolean disjunction, so that a match is made or it is not made. If not made, there is no resulting error because the machine cannot move forward. If we forget to put the period in when we give our computer a command, or we misspell a command, the computer registers an error term immediately and "refuses" to continue.

The human reasoner in the Chinese room might overlook such minor slip-ups and continue in any case, but this is because the human has some notion of the predication involved in having a relationship with another person. We are back to the question of empathy. This empathic understanding of the "other" allows one person to predicate and hence know the intentions of the partner in the relationship. One person knows what is "supposed" to take place and what is "not supposed" to take place in the relationship with the other person. The machine lacks this sense of oppositional possibilities and hence can never really play the role of the "other" as the relationship unfolds. What happens is what happens, and that is "it." Instead of *opposition*, a pattern of contrary positions, the machine deals in *apposition*, a pattern of placing items (meanings, etc.) "side by side." If we were to park two automobiles facing each other on a parking lot, we might say that they were parked "opposite to each other." The machine, however, would "see" or "grasp" only two automobiles parked side by side—appositely!—with more or less distance between them.

The upshot of this inability to reason oppositionally is that a machine cannot learn what was *not* input. If we send the Ten Commandments inward to a machine it would record ten ways in which to behave. A person, on the other hand, would have *at least* twenty possibilities suggested based on precisely the same input. Even if a machine is programmed to reason oppositionally, this will have to be accomplished based upon the software or the "rule book" in Searle's example. The hardware processing is never oppositional. As a result, the machine will be simulating oppositional reasoning with as little understanding of oppositional reasoning as Searle's closeted person has of the Chinese figure. Moreover, the machine will never be capable of reasoning to the opposite of the programmed injunctions, negating what it is instructed to do by deciding to affirm the contrary course. Searle's person, on the other hand, can always decide "No, I won't use this figure with the squiggle on the left-hand side, as the book says. I'll take this one with the squiggle on the right-hand side instead. Let's see what happens." In the process of moving locations from one side to its contrary, the output information will be fouled up. Opposition (negation) would be reflected in any such unwillingness to carry out instructions, of course. But the point is: The resulting errors in the processing of information would represent, not a mechanical failure, but an *intentional* deviation from the scripted action.

Searle's thought experiment suggests that there are significant gaps in the use of the computer as a complete model for the description of human behavior. And yet, there are many today who believe that the computer analogue is equal to the task of framing a fully suitable picture of human reason. It is my contention that, although computer technology does shed light on certain aspects of human reasoning, a major and fundamental aspect of such reasoning is left out owing to the technological limitations of the computing process. Computers do not predicate meanings; they match signals. Computers do not process or frame oppositional information, which is another way of talking about their inability to predicate.

It is not my intention to detract from those aspects of human reason that may be amenable to computer research. But my view is that a counter-balancing position should be advanced in the fields of psychology and computer science to offset the easy identification of human reason with artificial intelligence, network theories, information processing, and related endeavors in which the formulation of human reason does not include discussion or even minimal consideration of the predicational process. And yet, the program writing and calculations on which computer technology is based routinely refer to assumptions of the mathematical systems employed, as well as to the approach taken in the problem solution of a software package.

Finally, it is my hope that through the study of predication we will acquire a deeper understanding of the human being. Human beings are not always or only intelligent. There is stupidity in the world, artificial and otherwise. If we find that how people predicate what they come to know determines their level of intelligence, this would add considerably to our understanding of their basic natures. No genuine science of the person can ignore the weaker side of the human image. The role of error, of learning what was not taught, or presuming what was not intended, is clearly an aspect of human behavior. An understanding of predication and opposition permits the social scientist to paint a richer picture of what it means to be a human being, one that connects more directly with sociocultural outlooks such as we find in law, religion, and art. All such evaluative endeavors cry out for a depiction of the human being as one who predicates rather than simply mediates experience.

2.
Predicational Explanation Across the Ages

It is not hard to demonstrate that there have been intimations of a predicational style of explanation cropping up across the history of Western thought. This includes a conflict that arose in science concerning predicational versus mediational forms of explanation (for a similar conflict in Eastern thought, see Rychlak 1988:78–81). In the main, the conflict over explanation centered around the proper use of causation. We shall want to get a good sense of causal terminology and how it has changed over the centuries. This examination will necessarily bring in the other issues we found in our analysis of the Chinese room problem. Chapter 2 begins with the Grecian world outlook, moves to a survey of Newtonianism in the early rise of physical science, and then closes with a discussion of important changes that have taken place in modern scientific description. This historical background will prepare us for a better understanding of the scientific terminology being used in computer technology concerning parallels to human reasoning.

Predication and Opposition in the Grecian World

It was noted in chapter 1 that the Greek word *kategorein* means "to predicate" (Yartz 1984:147). Much of Greek philosophy, and indeed, of all philosophy, involves categorizing knowledge in some manner. In the Sophist dialogue, Plato (1952b) has the discussants saying that we know the quality of other people by the words that we use to describe them (p. 554). He goes on to name this verbal usage "predication" and then adds that we can "predicate many names of the same thing" (p. 569). Thus, whenever we make a statement about anything we employ nouns and verbs. One of the nouns serves as a subject of the spoken or written sentence, and the verb plus the other noun ("object") then serves a predicational role in what is expressed (p. 576). The goal of many Greek philosophers was to delineate a finite number of such categories or predicates, because then we could *immediately* know a great deal simply by applying these wide-ranging meanings to our experience of different things. Another way of referring to these highly abstract, broadly applicable predicates is as *universals*. It was because they believed that some such abstract predicates lent meaning to all of experience that the Greek thinkers sought to devolve meanings "from the universal to the particular."

It was Aristotle who was to wind this predicational view into a complex theory of human reasoning. I shall use him as our prototype philosopher who believed in human reason as a predicational process. Aristotle began his analysis on the assumption that human reasoning always moves from the broader to the narrower extension of meaning (Aristotle 1952a:8). He did not distinguish between human reasoning in general and the logical steps of the syllogism, which he invented (see Aristotle 1952e:143; 1952c:39). Structurally, a syllogism has three terms: (1) a *major* term in which the middle term is also contained; (2) a *middle* term, which is contained by the major and also contains the minor term; and (3) a *minor* term, which is contained or subsumed by the middle term. Figure 1 diagrams the relationship that is under consideration here.

Figure 1 presents the major term as a large circle, the middle term as a medium-sized circle, and the minor term as a tiny circle. This use of circles to represent predicational reasoning is adapted from the method of analysis introduced by Leonhard Euler (Reese 1980:160). Several references will be made to the logic of Euler circles in this volume. The arrows depicted in figure 1 refer to the direction that meaning extension takes in the syllogism. This is a sequacious flow of meaning (i.e., involving logical necessity). Aristotle stressed that sequacious meaning extensions always flowed from the wider to the narrower range of meaning (1952d:131).

Note the various orderings of the circles at the top of figure 1. On the left, the meaning is depicted as extending (via arrow direction) from "right to left" and on the right we see it extending from "left to right." What these two arrangements have in common is that the arrow indicates a meaning extension from the larger to the smaller circles. The arrangement in the middle of the upper portion of figure 1 depicts the three circles as if they were directly

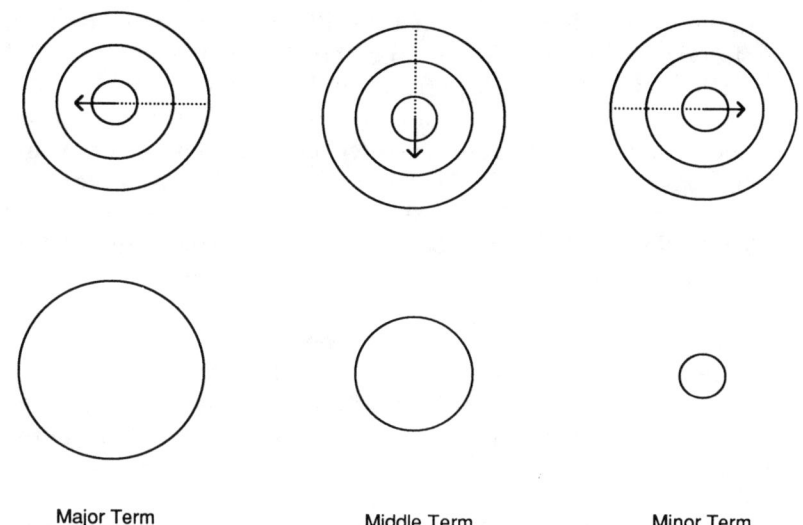

DIRECTION OF MEANING: FROM THE LARGER TO THE SMALLER REFERENCE POINT

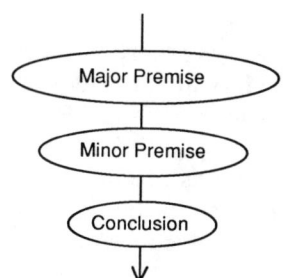

Figure 1. Syllogistic Reasoning

centered, one on top of the other. In this case, the arrow is extending forward, as if there had been a "bull's eye" through the circles —but once again extending from the larger to the smaller of the three. The direction of meaning flow is irrelevant, just so long as its course is always from the broader or wider expanse of meaning to the narrower expanse. This is the predicational "process" referred to in chapter 1.

The syllogism has often been presented in the form: "All men are mortal *(major premise);* this is a man *(minor premise);* therefore, this man is mortal *(deduction* or *conclusion)."* I have symbolized the three steps of the syllogism in this sense at the bottom of figure 1. Note that, once again, meaning extends from the broadly conceived major premise, which already encompasses the meaning of the minor premise, leading to a sequacious conclusion being drawn about a specific referent. From reasoning about the mortality of *all* men we arrive at the mortality of *this* man.

The premises involved in the syllogism also reflect predication. Aristotle defined a premise as "a sentence affirming or denying one thing of another" (1952c:39). When we say "All men are mortal" we, in effect, have the meaning of mortality as a wider referent—a a larger Euler circle — within which we situate the narrower referent "man." As Plato has suggested, any definition of a word, as indeed any sentence structure, already involves some such meaningful relationship in which a wider expanse is lending its meaning to a targeted, narrower expanse. Recall (from chapter 1) that this relationship is not simply "in" the words being used, but "in" the logical process known as predication. However, the meanings employed in relating concepts, one to another, have an important part to play in predication. Predication demands that we take meaning seriously.

Aristotle found that the philosophers before him had generally tried to find some "one" grand universal under which all knowledge could be predicated. Thales had postulated *water* as a universal substance, entering into everything. Diogenes gave this universal distinction to *air.* Some philosophers named more than one such universal substance, with *earth, air, fire,* and *water* leading most lists. Such grand predicates were referred to as "first principles" and the concept of a *deity* was also postulated to be one of these universals lending meaning to everything in existence (Aristotle 1952g:501).

Aristotle gathered these earlier speculations on universals together and, in effect, predicated them by subsuming them under *four different* causal meanings. The word Aristotle used for what we translate as "cause" was *aitiá*, which has the meaning of *responsibility*. This word was in general use, often expressed in legal contests where an effort was made to place the responsibility for wrongdoing on a defendant. Aristotle claimed that the true scientist always seeks to subsume the explanation of things under all four of these predicating causal meanings, because they are ultimately "responsible" for everything that exists. In a sense, he was asking the scientist to situate any concept within the overlapping portion of four broad Euler circles (Aristotle 1952d:128).

The first of these predicates is the *material cause*, which is the constituent matter "out of which a thing comes to be and which persists . . . e.g., the bronze of the statue, the silver of the bowl . . ." (Aristotle 1952f:271). I shall refer to the material cause as both matter and substance, but in strict Aristotelian philosophy the meaning of substance is more than this (i.e., combining form as so-called secondary substance; see Aristotle 1952h:644). But for our purposes the material cause is any constituent matter or substance that "makes things up." Mountains are made of earth and rock and people are made of flesh and bone.

The second grand predicate we might employ in accounting for anything is the *efficient cause*, or "the primary source of the change or coming to rest" (Aristotle 1952f:271). Efficient causes name the impetus in events, the instrumental push, thrust, flow, cueing, or triggering of motions in nature. The roots of mediational explanation reside in the efficient cause, because the antecedent impels the consequent along over time much as one billiard ball impacts upon and thereby moves a second billiard ball. Time's passage is fundamental to efficient causation, and hence we are likely to symbolize such motion as a left-to-right process, moving unidirectionally from location A to B.

The third predicate a scientist might employ is the *formal cause*, or the "definition of the essence, and the classes which include this (e.g., the relation 2:1 and number in general are the cause of the octave)" (Aristotle 1952g:533). By "essence" Aristotle had in mind the overall "synthesis of the whole" that an item of cognition takes on in its meaning (ibid.). For example, all people have similar forms in that they have heads, faces, torsos, legs, and so forth. Sometimes people look very much alike in these physiognomic characteristics, as in the case of identical twins. Yet, we who know these twins well can sense their essential differences even though we cannot name the precise discriminants that we are relying on.

Some Aristotelian scholars diminish the importance of shape per se in formal causation, placing their emphasis on form as that into which something is classified or made (e.g., Adler 1978:38; see also Robinson 1989:39). Nevertheless, since it is useful for my purposes to think this way, I shall interpret formal causes as referring to the pattern, shape, outline, or recognizable organization that occurs in the material substances of nature, as well as in the (efficient-cause) motions of passing events.

The fourth predicate to be employed for the existence or occurrence of anything is the *final cause*, or "the sense of [an] end or 'that for the sake of which' a thing is done, e.g. health is the cause of walking about" (Aristotle 1952f:271). This causal predicate brings us into that realm of purpose and intention that we found wanting in the strictly mediational, machine-like processing of the Chinese room (chapter 1). The Greek word for "end" is *telos*, and that is why we refer to theories that rely on final causes (choices, goals, aspirations, hopes, etc.) as *teleologies*. There are many forms that a teleology can take, including human, deity, or natural teleologies. It is all a matter of whether or not the theory presumes that events are created and/or moving toward an end, purpose, or reason through intentional influences of one sort or another.

There is an implicit tie between the formal and final cause (Aristotle 1952k:255). The formal cause as a pattern, blueprint, or plan is the "that" in the "that, for the sake of which" phrasing. Thus, the student attending college with an end in view of one day possessing a diploma has this latter end as the "that" for the sake of which he or she is currently behaving. This end is a purpose, which is pursued intentionally by the student. The formal cause is thus a necessary ingredient of final causation. It gives us an understanding of why a person is intentionally behaving—acting out a certain pattern—but there is still this overlying capacity that the person has to behave or *not* behave "for the sake of" this end. The student can always decide the end is no longer worth the effort and discontinue his or her studies.

Note that in talking about purposes and intentions we are necessarily considering the predications that people assume in their ongoing behavior. This is especially true when we say that they can behave "for the sake of" an end *or not!* How is it possible to describe people as behaving in this do/don't, either/or fashion? Here is where we begin to see the necessary tie of oppositionality to predication which was touched on in chapter 1. The Grecian world view was based in large measure on the interplay of oppositionality in all things. Anaximander held that the elements of the universe were in opposition to each other, so that air is cold, fire is hot, and so on. Heraclitus said that opposites could not exist on their own; we would not know what justice "is" unless injustices existed, and vice versa. Pythagoras believed that all things were compounded of opposite qualities. And Empedocles held that the elements earth, air, fire, and water were continually stirred by the opposites of "love" and "strife."

Socrates learned from the sophists how to capitalize on the oppositionality of all knowledge by devising his well-known "question and answer" didactic procedure known as the *dialectical method*. The concept of dialectic, which has a rich history of its own, is predicated on the identification and union of opposites (see Rychlak 1981a, chapter 9). In the Socratic method, the teacher puts a series of questions to the student. The original position taken by the student in response to the opening question was called the *thesis*, and the opposing position then defended by the teacher was called the *antithesis*. These contrasting meanings were thus generated and fundamentally related through oppositionality. The question-and-answer (dialectical) procedure brought out these two sides clearly and often suggested that only one of them was defensible or true. Sometimes a combination of the two (thesis and antithesis) was effected, bringing about a *synopsis* (Greek term used) or *synthesis* (modern term used) by taking the best or truest meaning from both sides. This unifying outcome would presumably be a step up the ladder of an ever-widening knowledge, pointing to the realm of universals. According to the Socratic theory of knowledge, it did not matter where the student and teacher began their search for universal truth. They might begin in error, but thanks to the fact that truth and error are oppositionally related, in time, through proper questions and answers, they could arrive at truth.

Aristotle, who was just as committed to oppositionality as his philosophical colleagues were (Ogden 1967:21), did not accept the Socratic assumption that if one began a line of study or reasoning in error, one would end in truth. Oppositionality had another role to play in human reason—relating to the manner in which we arrive at our major premises, our widest range of predication at the outset of a line of thought. Here is how he defined human reason:

> Now reasoning is an argument in which, certain things being laid down, something other than these necessarily comes about

through them. (a) It is a 'demonstration,' when the premises from which the reasoning starts are true and primary, or are such that our knowledge of them has originally come through premises that are primary and true: (b) reasoning, on the other hand, is 'dialectical', if it reasons from opinions that are generally accepted. (Aristotle 1952e:143)

Aristotle's empiricism is rooted in his theory of knowledge, which holds that in order to arrive at truth the scientist must *begin* in truth as derived from first principles or empirical observation (ibid.). The "primary and true" is the empirically observable or tautologically certain. It is not based on opinion or arbitrary interpretations —as is true in dialectical reasoning. This empirical thrust of looking "at" things gives theory in physical science an extraspective cast in which material and efficient causation is likely to be used, much in the vein of the Jones and Nisbett (1971) experiment. When reasoning dialectically, we are more prone to "look with" people, to try to understand their point of view (opinion), which amounts to a formal-final cause understanding of "that, for the sake of which" they are making their case. Furthermore, an element of arbitrariness always seems to occur in dialectical reasoning. One might, for example, take both ends of a dialectical position. Aristotle did not claim that dialectical reasoning was "all bad." There is an important role for it in rhetoric, in examining assumptions, and in discerning when a supposed syllogism is actually an enthymeme (an incomplete syllogism; see Aristotle 1952m:596).

To buttress demonstrative reasoning Aristotle also advanced a predicational principle that he felt could not be denied: ". . . the predicate cannot both belong and not belong to the subject at one and the same time with regard to the future" (Aristotle 1952b:28). We cannot say "Bridget is honest" and "Bridget is not honest [is dishonest]" in the same breath without contradicting ourselves. This principle, often expressed as "A is not non-A," has since been termed the *law of contradiction*, or sometimes the *law of noncontradiction* (in light of our rule versus law discussion in chapter 1, we might now prefer the "rule of noncontradiction"). The law of contradiction contrasts with the dialectician's principle of the *one and many* or *many in one*, which implies that all knowledge interconnects into an implicit unity, including opposite meanings such as A and non-A (Plato 1952a:612). The law of contradiction holds for both *contraries* (every science is good, no science is good) and *contradictories* (every science is good, some science is not good) [Aristotle 1952g:524]. Notice that negation is related here as well.

In pointing to contraries and contradictories Aristotle was recognizing the role that oppositionality plays in thought—one manifestation of which was dialectical reasoning. Indeed, this is how he arrives at his understanding of a human teleology. Although he made one of the first allusions to mind as a tabula rasa, a blank tablet on which experience etches its teachings (Aristotle 1952h:662), and he was attuned to the important influence of habit on behavior (Aristotle 1952m:612), Aristotle did not believe that such past influences could direct the course of reasoning in the present. He viewed the person as a predicator, as capable of reasoning "for the sake of" contraries and contradictions to past experience when the situation called for it. Learning cannot occur without premises that frame what is to be known in the first place (Aristotle 1952g:511). Learning moves from a wider realm of understanding to focus on the specific in a precedent-sequacious manner (ibid.:552).

Another way of expressing the relationship that Aristotle saw between oppositionality and predication is to consider the predicating Euler circle of figure 1 as having both an inside and an outside. We sometimes lose sight of this "outside the circle" realm, particularly in the classical syllogism about all men being mortal. Mortality would seem to cover everyone as a major premise except a deity. The non-mortal (outside the circle) in this case would be the deity. But in most instances of logical reasoning, the major premise, symbolized by the largest Euler circle, always has its contrary or negation delineated even if unstated. For example, if a number of smaller circles symbolizing human beings as well as other organisms were set within a larger circle symbolizing "flesh-eating organisms," we would be predicating the former by the latter. But since there are also non-flesh eaters, there is the "outside the larger circle" to consider here—and this outside area will always signify the meaning opposite to the predicating circle. In any act of predication, therefore, an opposite possibility is ipso facto implied. Aristotle was cognizant of this oppositional complication of any major premise, which is why he included dialectical reasoning in the human repertoire.

Memory for Aristotle was not a mechanical process of retrieving previous inputs. Memory involved *recollection*, which was an active searching for what was intentionally desired to be recalled (Aristotle 1952i). Aristotle spells out the role of predication in a context of knowledge when he asks and then answers the following question: "why does one thing attach to some other [in reason]? . . . We are inquiring, then, why something is predicable of something. . . . the inquiry is about the predication of one thing of another" (Aristotle 1952g:565). In his principles of mental association, Aristotle included not only similarity, contiguity, and frequency, but also contrariety! We pattern our thoughts by way of oppositionality. Our reasoning is directed through predication because we must, in effect, "take a position" on the meanings that we confront as they are oppositionally suggestive of alternative possibilities. We do not input singularities in the fashion of the Chinese room (chapter 1). We affirm "this" meaning as opposed to "that" meaning and behave "for the sake of" the former — or the latter — depending on the purpose we are choosing or intending to create (bring about, attain, express, etc.). Aristotle's free-will conception is situated on this line of argument, for as he said, "where it is in our power to act it is also in our power not to act, and *vice versa*" (Aristotle 1952l:359) and "the man is free . . . who exists for his own sake [his own purposes or reasons]" (Aristotle 1952g:501).

The Decline of Predicational Theory in Newtonian Science

Aristotle's predicational theorizing was extremely influential in the history of thought, but it was to run into difficulty around the seventeenth century with the first important developments in what was to be known as a Newtonian approach to science. A major reason for this difficulty had to do with the teleological aspects of predicational theorizing. We will want in particular to grasp the critique of Aristotle's final-cause usage leveled by Francis Bacon. The *Baconian criticism* is as valid today as it was centuries ago, and it has special significance regarding some of the claims made today by those who believe that the computer analogue is equal to the task of accounting for human agency.

Aristotle drew no real distinction between the creative actions of a person and the creative actions of "nature." Final causes or "ends" were to be seen in both human and natural actions (Aristotle 1952g:557). But in framing things this uniformly, Aristotle's explanations ran into difficulty. Thus, when he spoke of a human final-cause action, Aristotle took the *introspective* theoretical perspective, as follows:

> For consider how the physician or how the builder sets about his work. He starts by forming for himself a definite picture,

in the one case perceptible to mind, in the other to sense, of his end — the physician of health, the builder of a house — and this he holds forward as the reason and explanation of each subsequent step that he takes, and of his acting in this or that way as the case may be (Aristotle, 1952j:161–162).

Aristotle has us "looking with" the physician or the builder, just as in chapter 1 we looked with the person in the Chinese room, grasping the end (formal cause) for the sake of which (final cause) a personal line of behavior is being carried out. But when Aristotle next talks of the ends that nature is creating, his explanation takes on the *extraspective* theoretical perspective, as follows:

> ... the purpose of the blood in sanguineous animals is to subserve the nutrition of the body. ... the blood exists for the sake of nutrition, that is, the nutrition of the parts ... (p. 175). ... It is obvious also to sense that it is for the sake of the flesh that all the other parts exist. By the other parts I mean the bones, the skin, the sinews, and the blood-vessels, and, again, the hair and the various kinds of nails, and anything else there may be of a like character. Thus the bones are a contrivance to give security to the soft parts, to which purpose they are adapted by their hardness; and in animals that have no bones the same office is fulfilled by some analogous substance, as by fishspine in some fishes, and by cartilage in others (p. 179).

It was this extraspective employment of final causation that Bacon was later to attack. What did it add to our knowledge of the physical world to say that bones are "for the sake of" holding up the fleshy parts of the body, or that leaves are "for the sake of" shading fruit on the branches of trees (Bacon 1952a:44)? Bacon believed that by rushing to the telic form of description, Aristotle actually hampered the progress of empirical knowledge (p. 45). Bacon was careful to keep separate our knowledge of a person's behavior from our knowledge of a physical event. He accepted the use of final-cause description in areas of knowledge like metaphysics, but when it came to strictly physical study he did not see the need for such elaborations, noting that:

> ... for although the greatest generalities in nature must be positive, just as they are found, and in fact not causable, yet the human understanding, incapable of resting seeks for something more intelligible. Thus, however, whilst aiming at

further progress, it falls back to what is actually less advanced, namely, final causes; *for they are clearly more allied to man's own nature, than the system of the universe*, and from this source they have wonderfully corrupted philosophy. (Bacon 1952b:111; italics added)

It seems that Bacon was amenable to final-cause description in the understanding of "man's own nature," which suggests that he would accept an introspective formulation of such causality. As a matter of fact, Bacon did accept the use of final-cause description in metaphysical analysis (which is predicational). There is a submerged theological issue in all of this. Aristotle's "nature" was actually a reflection of the deity's creative intention. He spoke of the "divine science" and of the importance that God as a first principle has above all other principles (Aristotle 1952g:501). Subsequent theologians like Anselm and Aquinas built on this theme, advancing the deity conceptions of a First Cause and the Divine Plan. This suggests that Aristotle's natural teleology is at heart a deity teleology. If so, then we have an introspective formulation after all. But if we presume to see a God's predicating plan (formal cause) for the sake of which (final cause) the universe is under creation, do we not claim to "know" God's intent? Farrington (1949) notes that Bacon definitely believed that Aristotle had committed precisely this sin of intellectual pride, in which "the presumptuous endeavor [is made] to conjure the knowledge of the nature of things out of one's own head instead of seeking it patiently in the Book of Nature" (p. 148).

Bacon's recommendation is that physical scientists merely observe extraspectively what is taking place in nature, describing events according to material and efficient causation. He was not thinking of describing the minds of human beings, of course. There is another significant reason for the decline of introspective, predicational theorizing to be noted in the rise of science during the seventeenth century. I refer here to the unfortunate incident of Galileo and the churchmen of the Inquisition (Burtt 1955). The latter individuals realized that a heliocentric (sun-centered) theory of the universe was possible to conceptualize and even prove empirically through mathematical calculation and prediction of the course of heavenly bodies. The churchmen viewed such formal-cause "mathematical suppositions" as intellectual exercises, suitable for discussion among scholars but not representative of the "reality" of the heavens. Since the Ptolemaic geocentric (earth-centered) theory was not in conflict with church dogma—meaning God's predicating intentions—the churchmen naturally preferred this formulation to Galileo's (even though it was not as mathematically precise as the latter's theory).

Galileo was asked and then forced to relent on what was "really the case" and what was simply a mathematical formulation of the imagination. The reality was as Biblical accounts depicted—that is, the universe is geocentric. The important confrontation for the subsequent theories in human sciences was not the heliocentric versus the geocentric issue. The important confrontation was *teleology* (with no distinctions drawn between human and deity) and *mechanism*. The mechanism of Galileo was based on his empirical observations and mathematical calculation of the patterns of celestial motion. The churchmen had such patterns created by a deity whose "that *(Divine Plan)* for the sake of which *(Divine Intention)*" was revealed and hence not open to question. Here, therefore, is another manifestation of the kind of physical description that the Baconian criticism was aimed at: the theologians were placing superfluous interpretations on the workings of the universe by bringing in a predicational account. Galileo was dealing exclusively in the empirical facts, unfolding over time in a marvelously precise, efficient-cause fashion. Conclusion? Theologies were teleological, metaphysical speculations that had *no place* in the scientific description and understanding of the physical universe. Scientists must describe "how" the physical universe works and not become embroiled in questions of "why" it works as it does.

Not only was final causation reduced in influence, but formal causation was as well. The obvious formal causation involved in mathematical calculation was overlooked. Newton believed that geometry was itself a reflection of the universe's mechanics (ibid.:215). If a mathematical pattern was identified in natural events it was presumed by the Newtonians to be a reflection of an underlying efficient causality rather than vice versa—in which case the mathematical (formal-cause) assumptions made would be determining what was "being seen." The concept of *reductionism* was now advanced as an ideal. The natural scientist was to limit the range of causal description to material and especially efficient causality. Indeed, the very meaning of "natural" in both Newtonian "natural science" and Darwinian "natural selection" is "non-teleological."

Newton said that he framed no predicating hypotheses in his work as a scientist. He simply tracked the immutable, efficient-cause patternings of nature, extraspectively taking place "over there," in the reality of the atomic substrate. Since this time in history, "determinism" has come to mean *only* efficient-cause determinism. Efficient-cause determinism reached its most elevated and eloquent expression in the famous remark of Laplace, the Newtonian, who said "that a superhuman intelligence acquainted with the position and motions of the atoms at any moment could predict the whole course of future events" (ibid.:96). Interestingly, this view of nature can be consistent with a deity teleology. In fact, there were physicists following Laplace who rejected such a hard determinism precisely because it seemed to be predicated on a belief in the rational powers of a deity who had set the atoms in place to begin with (creation).

But the important point for our purposes is that in the rise of Newtonian science there was no real opportunity for a predicational model to be used. This was not a problem for the physical scientist. Who needs to take the point of view (i.e., predicating assumptions) of Mars as it circles about the Sun each day? Who needs to understand the viewpoint of the stomach as it digests food following a meal? The Baconian criticism is sound. It adds nothing to our understanding of such physical events to ascribe to them some form of predicating reason for the sake of which they are being carried out. In the closing decades of the nineteenth century an extension in science was made from the study of strictly physical bodily processes to the study of *mental* processes. In this endeavor, some of the points made by Bacon concerning the compatibility of final causation with human nature were overlooked. It *does* add something to our understanding of human beings to be aware of their introspectively formulated predications regarding life.

In the main, the British philosophy was to underwrite an extraspective view of human behavior. Bacon's empirical approach was enlarged upon by Hobbes, Locke, Hume, the Mills, and others. Cognition was explained in terms of a frequency and contiguity principle. People thought about what had frequently entered their tabula rasa mind (efficient-cause inputs), associating to other such contents in convenient proximity. Mind was a posteriori. Continental philosophy continued to defend, at least in large measure, the more introspective view of mind with the major champion being Kant, whose view of mind was a priori. Whereas Locke had argued mediationally that the mind is tabula rasa and takes in its ideas from external experience in a fundamentally passive manner, Kant argued predicationally that ideas are conceptualizing or "constructive" processes that give meaning to the unstructured sensory noise entering from experience. Kant reminds us of Aristotle in his definition of reasoning as "the faculty of deducing the particular from the general" (1952a:194). The role of predication in human reasoning is here given central emphasis. Kant also had oppositionality functioning within mind by way of a transcendental dialectical capacity of reason to rise above what "is" being thought about to see indications of what "is not" being thought about (ibid.:229). We shall have occasion to contrast the Lockean and Kantian conceptions of human reasoning at several points in the remaining chapters of this volume.

The influence on American academic/scientific psychology was to be almost completely Lockean. The founding fathers of psychology departments in the late nineteenth and early twentieth centuries (e.g., Thorndike, Hall, Cattell, etc.) took their lead from Great Britain. Although William James espoused teleology in his philosophical writings, his psychological writings did not lend theoretical and methodological support for such a view of the person (Dooley, 1975). Those who did establish scientific psychology embedded it in a mechanistic formulation from which it has never recovered. John B. Watson, the father of behaviorism, asked his followers to *"try to think of man as an assembled organic machine ready to run"* (1924:216; italics in the original). Edward C. Tolman (1932/1967) advanced a "purposive behaviorism" by suggesting that rats exploring mazes could frame a "means-to-end" cognitive map of such mazes. The only problem with his formulation is that Tolman construed such cognitive maps, not as predicating frameworks brought to bear in a Kantian fashion, but as intervening variables taken in from reality in the mediational sense (chapter 1). Thus, Tolman defined mental processes as "functional variables which *intermediate* [italics added] in the causal equation between environmental stimuli and initiating physiological states or excitements, on the one side, and final overt behavior, on the other" (p. 2). What we have here as "purpose" is an input from the environment, like one of the already formed Chinese figures (of chapter 1) functioning as a mediator in the ongoing efficient causation of nature.

Much of the effort in research on lower animals in psychology was aimed at discrediting final causation in the description of human behavior. After all, we cannot speak with a white rat. Is it possible that we want to argue that white rats frame predications?

(In chapter 7 we shall find that this suggestion is not so silly as it once seemed). Psychologists of this period joked about the rat, sitting at a choice point in a maze, trying to decide which direction to take. Rather than attempt to take the rat's viewpoint, better to stand off to one side and describe what is taking place in exclusively material/efficient-cause terms. This Newtonian attitude permeated psychology over the first two thirds of the twentieth century. We get a fine example of the denigration of telic description in the following 1937 quote from Clark L. Hull, a giant in the behavioristic tradition:

> We may start with the assumption that every drop of rain in some way or other gets to the ocean.... Anthropomorphizing this condition we may say that it is the *purpose* of every drop of rain to get to the ocean. Of course, this only means that virtually every drop *does* get there eventually.... Falling from the cloud it may strike the leaf of a tree, and drop from one leaf to another until it reaches the ground. From here it may pass under or on the surface of the soil to a rill, then to a brook, river, and finally to the sea. Each stage, each fall from one leaf to the next, may be designated as a *means* toward the final end, the sea.... Human behavior is merely a complication of the same factors. (1937:2)

The effort here to account for teleology through natural laws confronts the same problem that we can see in Tolman's purposive theorizing. Both Hull's and Tolman's formulations of purpose are subject to the Baconian criticism! If we can explain an event through sheer mechanical forces or frequency principles then why should we bother with an intentional conception like purpose? What does it add to our understanding of the process underway? Of course, as we will learn in chapter 5, the conditioning theories on which Tolman and Hull based their explanations really do not account for unpredicated learning as was once believed. But the thrust of the Baconian criticism for the mechanistic theorist who relies on a mediational view of behavior is that he or she should avoid purposive constructs altogether. One psychologist with the intellectual integrity (a concept he would doubtless reject) to do so has been B. F. Skinner. Following one of his debates with Carl Rogers, an exchange occurred that is relayed to us by the latter as follows:

> A paper given by Dr. Skinner led me to direct these remarks to him: "From what I understand Dr. Skinner to say, it is his

understanding that though he might have thought *he chose* to come to this meeting, might have thought he had a purpose in giving this speech, such thoughts are really illusory. He actually made certain marks on paper and emitted certain sounds here simply because his genetic makeup and his past environment had operantly conditioned his behavior in such a way that it was rewarding to make these sounds, and that he as a person doesn't enter into this. In fact if I get his thinking correctly, from his strictly scientific point of view, he, as a person, doesn't exist." In his reply Dr. Skinner said that he would not go into the question of whether he had any choice in the matter (presumably because the whole issue was illusory) but stated, "I do accept your characterization of my own presence here." (Rogers 1963:271–272)

We see here all four of the issues delineated in chapter 1. Skinner is simply conveying influences sent his way by his environment, in mediational fashion. He has no meaning to predicate but is shaped by these efficiently caused determinants. He is not a "person" because he has no originating source of control. He cannot think to the opposite of what his past life has formed him into being and behave in the contrary fashion that Aristotle said was possible. He is shaped unidirectionally by his past experience. In denying his personhood, Skinner as scientist stands off to one side and observes himself as "that, over there." This extraspective style of explanation was written into the very core of scientific psychological description by the reductive theorist Stevens, who said: "Psychology regards all observations, including those which a psychologist makes upon himself, as made upon the 'other one' and thereby makes explicit the distinction between the experimenter and the thing observed" (1935:517). As we shall see in the final section of this chapter, modern physical scientists have found it impossible to live up to this "principle of extraspection."

The Rise of Predicational Theory in Modern Science

In a fascinating manner, and thanks to empirical study, modern physical scientists are bringing themselves back into the research process in a way that clearly reflects predication. We witness two definite developments taking place in how science is currently being understood: (1) the formal cause is replacing the efficient cause as the ubiquitous predication that scientists employ in the understanding of nature, and (2) the recognition of Kantian a priori influences on scientific thought has made room for final causation in the new understanding of the scientist as a *participator* in the knowledge framed in observation and experimentation.

The Newtonian dream of tracing events in uniformly measured steps of efficient causation has long since been abandoned in modern science. Units of measurement vary, depending on location of the observer in a field (a wider context!). It is even possible to think of such familiar efficient-cause movements of passing through past, present, and future time as existing "all at once," as a mosaic pattern (formal cause) with distinctive features known by these names (de Broglie 1949:114). What one experiences as past, present, and future is dependent upon the slice of space-time within which an observer frames the predicate assumptions about that which is being "observed." Although he believed that there was an independent reality that scientists address in their studies, Mach was among the first to point out a phenomenological—that is, an introspectively framed, predicational—aspect to the mathematical schemes that the scientist frames in an a priori fashion. Thus, Mach observed:

> Different [a priori] ideas can express the facts with the *same* exactness in the domain accessible to observation. The *facts* must hence be carefully distinguished from the *intellectual* constructs the formation of which they suggested. The latter —concepts—must be *consistent* with observation, and must in addition be *logically* in accord with one another. Now these two requirements can be fulfilled in *more than one* manner, and hence the different systems of geometry [e.g., Euclidian, Cartesian, etc.]. (Bradley 1971:83)

The interest here is shifting from the accuracy of tracing an independently functioning Newtonian reality to the alternative "points of view" that one might take in construing this "reality." Heisenberg found that it was not possible to measure both the position and the velocity of an atom's electronic motions without thereby influencing an electron's speed or direction of movement. This was not a problem of instrumentation but was at heart a conceptual limitation in the study of natural events. The scientist is required to choose whether to track the speed or the location of the electron and cannot predicate both aspects with accuracy in the same experiment. A similar choice is involved in the concept of light, which can be proved to be either a wave or a series of particles, depending on the predicate assumptions we make and the resultant experiment that we conduct to prove our case.

This is a good point at which to observe that the logic of empirical study is flawed—not fatally, but in a way that limits the certainty with which our explanation of empirically proven facts can be believed in. We never achieve logical necessity in the proof garnered by a scientific experiment. This is because we always commit the logical error that Aristotle pointed out long ago, of *affirming the consequent* of an "If, then" line of argument. For example, if we were to say "If a person, then a mortal being" and go on to point to some target in experience and say "That is a person" it would follow necessarily that "That is a mortal being." This is because we had affirmed the so-called antecedent term in the statement "If a person *[antecedent]*, then a mortal being *[consequent]*."

Stated in terms of our Euler circles, since the smaller "person" circle is contained within (hence predicated by) the wider "mortal beings" circle, it follows that anyone placed within the former circle will be encompassed by the meaning of the latter circle as well. If, however, we had pointed to some target in experience and stated "That is a mortal being" it would *not* follow necessarily that "That is a person." In this case, we would have affirmed the consequent term (mortal beings), and so we no longer have the certainty of what meaning is being encompassed by what other meaning. In the Euler circles sense, we have affirmed the larger circle, the larger range of meaning within which are situated circles other than the one we are targeting (i.e., the person). Hence, pointing to a "mortal being" does not mean we are necessarily pointing at a person in the wide expanse. We could be pointing at a rabbit or a fly.

In like fashion, when conducting an experiment the scientist is following the logic of "If my theory is correct, then my observations or experimental results will array as I predict them, in A, B, C fashion." Following data collection the scientist might indeed find that the results arrayed as predicted, in A, B, C fashion, and conclude thereby "My theory is certainly correct, based on the evidence." The scientist has, in effect, affirmed the consequent of a logical sequence and to that extent has committed a logical fallacy. All the scientist can legitimately say is that "My findings are consistent with my theoretical line of thought" and recognize in the process that, as Mach has taught us, *other* theories might equally account for the A, B, C array of empirical observations (i.e., facts).

Another way of saying this is that the empirical findings act as a predicating meaning for our theory, but there are always going to be other theories that can take meaning from this data array as well.

Now, this appreciation of how alternatives are germane to scientific experimentation did not hold back the march of modern science. Einstein, in particular, was to instruct us in the role that the observer's predicate assumptions play in what can be observed. Though he believed in an independent reality, Einstein also appreciated the role that the scientist qua predicator played in framing this reality. Citing Kant as his precedent, Einstein notes that there are concepts "which play a dominating role in our thinking, and which nevertheless, cannot be deduced by means of a logical process from the empirically given" (Holton 1973:279). In contrast to Newton, Einstein placed the scientist introspectively at the center of the scientific process. Newton's laws did not assume that the observer was a "physical being." Objective description was defined precisely as the absence of any reference to its author. For "nonphysical" intelligent beings capable of communicating an infinite velocity, the laws of relativity would be irrelevant. The fact that relativity is based on a constraint that applies only to physically localized observers, to beings who can be in only one place at a time and not everywhere at once, gives Einsteinian physics a "human quality" (Prigogine and Stengers 1984:218).

Bohr also looked at the scientist's role from the introspective perspective. He fashioned a *principle of complementarity*, in which it was held that separate and distinct experiments—such as those on the nature of light—can lead to mutually exclusive findings yet retain validity. It is not for the physicist to decide what the ultimate reality "is." All the physicist can deal with are probabilities and/or correlational data observed under the specified conditions of a given experimental approach (Zukav 1979:37).

The talk of probabilities and correlations strikes at the heart of Laplacian certainty in the efficient-cause bumpings of atoms, even as it must be appreciated that the formal cause is taking ascendancy in Bohr's characterization of the scientist's role. That is, probability refers to the *patterned* ratio of specified items to a population estimate including other items (e.g., the ratio of x to $x+y$ becomes $x/x+y$). Correlational relations are also *patterns*. Of course, the situation in the subatomic realm becomes highly complex, because we begin thinking in terms of individualized "probabilities of probabilities" taking place.

It was in the subatomic realm that some of the clearest indications of the primacy of formal-cause description were to be seen. It was becoming apparent to the physicists early in this century that they could not hope to "picture" the world through mechanisms of the sort that Newtonianism had proposed, such as *ether* (Cassirer 1950:110). Subatomic particles are not "things" in the palpable sense of a material cause. Nor do their motions follow the unilinear course suggested by the tracking of an efficiently caused sequence of events. Subatomic particles make jerky movements, jumping across units of uniform, linear measurement. Indeed, efficient causality *breaks down completely* in the realm of the subatomic, where physicists are prone to speak of particles as "complex structures" (Bohm 1957:33) that change in *patterned organization* without discernible efficient cause sequences intervening.

Thus, when an electron changes orbits (or shells) around the nucleus of an atom, there is no way *in principle* to observe the electron moving from one orbit (shell) to the next in efficient-cause fashion. All we can observe is the changing *pattern* of what Bohr called a given "stationary state" of the atom from one organization (state, pattern) to the next (state, pattern) (1934:108). And time is not a factor in such changes, which occur instantaneously. Each of these states or patterns must be considered an individual process, with its unique probabilities of occurrence; the change from one stationary state to another is not and never will be amenable to "detailed description" (p. 109). To account for all of this, Bohr relies on the formal cause as pattern to predicate his understanding of atomic dynamics. He addresses the fact that efficient causation will never be useful as a predication in the subatomic realm and then adds the interesting opinion: "We are here so far removed from a[n efficient-] causal description that an atom in a stationary state may in general even be said to possess a free choice between various possible transitions to other stationary states" (ibid.).

I do not mean to suggest, of course, in citing this comment that Bohr was assigning purpose to atoms. But eminent physical scientists early in this century were willing to draw an analogy to human final-cause concepts of this sort when psychologists of the same period found such commentary totally unacceptable. (For more on this, see Feuer 1974:ch. 2.)

There are proven examples of subatomic particles in one area of the field somehow influencing particles in another area that is far beyond the influence of so-called local (i.e., efficient) causes (Schrödinger 1935). Indeed, some of the subatomic particles in a field seem to complement each other, so that if one electron in a two-particle system of zero spin is made to spin right its opposite number will immediately spin left; if we pass these electrons through a magnetic field and one therefore spins down its opposite number will spin up (Zukav 1979:284). We are dealing here in fantastic patterns. It is unquestionably clear that with the rise of contemporary science the formal cause has assumed ascendancy over the efficient cause. Einstein's famous formula, $E = MC^2$, demonstrates most clearly how energy/force *[E]* (i.e., efficient causation) and mass/matter *[M]* (material causation) are two ways of expressing the same patterned totality (formal causation) in relation to a grounding standard, that is, the speed of light *[C]* (see Kuhn 1977:26–27).

One of the more dramatic examples of subatomic patterning is to be found in the recently established Bell's theorem (Davies and Brown 1986), which states that when two particles are emitted in opposite directions and the properties of one of them are measured, the properties of the other will be found to be correlated or linked to the first when it too is measured. Even if the distance between the two particles is that of light-years, the patterned relationship will hold. Such findings suggest that physical events occurring at subatomic levels have implications for the broader reaches of the macroscopic world of events as well (Stapp 1975). Although it has been common for advocates of a more Newtonian view of human beings to suggest that subatomic theories have little or no relevance for our everyday, macroscopic world (see Dennett 1984:67, for an example of this attitude), the drift of speculation in physics today seems clearly to be that there are direct theoretical links between the findings at the subatomic level and the actions of human beings (see, e.g., Bohm 1987). The linking tie here is clearly that of formal causation — the influence of a wide-ranging pattern on the elements within its purview.

We might find in the contrary actions of subatomic particles some evidence for oppositionality "in nature." Today there is also speculation in physics on matter and antimatter. We have entropy (disorder, sameness) and negentropy (order, difference) being discussed. But this would seem to be pressing the point, particularly since we see dialectical or oppositional reasoning as making greatest sense as an introspectively construed process. In light of this latter suggestion, it is interesting to note that in the cognitive activity of famous physicists we frequently find significant indications of oppositional strategizing taking place. It is known, for example, that Bohr was heavily influenced by the dialectical aspects of Kierkegaardian philosophy (Feuer 1974:ch. 2). Bohr apparently held to a dialectical interpretation of truth in which there were both trivial opposites, suggestive of nonsense, but also profound oppositions that could not be dismissed just because they violated the law of contradiction. Bohr's style of working was to pace up and down, arguing with both himself and a fellow physicist whom he had persuaded to assist him in thinking through some problem. He constantly searched for contraries or contradictions and it is said his persistent attacks on the received views of physics often left his colleague, who was in the position of defending the status quo, exhausted at the end of a creative session (Holton 1973:148).

Holton has pointed to Einstein's brilliant exploitation of polarities in his theoretical efforts: "The most evident example [of polarity] is the presence and use of contrast in the original relativity theory paper itself; we find there both the positivism of the instrumentalist and operationist variety, which Einstein uses in defining the concepts, and, on the other hand, the rational realism inherent in the a priori declaration of the two basic principles of relativity" (pp. 361–362). Critics charged that Einstein had taken both a rationalistic and an extreme empiricistic position at the same time— a charge to which he agreed. Further evidence for Einstein's dialectical reasoning can be seen in his contribution to the wave-particle duality issue regarding light. Indeed, his famous formula (cited above) combines the seeming opposites of kinetic energy and stationary mass.

The point being made here is that even if we do not wish to attribute oppositionality to nature per se, there is ample evidence that physicists, as human reasoners, have relied on the insights to be gleaned in dialectical patterns of *meaning* that they create in their cognitive efforts. Note that here again we return to a formal-cause conception, because if meanings are united oppositionally the resultant organization is obviously *not* a building block arrangement of unipolar singularities "adding up" to this totality— as the British associationistic viewpoint contends. If we think of reality as patterned cognitively through opposition—both trivial and profound meanings resulting, in the Bohrian sense—then we have a basis for thinking of the physicist qua human reasoner as a predicator. This human reasoner can affirm the meanings that may or may not be "in" reality at present (i.e., contradicting what "is" the case) but that may be "put onto" reality speculatively, as a possibility worthy of further investigation and/or creation.

Kuhn's (1970) widely cited historical analysis in which so-called "paradigms" are found to influence how a scientist in any era will think about data, study it, and write up the empirical findings rests ultimately on a formal-cause conception. Holton (1973:65) refers to these precedents as "themata" and believes there are really not too many such patterned assumptions that have been used in science to date. Pepper (1970) has referred to such precedents as "root metaphors." The dynamic process of how it is that scientists rely on paradigms, themata, or root metaphors is surely consistent with a view of human reasoning as predicational. These formal-cause patterns that influence a line of thought function as the "that" (formal cause) "for the sake of which" (final cause) the physicist fulfills a professional role.

It should not be thought that modern physics was the only science to recognize the central role of formal-cause conceptions in its subject matter. Prigogine and Stengers have shown how chemistry as a discipline cannot be treated in mechanical (i.e., efficient-cause) terms (1984:136–137). We cannot think of chemical actions as reversible, as when one throws a machine into reverse to bring it back to the same point at which it was before. Irreversible processes are stochastic and emergent, so that what they become is not traceable to what they previously were. Processes such as chemical clocks work "as a whole" (p. 148) in that molecules form into concerted patterns suggesting that a kind of precedently organizing flow of communication underlies them. Irreversible processes can even bring patterned order out of previous chaos. Hence, the past does not "shape" the future in the unidirectional, efficient-cause manner called for by the Newtonians.

In the realm of mathematics we find the emerging field of "chaos" suggesting that out of randomness and unpredictability patterned order can occur. Structures arise from randomness and patterns emerge from the unpredictability of nonlinear systems (Gleick 1988:44). References to a form of "stable chaos" (ibid.:55) in the functioning of self-organizing systems challenge our traditional conceptions of natural (Newtonian) laws, which are supposed to be stable and always predictable (nonchaotic). But chaotic outcomes in all corners of the natural order are to be found, and they are both stable and structured. An oppositional contrast is suggested in the aesthetics of such natural products, as follows: "Our feeling for beauty is inspired by the harmonious arrangement of order and disorder as it occurs in natural objects—in clouds, trees, mountain ranges, and snow crystals" (ibid.:117).

In biology we frequently find life itself being described as due to patterns of logic and communication, both between and within living organisms (Jacob 1976). Jonas (1966) argues that the most important feature of any living entity is its metabolic capacity to maintain an identity of form over time. Still other biologists speak of life as a process of centeredness or inward harmony in an evolving organism (e.g., Portmann's work as presented in Grene 1965). Biologists also like to stress the fact that living systems have a past in that their form has taken shape over long periods of selective evolution. This form has survival value and hence takes on significant importance in any consideration of the total biological system as it is situated in its environment. The form transcends the individual organism taking influence from it. Sheldrake (1989) refers to such forms as morphic fields, which resonate upon the structure and the behavior of living organisms: "Morphic resonance involves the transmission of formatic causal influences through both space and time" (p. xix). A comparable notion of "formative" causation in physics is suggested by Bohm (1980:13).

We see a changing role and self-image for the contemporary scientist in all of this. Scientists no longer trace smaller and smaller elements in hopes of getting to that basic substrate at which the blind forces of nature supposedly "whip up" such elements into lawful Newtonian regularities. Scientists today are beginning to suspect that there may *first* be (precedent) patterns or orders in nature—usually described as "fields"—and only secondarily does the motion of events come about as a reflection of this existing organization. More amazingly, some of this order is supplied by the conceptual *participation* of the scientist with nature. No longer is "nature" being construed as a separate and distinct "other" as the principle of extraspection calls for. Scientists engage in a dialogue with nature, and their predications influence what will emerge from this dialogue. As Prigogine and Stengers sum it up: "Out of the dialogue with nature initiated by classical [Newtonian] science, with its view of nature as an automaton [mechanism], has grown a quite different view in which the activity of questioning nature is part of its intrinsic activity" (1984:301).

It is evident that the four issues raised by the Chinese room problem of chapter 1 have been with us for a long time. The slipping and sliding back and forth from an introspective to an extraspective understanding of what one is attempting to describe generates much confusion. Introspective accounts invite formal and final causation, since they invariably take on predicational overtones in which the meaning under affirmation is the focus of concern. Extraspective accounts invite material and efficient causation, in which a succession of palpably observable items is moved along unidirectionally in the mediational sense. Although there have been extraspective formulations of a dialectical nature (e.g., Hegel, Marx; see Rychlak 1981a:283–290), the contribution that we find such oppositional reasoning making to an understanding of human cognition is totally introspective, as in the formulations of Kant. Meaning is an essential ingredient here, in that it is through a transcending dialectical capacity that the human being can derive implications to the opposite of what he or she is now thinking.

Extraspective formulations are more likely to generate a demonstrative strategy of explanation, as in the British tradition where sheer frequency of contact with an item takes precedence over meaning per se. That is, meaning, a formal cause concept of patterned relations, is replaced by a tabulation of efficiently caused contacts between items—termed an "association." This tabulation of contiguous items is what matters in the ongoing, linear mediational process that is said to result. Newtonian physicists did not attribute meaningful understanding to the stars, and Newtonian psychologists did not attribute meaningful purpose to human beings. The Baconian criticism was seen to hold up rather well in countering the latter efforts to reduce a final-cause conception (purpose) to a string of efficient causation.

But the main lesson of this chapter is that traditional Newtonian mechanism has proven inadequate to deal with the fundamental substrate of material reality, to which it had hoped to reduce everything. Instead of finding that a billiard-ball kind of (efficient) causation is at the base of physical matter, scientists have found a patterning of events, and most profoundly of all, a winding of their own mental patterns into these events as participators in creating the knowledge that results. Modern scientists fully recognize their role as predicators of that which they study. Because formal causation is the "that" in the "that for the sake of which" phrasing of final causation, it is a perfect link between the scientist as observer and the data under observation.

Hence, we can view the construing scientist as framing a "that" for the sake of which he or she then brings to bear a line of theoretical explanation and empirical study. This formal-cause pattern may actually be observable in a controlled experiment, as in the case of observing the phenomenon of light. Another scientist, looking at the identical phenomenon from a different "that" assumption, is also bringing to bear a line of investigation. Since part of what will be found depends on the meaning of the "that" under predication by these respective scientists, it is not a contradiction of the merit of science to find that two different but complementary findings may result: light as particles, light as waves. Different predicating assumptions can result in different "realities."

The Baconian criticism does not hold in this instance because the scientist's precedent assumptions *make a significant difference* in the kind of knowledge that results, as well as in our understanding of the nature of the process that brings this knowledge about. We cannot understand what has been found empirically without taking such precedent (formal-final cause) meanings into consideration. The same can be said for any attempt to account for a human being. We require all four of Aristotle's causal predicates to do the job. People are made of flesh, bone, and blood (material-cause predicates). They expend energy in different physiobiological processes (efficient-cause predicates) as they behave. They take on patterned shapes and habitual styles of behavior that are readily discernible by the interested observer (formal-cause predicates). And, we now argue in opposition to the Baconian criticism, they have plans and intentions "for the sake of which" (final-cause predicates) their behavior is determined. These plans and/or intentions are "thats," hence, formal-cause predicates as well.

Bacon acknowledged a role for introspective formulations like purpose, as in his recognition that formal and final causation entered into metaphysical analyses. Hence, I think that if he were present today, in this age of the scientific study of human beings, he would not object to the use of formal-final cause description in the human sciences—where they do make a difference! Stated another way, his criticism holds for the extraspective form of telic description that Aristotle employed but *not* the introspective variety! And predication is in its essence an introspective formulation of human reason. There are significant implications here for artificial intelligence, which lays claim to capturing such traditionally introspective conceptions as purpose, agency, and intention in the behavior of machines. We will want to keep the Baconian criticism in mind as we delve deeper into the precise nature of artificial intelligence. Chapter 3 begins with a consideration of what it means to say that computer technologies "simulate" human reason or cognition.

3.
The Many Faces of Cognitive Simulation

The considered opinion seems to be that the cognitive revolution we are studying began in the 1955–1960 period, although it had mathematical and technical precedents trailing back to the nineteenth century (for historical overviews see Gardner 1985; Newell and Simon 1972:873–889). Gardner (1985) virtually traces the specific onset of the revolution to an institute sponsored by the Rockefeller Foundation that was held at Dartmouth College in the summer of 1956. One of the organizers of this conference, John McCarthy, is given credit for coining the phrase "artificial intelligence" (AI) [ibid.:138–139]. Others attending included Marvin Minsky, Allen Newell, Claude Shannon, and Herbert A. Simon, all of whom were to become leading figures in AI. Simon was the first to see the immense possibilities that AI held for psychology. In 1957 he predicted that "within ten years most theories in psychology will take the form of computer programs, or of qualitative statements about the characteristics of computer programs" (Dreyfus 1979:82).

Newell and Simon (1972) thought of their work as the study of "complex information processing," as well as the "simulation of cognitive processes" (Simon 1985:7). This idea of a *simulation* (a pretension, having the external characteristics of) was central to Simon's theoretical outlook. The artificial "thinker" (computer) could be studied as it simulated the natural "thinker" (human being). In time, Simon was to list four criteria for identifying artificial objects: Artificial things (1) are synthesized by human beings; (2) imitate natural things but lack something that they have; (3) can be characterized in terms of functions, adaptations, and goals; and (4) can be discussed in terms of imperatives, as well as descriptives (p. 8). With these points in mind, Simon concludes that "psychology is a science of the artificial" (p. 89).

Initially, Minsky and his colleagues did not claim to be simulators of human reasoning. Their professed goal was to build machines that were intelligent without claiming to make them humanoid (Dreyfus 1979:18). However, as the years slipped by, Minsky has also seen the implications that AI holds for psychology, so that today we find him proposing theoretical accounts of the human mind drawn from the theories of AI (e.g., Minsky 1986).

Psychologists were much quicker to follow Simon's lead if not to fulfill his prophecy. Miller, Galanter, and Pribram published *Plans and the Structure of Behavior* in 1960, and this important effort showed many psychologists how to adapt the language of AI to the study of human behavior. Mandler (1985:16) has suggested that the reason AI theory was so readily accepted at that time in psychology was that behaviorism was "dying." He also observed in passing that there may be a fundamental affinity between the older S-R models and the input-output models of AI (p. 21), making it easy for psychologists to switch terminology from what we now recognize as one efficient-cause concept to another.

We should not get the false impression that all cognitive psychologists were ready converts to AI theory. There have been detractors as well as supporters of the computer analogue in cognitive psychology. On the positive side of the ledger we have Mandler (1985), who says that the present cognitive psychology or human information processing (he equates the two, see p. 21) "is or is well on its way to becoming mainstream psychology" (p. 17). Massaro has suggested that "at a fundamental level, the computer metaphor represents a solution to the mind-body problem" (1986:73). And Anderson believes that using a computer analogy enables the psychologist to view the cognitive system as "a rich and complex programming language with many hardwired features" (1983:41).

But on the negative side of the ledger, Neisser has suggested that "Unlike men, 'artificially intelligent' programs tend to be single-minded, undistractable, and unemotional" (1967:9). Neisser goes on to suggest that if his account of cognition is correct it will not be simulated for a long time to come. Coulter has concluded that the computational approach of AI to the study of cognition "is misleading as a source of conceptual tools and either false or incoherent as a way of overcoming the classical problems of the behavioural sciences with the concept of the mental" (1983:161). And, as we noted earlier, Tulving has criticized the computer as a complete model for human beings because it lacks episodic memory (1983:53).

These are trenchant criticisms, and they suggest that at least some cognitive psychologists believe that the tables have turned on them. It is becoming difficult to tell the simulator from the simulated. Is the machine simulating the human being, or is it the other way around? If Simon and Mandler can so confidently state that information processing or AI theory "is" or soon will be all that there is to psychology, then it follows that the machine and not the person is the "simulated." Psychologists will routinely predicate their explanations of human behavior on AI concepts to meet the descriptive requirements of their science. There are obvious dangers here, and not the least of the problems likely to arise is a recrudescence of the grounds for leveling a Baconian criticism at psychology. For example, if psychologists attempt to explain something like human agency or free will in terms of extraspectively framed AI concepts, then it would follow that they would be doing what Aristotle did in ascribing final-cause characteristics to a natural process like leaves, supposedly purposively shading fruit on the limbs of trees. Does the ascription of teleological functions really add to our understanding of how the AI machine works? If not, then we are subject to the Baconian criticism.

Of course, the AI enthusiasts may claim—as indeed they often do claim—that the computer *is* a teleological device (see chapter 6). There may be aspects of the computing process that account for what agency is supposedly all about. Doubtless Massaro had such an idea in mind when he suggested that the computer metaphor has solved the mind-body problem. Claims of this type must be studied in detail before we accept them as valid. It therefore behooves the serious student of human nature to look carefully into the whole question of the suitability of the computer analogue in human description. We begin this effort with an examination of the first question that should occur to the cognitive theorist considering employment of the computer as a model for the person: "What are we specifically simulating when we rely on the computer analogue of AI?" There are five corollary questions flowing from this general query. These five issues will be used as the framework for chapter 3.

Are We Simulating the Bios or the Logos?

Massaro has hopes for a solution to the mind-body problem because he believes that the computer analogue requires both a physical and a psychological description for it to be fully encompassed (1986:81). The physical side to the computer is its *hardware*, the electronic transistors and switches that go to make it a machine. When Charles Babbage (1791–1871) first designed a thinking machine, his mechanical rather than electrical design was influenced by the even earlier weaving looms, which relied on various punched cards to "direct" the actions of the loom in the sense that they dictated the pattern of weaving that the various threads would combine into. Babbage believed that a single machine could be manufactured that would calculate any set of mathematical operations. Such a general-purpose computer would be capable of playing chess. Time was to prove him correct, for in the 1930s Alan M. Turing proved mathematically that Babbage's chess-playing machine was feasible (Dorf 1974). John von Neumann added the concept of a stored program that could be housed in a computer's internal "memory." The unique contribution of the program, its particular directedness on the course of information processing was termed the *software*.

If we think of the computer's hardware as simulating something about human beings then we must be thinking of the biophysical aspects of the human body—or the *Bios*, as we may call it. Our theoretical formulations would rely in large measure on predications based on material and probably efficient causality. But what about the software that directs the electromechanical processes of the hardware? In this case we would probably be dealing with an effective procedure or *algorithm*, which is a rule or set of rules enabling the solution of some delimited task (e.g., a formula for calculating the mean of a distribution of test scores). Is this rule-following process to be understood in the same sense as the *Bios*? Massaro admits that even if we knew the neurophysiologic mechanism of something like the brain, this would not tell us a great deal about the algorithms that the brain might be using to solve problems (1986:81). He concludes: "Thus, it is meaningful to understand the software or programming level regardless of the biological or electronic structure it is instantiated on" (p. 82). A moment's reflection will establish that the software deals with the plan, strategy, or "that (reason) for the sake of which" the AI processing is being carried out. As such, the software is necessarily predicated by formal and final causes, which sets it off from the hardware. But whose formal-final causes are these—the software's per se or the *author* of the pattern electronically recorded on the tape of the software (i.e., a person's intentions as designed into the software)?

Given this distinction between the software as a product of a person's intentions and the software as a patterned director of machine processes, we might wonder how much of a solution to the mind-body problem the computer analogue really is. Software seems more in the realm of the logical—or the *Logos*, as we might call it—than in the realm of the physical *Bios*. And the field of psychology is battle scarred by the historical debates over which one of these two realms of explanation takes precedence in the understanding of human behavior—mind *(Logos)* or body *(Bios)*. The question posed by this section takes us back onto this battleground by asking which of these two relatively independent processes are we primarily simulating in AI. We might say that the *Bios* is under simulation because obviously there is far from a correspondence between the computer as a technological device and the physicochemical structure of the central nervous system, which may "work" more like an analogue than a digital computer (not to mention the possible role of chemical reactions in neural transmission going completely beyond computer technology; see Dreyfus 1979:161).

Even so, a cognitive network theorist like Anderson takes inspiration from a belief that his theoretical concepts are at least suggested by the structure of the nervous system. In presenting his activation conception, Anderson argues as follows: "There are numerous reasons for believing in a spreading activation mechanism. One is that it corresponds to our understandings of neurophysiology. The neurons and their connections can be thought of as a network. The rate of firing of a neuron can be thought of as the level of activation" (1983:86). It is clear that Anderson believes his job as a psychological scientist is to simulate the *Bios*. Setting aside now the fact that many experts in neurophysiology would reject Anderson's equating of neurons with programmed networks (e.g., Granit 1977:206; see also chapter 8), there is another point to consider regarding what we are out to simulate in AI. Thus, Hofstadter, a leading spokesperson for AI, tells us that at least some of his colleagues have no desire to tie their simulations down to the *Bios*:

Artificial Intelligence research is not aimed at simulating neural networks, for it is based on another kind of faith: that probably there are significant features of intelligence which can be floated on top of entirely different sorts of substrates than those of organic brains.... The idea that, if AI is to be achieved, the actual hardware of the brain might one day have to be simulated or duplicated is, for the present at least, quite an abhorrent thought to many AI workers. (1980:572)

This reference to "simulated or duplicated" is pregnant with implications for the AI theorist. To duplicate is *not* to simulate but to recreate the very thing that is under scrutiny. As Massaro observes: "A model should represent the phenomenon of interest in an informative manner. It should not be identical to the phenomenon; if it were, then it would no longer be a model but would be the phenomenon. We want a model or simulation, not the actual phenomenon or a duplication" (1986:80). Given this understanding of a model, an interesting problem arises for Simon (1985): he first notes in agreement with Anderson that certain properties of the computer's mechanical devices are "shared by the human central nervous system" (p. 24). But then later, in discussing how human beings solve a cryptarithmetic task that he uses in his research, Simon finds himself in another realm of study for he notes that as we observe the learning strategies of people in this task: "We should certainly be unlikely to learn anything specific about the neurological characteristics of the central nervous system, nor would the specifics of that system be relevant to his [the subject's] behavior, beyond placing bounds on the possible" (pp. 71–72).

If all the central nervous system can do at this point is to set limits on the reasoning capacity (e.g., a brain-damaged person would have difficulty completing the task), then is not Simon admitting that he is studying a *Logos* rather than a *Bios* process? And if a person uses some discernible logical strategy to solve a problem, and a machine is then made that duplicates this problem-solving strategy, is the machine simulating the *logic* or the *mechanical processes* acting as instrumentalities to carry out the logical progression? Simon has told us (refer above) that an artificial process merely imitates what it is simulating but that there are always one or more things *lacking* in this simulation. But what is lacking in the logic of a machine's "reasoning" that is present in the human being's reasoning processes? It is the thesis of the present book that there are decided omissions in the computer analogue when compared to human reasoning, but strictly speaking, when we consider just the *Logos* in the way that it is studied by AI theorists, we could say that there is none of the simulation occurring here that is true in the realm of the *Bios*. In the realm of the *Logos*, there is only duplication taking place!

All of which focuses our attention on the matter of what we take to be the *process* under study in AI and what we take to be the *content(s)* of that process. When Minsky says "Whenever we speak about a mind, we're speaking of the processes that carry our brains from state to state" (1986:287) he must be viewing the *Logos* as a content of the *Bios* process. This assumptive predication frames his entire approach to an understanding of cognition. Yet, there is nothing discernible that ties the *Bios* to the *Logos* in the manner suggested by Minsky. Clearly, the logical (including the psychological) is *not* merely a content within the biological processes of the body. We can enumerate the course of a logical process through concepts such as predication, deduction, inference, tautology, and so forth, without reference to biological processes like the firing of cortical neurons. Indeed, the logical process would be unaffected by the nature of the biological process. This establishes that the *Bios* does not "produce" the *Logos*.

The physical being of a person surely makes the recognition of what we call mind possible, and, as Simon has noted, sets certain limits on what we can do with this *Logos* process. We require cortical neurons, as well as other bodily structures, in order to be capable of functioning in the (psycho-) logical realm, just as we require limbs to climb or teeth to chew. But logical processes also make possible the knowledge of physical structures like neurons in the first place. To rank one process over the other simply reflects the bias of the theorist in question. It is not only possible but also necessary to think of the *Logos* as a separate process, having its distinctive contents that are open to study in a manner directly comparable to the process we have been calling the *Bios*. It seems only reasonable for AI theorists to get clearly in mind which of these processes they are going to study and whether this study is a simulation or a duplication of human behavior.

Before leaving this section I should comment on the fact that the use of algorithms can give one the impression that a machine processing them is predicating rather than simply matching information. For example, suppose we wrote the following algorithmic rule into a program for the machine: "If the first number in a series of numbers is larger than the second, add the first to the second; if the first number is smaller than the second, subtract the first from the second." In carrying out this effective procedure the numbers processed might be low in value (3, 4, 8, 6, etc.) or high in value (1023, 1384, 1575, 1126, etc.). It might appear, therefore, that this is an example of a broad principle (the algorithmic rule) being applied in turn to specific instances of low and high numbers, respectively. Is this an example of predication? No, it is an example of "matching."

Actually, what we have here is a repetition or *iteration* of the *same* effective procedure without any predicating sense of its negation or the broader possibilities open to its change. The same algorithm is being *matched* to different numbers. We could write a similar matching procedure into the rule book for the person in the Chinese room. We could instruct the person that when two squiggles follow one squoggle, go to the basket in which there are now three figures combined into one unit, as a squiggle-squiggle-squoggle. And if the first is a squoggle followed by two squiggles, go to the basket holding figures with a lone squiggle affixed. These combinations could then be applied to longer or shorter strings of different types of Chinese figures, reflecting greater or lesser complexity. It makes no difference because the effective procedure is identical in each of the applications. No predication is involved. A "position" is not being taken within an oppositional context. A matching procedure is all that controls the sequence of events. This takes us to our next question.

Are We Simulating the Meaning of Information or the Control That Such Information Has on Behavior?

This question takes root from ideas advanced by two of the founders of information-processing theory, Claude Shannon and Norbert Wiener. As noted earlier, Shannon drew a clear distinction between information per se and the engineering process of a machine; the one need not have any relation to the other (Shannon and Weaver 1962:3, 99). Engineering processing deals in *bits*, or the halving of information per se. There is a reduction in uncertainty here, a halving of the possible routes that a signal might take in a network. Each bit tells us the amount of information needed to select one electrical signal from two equally probable. To speak of bits of information in this sense has to do with the control of information flow and *not* with the particular meanings under predication or the meaningful elaboration of that flow (Dreyfus 1979:165).

Wiener coined the term *cybernetics,* which is based on a Greek root meaning "steersman," for he wanted to convey the fact that a machine with input, output, and feedback capacities could direct or control its behavior. In fact, such a machine could also control the behavior of others through communication. Communication and control are very much alike, says Wiener, because: "When I control the actions of another person, I communicate a message to him, and although this message is in the imperative mood, the technique of communication does not differ from that of a message of fact. Furthermore, if my control is to be effective I must take cognizance of any messages from him which may indicate that the order is understood and has been obeyed" (1954:16).

Wiener goes on to say that the aim of cybernetics is to develop a theoretical language and techniques of investigation enabling scientists to study the problem of "control and communication in general" (p. 17).

There is potential for confusion here in the study of people, because in communicating with others, human beings employ a symbol system, a language that encompasses certain rules of syntax but also semantic (meaning) considerations including logical relationships. But now, if all that mentation comes down to is the processing of bits of information, regardless of what meanings are being decided on for inclusion and elaboration, then we find ourselves raising the question of this section. What are we simulating—controls over behavior or the framing and extension of meanings? Do language terms reflect meanings that are predicated by the language user? Or are language symbols merely mediating signals without meaning? Harking back to our process versus content distinction, is language a process per se, with its distinctive contents framed as meanings in the words and sentences used during linguistic expression? Or is language simply a content of some "other" process, such as an underlying mechanical process that controls it without taking meaning into consideration?

Stich vigorously defends the latter thesis: "As I see it, the notion of 'content' [meaning] or the folk psychological strategy of identifying a mental state by appeal to a 'content sentence,' despite all its utility in the workaday business of dealing with our fellow creatures, is simply out of place when our goal is the construction of a scientific theory about the mechanisms underlying behavior" (1986:5–6). Stich is particularly critical of the "folk" psychological notions (content sentences) encompassing intentionality (p. 6). On the other side of the coin, Weizenbaum has stressed that in writing a machine program to simulate human conversation the basic task involves guessing the intentional content of the ongoing dialogue (1976:190). From this perspective, the meanings under extension dialogically are of primary importance.

To demonstrate how this matter of control versus meaning expression is reflected in the cognitive literature, we can point to the concept of a "plan" proposed by Miller, Galanter, and Pribram (1960). These authors suggest that a plan *"is any hierarchical process in the organism that can control the order in which a sequence of operations is to be performed"* (p. 16; italics in the original). As we read their account, it becomes ever clearer that our cognitive scientists are more concerned with plans as controlling guidance mechanisms (ibid.:37) than as meaningful strategies to be used heuristically in organizing experience. They begin with the presumption that a plan "for an organism [is] essentially the same as a program for a computer" (p. 16). Plans are frozen structures guiding the person's behavior, and an intention is the uncompleted parts of a plan *"whose execution has already begun"* [italics in original] (p. 61).

A predicational theorist thinks of intentions as formal-final "causes" and not as the "effects" of a controlling plan. Intentions are preliminary to the framing of a plan, which is a formal-cause pattern or rule reflecting the precedent intended meanings of the creative agent after they have been perfected and sketched into a final strategy for action. The execution of the plan would therefore be an instrumentality or efficient-cause enactment of what the plan's framer had meaningfully intended (which could be thought of as a *Bios* enactment of a *Logos* product). But Miller, Galanter, and Pribram are trying to stay within the strictures of the computer analogue. Plans as programs are always "given," so that what the machine is to do in light of these programs/plans becomes a fait accompli. The plans (programs) are never intended. We may think of the plan as a formal-cause pattern in this case, but the way in which it is carried out makes intentionality an instrumentality, an efficient-cause sequence of linear actions in the style of the mediational process.

In chapter 1 the distinction between a law and a rule is drawn. This distinction has relevance for the present question. Though both rules and laws are formal-cause (patterned) conceptions, they are not the same thing. Laws seem more related to the *Bios* realm and rules to the *Logos* realm. Also, we are unable to control or manipulate logical processes in the same way that we control processes in the biophysical realm. Predicated meanings (contents) can be supplanted, but the precedent-sequacious force of deduction, inference, and so on (process), is not amenable to control in the way that we direct our automobiles about or take medications to correct a physical ailment. People rarely reach their normal, spontaneous decisions in the same way that a mathematician or statistician would decide things, and they can easily be led astray by irrelevancies in framing grounds for a decision, but there is always a detectable and unmanipulated logical order to be seen in their erratic and unsound course of mentation (Kahnemann, Slovic, and Tversky 1982). Often, this logical order of reason is dialectical (Lamiell 1987). The controls applicable to the *Bios* are irrelevant to the *Logos*, owing to the fact that we are considering totally different realms of determinism, the former relying on material/efficient and the latter on formal/final causation (for a discussion of determinism in light of causal meanings, see Rychlak 1981b:262–268).

The law-versus-rule distinction also has important implications for how we describe mechanical processes taking place. Laws move us to an extraspective perspective, since they are such ironclad regularities. Rules, on the other hand, invite an introspective understanding since they are more likely to be relative formulations, based on certain assumptions or viewpoints. Thus, the planets move about the sun in their orbits, says Dreyfus (1979:167), but though they can be conceptualized and tracked in terms of mathematical equations (rules) this does not mean that they are "computing" differential equations as they carry forward their lawful regularities in space. The same holds true for our brains. They may function according to biochemical laws *(Bios)* [Bunge 1980:161], but the thought being conducted in light of such inflexible regularities may be more akin to rule following *(Logos)*. Transferring this line of argument to the computer, we would expect to find a role for meaning and rule following in the software but not the hardware, just as we did in the person's rule following but not the machine-like processes of the Chinese room. If the software is indeed rule following then there should be some interest among the AI fraternity in such simulations. This takes us to our next question.

Are We Simulating the Complete Logic Employed by Human Beings? Are the Speed and Accuracy of Logical Reasoning a Vital Simulation?

Overlooking now the fact that logical processes in computer simulations are *not* being simulated but rather being duplicated (refer above), there is still a legitimate question to consider regarding the specific nature of the logic being duplicated by the computer. We all know that computers "compute," which means that they employ some kind of mathematical rule-following process (the algorithm) to accomplish their simulations of human thinking. In chapter 1, we traced the mathematics lying at the root of computer processing to George Boole (1815–1864), who in effect analogized between the symbolic calculations of algebra and such logical processes as syllogistic reasoning (Boole 1854/1958; Gardner 1958:143). Though Boole did not think of logic as a branch of mathematics, in due course and thanks to his lead, Whitehead and Russell (1963) were to prove that mathematics and logic were tautological activities. The question arises, what kind of logic are we talking about here?

In my presentation of Boolean disjunction (see p. 12), I noted that classes are always divisible into one or the other, and never "both." This makes it possible to equate a decision such as "true-false" with the electronic switch that is either "on" (true) or "off" (false). This was Shannon's (1938) insight. Subsequently, McCulloch and Pitts (1943) argued that the all-or-none firing properties of nerve cells could be construed in this binary fashion. An active or firing neuron was "on" and an inactive neuron was "off." McCulloch and Pitts perfected the neural network conception and tried to directly map the logic of the machine on the structure of the central nervous system (leading to the kind of confidence placed in the computer analogue as a map for the central nervous system that we saw Anderson expressing, above).

It is ironic that whereas the word *algebra* is a derivation from the title of a famous Arabic text bearing the meaning of "science of the reunion and the opposition" (Eves 1953:195), in Boolean algebra we are presented with a style of thought that separates one classification *(x)* from another *(y)* without consideration of an implicit bond of opposition that would unite the meanings of both classes (*x* delimiting the meaning of *y* and vice versa). Boole's interpretation of disjunction is, in effect, a reaffirmation of the law of contradiction (see p. 22). It is clear, therefore, that the binary strategy flowing from Boolean algebra is what Aristotle would have called a *demonstrative* style of reasoning (see Boole 1854/1958:49). The major premise is either taken on as a true premise (an "on" switch in the machine or an active firing in the neural network) or it is dismissed as a false premise (an "off" switch in the machine or an inactive neuron in the network). The term "digit" of the phrase "digital computer" is taken from the Latin for "finger," implying that a discrete unipolarity in meaning can be pointed to as a singular instance (either/or) in every case. There is no tie of Socratic oppositionality to unite the true (on, active) side to the false (off, inactive) side as implicitly contrasting meanings (x and y jointly). The one-and-many principle is consequently dismissed in this formulation. As we have already found in chapter 1, Boolean mathematical theory and the computing logic that is based on it is *never* in the *dialectical* mode.

Most definitions of the basic logical process draw from the concepts of inference (Reese 1980:309) and implication (Quine 1981:135), each of which has to do with how the person frames the premises and extends meanings based on such precedents. Inferences or implications are always extended from some precedent organization of meaning, and logicians are frequently concerned with the validity of such—ultimately, predicating—meanings and the course of reasoning that they influence (imply, infer). Indeed, the very word *logos*, as coined by Heraclitus in the B.C. world, conveyed this sense of an organized pattern of meaning or "rationale" through which experience could be understood. A demonstrative logic is based on the assumption that predications fall into distinctive, unipolar meanings, like separate camp grounds where one might pitch a tent. You cannot pitch your tent in two locations at once.

On the other hand, a dialectical logic presumes that what is affirmed as a premise has been drawn from a complex of meanings united at some point through oppositionality. The *psycho*-logic of dialectical reasoning has it that a tent *can* be pitched on two locations at once. All we have to do is fold the location "there" onto the location "here" to unite them on common ground, much as we would fold a map over to bring New York and London together between our fingertips. This maneuver may be impossible in the real world, but it is always a possibility in the dialectically free thought of imagination. Einstein's concepts as framed by his notorious thought experiments were often of such fantastic magnitude, resulting on several occasions (but not all) in a new and valid understanding of the "real" world (see chapter 2). If people do reason according to a dialectical logic, drawing meanings from oppositional precedents, negating realities and proposing fantastic alternatives, then how is a psychologist to react when told by Mandler and Simon (refer above) that the demonstrative formulations of AI are the sum total of human logical reasoning? Aristotle believed that all people reason *both* demonstratively and dialectically. If we follow his lead then there seems to be a logical mode of thought missing in the grand design of AI.

How would the "1, 0" binary logic employed by a computer deal with something like opposition? Where would an exclusively demonstratively reasoning organism/machine locate the oppositionality that is fundamental to dialectical reasoning? Figure 2 presents a schematization contrasting the Boolean either-or (1, 0) form of disjunction with a non-Boolean interpretation of disjunction (encompassing "both").

Taking up the Boolean formulation at the top of figure 2 first, note that we have a small circle labeled A. Let us think of this as an affirmed item of meaning. The complement to this item is all those items that A is not, that have not been affirmed. In either-or logic, we would combine all non-A items under a common designation, symbolized by the larger circle containing several items that are *not* A. The demonstrative reasoner holds that oppositionality is one of these several items (meanings, etc.) that have *not* been affirmed as A (all those items that are non-A). Hence, to give a simple example, if A represented the word "good" then any of a number of other words might appear in the complement grouping. The word "morning" might be represented by B and "bad" would be represented by opposite-A. Hence, if we were to combine good (A) with either morning (B) or bad (opposite-A) the very same kind of process would take place in the cognizance of the reasoner. On this demonstrative formulation, "good-bad" has no special status; it is formed identically to the "good morning" combination. (I discussed this same issue less technically in chapter 1).

Dropping down to the non-Boolean disjunction in figure 2, we find that the opposite-A meaning is *not* a member of the complement grouping, for it is intrinsic to the "both" combination. As the many-and-one thesis suggests, there are always going to be meanings that delimit each other even as their significations are contrary, contradictory, or negational. Thus, in the non-Boolean view of disjunction we would find oppositionality located within the

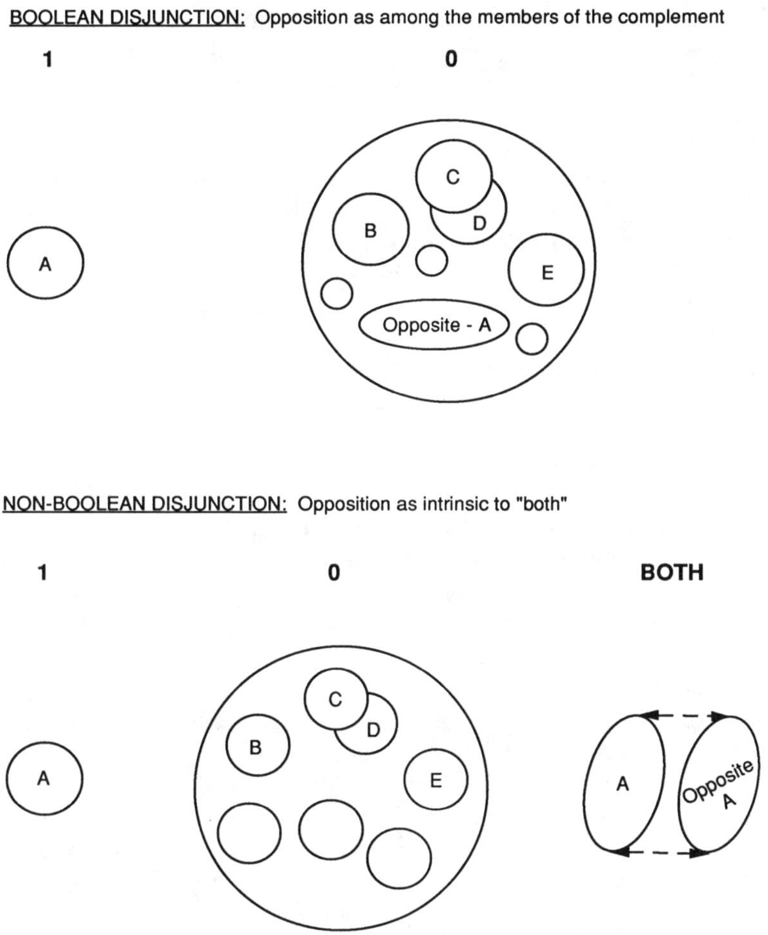

BOOLEAN DISJUNCTION: Opposition as among the members of the complement

NON-BOOLEAN DISJUNCTION: Opposition as intrinsic to "both"

Figure 2. Boolean Versus Non-Boolean Disjunction and Opposition "both" designation (we are not considering the case of "neither *A* nor opposite-*A*" at this point, but this negation would itself reflect oppositional or dialectical reasoning). In this case, "good-bad" would indeed be given a special status and would not be construed as taking place in a manner identical to the "good-morning" combination. The intrinsic tie of *A* to opposite-*A* provides us with a completely different view of the cognitive process than we are given when we follow the either-or logic that is ensconced within the hardware of the binary computer.

For example, let us take the case of sorting items out on a table top. We place item *A* on "this" side of the table and all those items that are not *A* on "that" side of the table. We might argue that one of the non-*A* items on "that" side of the table happens to be an opposite-*A* (i.e., the opposite of *A*). Although the computer, or a computer programmer reasoning in the demonstrative mode may simulate or account for opposition in this fashion, anyone reasoning in the dialectical mode would quickly recognize the inadequacy of this portrayal. As we noted in chapter 1, this placing of items on the table top is actually a form of *apposition* (putting things side by side) rather than *opposition*. The fact that opposite sides of the table are involved arises *only* in the cognizance of the person doing the sorting. Even if we wrote "good" *(A)* on a slip of paper and "bad" (opposite-*A*) on a different slip of paper, and then arrayed the slips on opposite ends of the table top, this would not capture opposition. We shall never locate the meaningful opposition "on the table top" because it has provided the very context within which items have been sorted out in the first place. Opposition is fundamental to the *Logos*, and it is through the predicational process that we bring it into our understanding.

We have a related question for this section, having to do with the speed and accuracy of human reasoning, as in the solving of problems, committing things to memory, and the recalling of such memories at a later date. Cognitive psychologists frequently use "speed of processing" (encoding, retrieving, etc.) as a dependent variable signifying the effectiveness of learning or nodal proximity in an associative network (for numerous examples, see Anderson 1985, Howard 1983). The rationale seems to be that easy-to-learn tasks are done quickly, and ideas that lie close together in a nodal network will connect rapidly as a neural impulse traverses the shorter internodal pathway. Ease of solution ties into the matter of how accurately a task is accomplished. It is significant to observe in this context that AI is dedicated to intelligence, and not to stupidity. Yet, if we are to study the full range of human behavior, it would seem that both slow and stupid behaviors require simulation in addition to rapid and correct behaviors.

Actually, speed and accuracy are characteristics of the hardware and not the software—at least, not the creation of the software. Computers carry out fantastic calculations in the blink of an eye. But the software programs that direct the steps of this process are usually achieved through a slow, grinding process of trial and error, with many false starts and repeated ad hoc corrections after completion. There are "bugs" or unforeseen problems in any new program, and the notorious "virus" can also occur, in which case a programmer, either through some colossal blunder or with hostile intent, inserts an instruction routine into a system that copies itself repeatedly to severely curtail or shut down data processing entirely (see Elmer-DeWitt 1988 for a description of a nationwide "infection" of this type).

Both Hofstadter (1980:306) and Minsky (1967) have cautioned that programs can sometimes get away from the programmer in large-scale projects where ad hoc solutions for old problems mount up, new programmers appear on the scene who know nothing of the grounds for the solutions effected, and before long there is a genuine lack of human intelligence concerning precisely how the artificial intelligence software is doing the job it was written to accomplish. Looked at from the perspective of software creation, the criteria of speed and accuracy do not seem to cover the field of human intelligence by any means. We move next to another form of simulation that is frequently cited in the AI field.

Are We Simulating a Deception, the Artfulness of a Program, To Convince Us That We Are Communicating with a Flesh-and-Blood Person When We Are Not?

One of the most common simulations attributed to the computer is based on the Turing test that was described earlier. As Weizenbaum correctly observed (p. 52), the Turing test relies on the ability of a program writer to anticipate the verbal interactions (questions, comments, etc.) of a person expressing certain intentions in the ongoing conversation with the machine. The programmer has to play two roles in the anticipated course of meaning expression, so that a convincing or even a misleading reply will be forthcoming at the proper point in the conversation. Recall that in the original test, an interrogator *(C)* is attempting to decide the sex of two individuals *(A* and *B)*, when in fact one of them is a machine *(A)*. The program writer, the human being who is strategizing this exchange in the first place, must predicate the task rather thoroughly by anticipating the sorts of questions likely to be put by the interrogator and devising clever answers in reply.

The interrogator, who is also a human being, can be expected to frame predicate assumptions regarding the plausibility of such answers, the continuity of the ongoing exchange, the implications and inferences of what is being stated, and so forth. This can all be anticipated in imagination by program writers, who in effect place themselves in the role of the interrogator as the program is being written. In line with earlier comments, the simulation here is clearly in the realm of the *Logos*, but there is an additional feature of deception and possibly also gullibility on the part of the interrogator-observer. If *C* predicated the task as "identify the machine" rather than "identify the sex of the participants" we might witness a completely different line of questioning taking place, which in turn would require the programmer to anticipate a number of different contingencies in the program to be written.

One of the discoveries made by those who have written programs aimed at interacting "conversationally" with human beings is that there is an amazing readiness on the part of people to anthropomorphize such programs. This tendency to treat a machine like a human being is so pervasive as to be termed a *reverse Turing test*—which we might define as follows: "Can a machine interacting with a human being avoid being anthropomorphized?" Anyone who doubts this reverse Turing test should spend time listening to those who teach courses in computer use. It is routine in such courses to hear the instructor say that the computer "wants to" do this, or will "not allow" certain alternatives to be exercised in the procedure under study. It is notoriously difficult speaking about the logical application of programs without seeming to anthropomorphize the computer in this fashion.

Why is this? Because the computer is a substantial item, a "thing" that presents the logical meanings of the program instrumentally (automatically, mechanically). What the person who is anthropomorphizing the computer is actually doing is referring to the meanings conveyed instrumentally by this machine's electronic devices, even though as Shannon has taught us, the engineering features of such devices are completely unrelated to the meanings they may or may not be conveying. Rather than refer to "the person who programmed this computer" at every turn it is easier to refer to "the computer" per se, as if the latter were predicating the meanings conveyed rather than the former. A program of conversational exchange is only as effective as the person who wrote it, who anticipated what would take place, and thought up suitable "dodges" for the program to take when an unanticipated embarrassment arises in the course of the exchange (Winograd 1980:212).

One of the more remarkable demonstrations of a reverse Turing test occurred when Weizenbaum (1976) wrote his DOCTOR program (initially named ELIZA). The script for this program was designed to play the role of a Rogerian psychotherapist who was engaging in an initial interview with a client. The person interacting with the program sits at a computer; types statements into the keyboard, which transmits to the computer's screen; and then reads the replies of the program on the screen as well. Since the Rogerian takes a so-called nondirective approach to the client, the strategy followed in this program is to rephrase statements, offer broad leads, and generally keep the conversation going based on what the human being offers as input. For example, if the person types in "I'm feeling upset" the computer would reply "Why are you feeling upset?" and so on. If something unanticipated arises, the program might direct a general lead back such as "And how did that make you feel?" or introduce a new direction such as "Tell me about your father." Once again, the program is only as good as the anticipated course of interaction written into it.

Weizenbaum did a masterful job, but even he had the unexpected verbal reply confound the program from time to time. For example, Dreyfus tells of an occasion when he was interacting with DOCTOR and was asked by the program how he felt, replying "I'm feeling happy" and then quickly adding "No, elated." At this point, DOCTOR replied with "Don't be so negative" (Dreyfus and Dreyfus 1986:71). The reason this "error" occurred is that the program followed the rule of outputting this rebuke when a "no" was input. We might observe in passing that Dreyfus' negation of an initial predication could be viewed as reflective of the dialectical mode of reasoning, a mode of logic that we now appreciate is foreign to the computer. Imagine if Dreyfus had typed "I feel terribly good" or "It's a sin to feel as good as I do." Contradictions such as these are difficult to deal with in a binary logic, and we shall meet them again when we discuss context effects in chapter 4.

In the main, DOCTOR has proven remarkably effective. People enter into the flow of conversation with the program and find their most intimate thoughts being examined and extended (as paraphrases and elaborations of what they introduce into the "conversation"). In fact, to his dismay, Weizenbaum (1976) found that people became emotionally involved with the program. His secretary, who had seen him working on the program for several months, actually asked him to leave the room once she had begun exploring her more intimate thoughts with this nondirective script (p. 6). Thanks to this tendency to humanize the computer, several psychiatrists even suggested to Weizenbaum that DOCTOR might be perfected into a form of automatic psychotherapy that could be used in general practice (p. 5). Weizenbaum was considerably sobered by his experiencing at first hand the "reckless anthropomorphization of the computer" (p. 205).

Now, whether people fail to recognize when a computer is actually involved in a typed interaction (Turing test), or whether they assign human characteristics to a machine in such an interaction when this is not warranted (reverse Turing test), we must ask ourselves what is actually at play here. Obviously, any simulation taking place at this point has *nothing* to do with machinery (hardware, the *Bios*). We are now in the realm of how it is that people frame their meaningful understanding of what is taking place in their experience. This is a predicational process, a search for the rational (or irrational) reason. A "test" of rationality here can only mean something like assessing the precedent assumptions framing the reply to a question, following a logical sequence that makes sense, or being thrown off course for some ulterior purpose that can be speculated on. We will not find the precedents to such predicate activities *in the machine* but always *in the psycho-logic of the programmer*. There is one more question to raise concerning computer simulation.

Are We Simulating the Way in Which Cognitive Representations Arise and Function in the Human Intelligence?

A word that we frequently see used in the AI literature is "representation." The vaunted intelligence of a computing machine rests in large measure on the fact that it can input and store a copy or representation of its environment, enabling it to adapt to or actually bring about changes in that environment based on programmed strategies (Miller, Galanter, and Pribram 1960:12; Newell and Simon 1972:3). The concept of "information" as used by those who are not strictly electrical engineers invariably borrows from this notion of representation. Representations as plans, schemas, scripts, and so on, are what the AI system processes. As Mandler has said: "Representation and process are the primary foci of all the cognitive disciplines, and it is symptomatic of our acceptance and their importance that we rarely hear anybody question these two foundations" (1985:10). Gardner traces this universal reliance on representation to the biological substrate: "All cognitive scientists accept the truism that mental processes are ultimately represented in the central nervous system" (1985:40).

A representation is a patterned likeness, suggesting that it is not "the" original item being copied but a product of the original item from which the likeness is drawn. We can now ask the question: Where in cognition is the original item to be found that provides the pattern for a likeness? Is this item external to the cognitive process that patterns it, or is it internal to the cognitive process, as a feature of its functioning from the outset? As we recall from chapter 1, a mediational model of behavior places the ultimate sources of a representation external to the cognitive process. Kant suggests that human beings are equipped with a priori categories of the understanding that *predicate* experience from the outset. On Kant's model, the representations in mind would be "produced" by the precedent (a priori) categories rather than by the a posteriori shapings of the environment.

This issue of precisely how representations are formed is not always confronted in AI writings. The fact of their existence seems to be sufficient evidence for the AI theorist that people "process information." We may read that computers model or represent their environment in some way that is not yet completely understood (Boden 1981:134). The representations may be said to involve a symbol system, and as we shall see in chapter 4, it is common to equate such symbolic representations with language (Boden 1977:15). Languages are learned and hence represent a posteriori knowledge. But occasionally the case is made for innate, a priori representations in a more Kantian vein (e.g., Fodor 1975). In fact, Kant is frequently invoked in the literature of AI (see, e.g., Johnson-Laird 1983:402–403; Pylyshyn 1981:170–171). If an AI theorist is working in the realm of the *Logos*, a Kantian formulation encompassing predications surely makes a good deal of sense. The person's most fundamental premises (encompassing predications) act as introspectively conceived prototypes "for the sake of which" (formal/final causation) experience is formulated into a cognitive representation. But if the AI theorist is trying to simulate the *Bios* (material/efficient causation), a more extraspective stance is going to be taken with the result that cognitive representations will be characterized as input from environmental sources. Not infrequently, the representational process is described as a computational process (e.g., Johnson-Laird 1983:12).

Dreyfus has pointed to a "knowledge representation problem" for computer programming, which arises from the fact that information is always contextually situated (1979:33). (We are dealing now with the processing of meanings and not simply electrical impulses.) What something means "depends" on how the situational circumstance is formulated. As Winograd expressed this issue, "Every speech act occurs in a context, with a background understood by speaker and hearer" (1980:231). Contextual factors are always of a wider compass than the specific information being targeted and therefore they meet our understanding of predication. In the example of the DOCTOR program, if people could be expected to answer a query about how they felt with "I feel terribly good" the machine program would require specific directives indicating that on occasion a negative meaning like "terrible" can be combined with a positive meaning like "good." The machine program is exceedingly literal because its scope is so narrow thanks to the matching procedure that it follows. This literalness of program writing takes us into the topics of chapter 4.

Our search for the meaning of cognitive simulation has been mildly frustrating albeit instructive. We have learned that it is not possible to say unequivocally what machine "simulation" means when applied to the characterization of human experience. Some of the so-called simulation depends on a logical line of reasoning, devised through careful foresight by a human being who is not limited to the demonstrative reasoning of the computer, with its Boolean restrictions on oppositionality. In concrete terms, the Turing test could not *simulate* if it were not itself founded upon a *duplication* of the logic in discourse. It is the dialogical cleverness of the programmer, anticipating the likely intentions of a fellow human being, who makes the simulation possible as a kind of language game. Computer reasoning is necessarily a fait accompli. It is "over" before it is "begun," and if the enactment of the program does not occur as expected the computer either stops working or begins to spew forth non sequiturs. Human reason has a priori features that the machine never "grasps."

The question of meaning, which is secondary to the strictly

engineering aspects of the hardware, seems to be of utmost importance in the interpretations made by people of what the computer is conveying. We found that a reverse Turing test is readily discernible in the fact that people feel compelled to anthropomorphize anything that seems to be expressing meanings as the computer does. This is just like the case of a Chinese person, standing outside the Chinese room, receiving meaningful answers to questions when the person inside the room has no meaningful intention contributing to the conversation. The former would be "anthropomorphizing" the latter, thinking that the questions sent inward were under intentional/selective reply when in fact they were "answered before they were framed" by the delimitations of the (programmed) rule book.

It is this side of human reasoning, resulting in the selective affirmation of a precedent meaning, that computer simulations never portray. Computers "match" categorical information through rule following, so that they can appear to be enacting a predicational process. But matching is not predicating, for there is no sense of the broader context in a matching. An important and essential feature of this broader context is the meaning opposite to the one under affirmation in any predication. A predicational process is always cognizant of what it is *not* meaningfully affirming and extending—the "outside of the largest Euler circle," so to speak. As "matchers," computers never have this oppositional "cognizance."

I conclude, therefore, that if the computer analogue is supposed to represent a simulation of the human being's cognitive processes, it is an incomplete model. To use the language of the final section of this chapter, the computer analogue is not a suitable representation of the full range of human reasoning. It is not wrong, but only half right, simulating the demonstrative but not the dialectical aspects of cognition. It imitates what we humans do *after* we have come to a predication encompassed in a premise (assumption, belief, etc.) on which we then act. We shall move ahead now in chapter 4 to a consideration of the efforts made by the AI fraternity to write a complete psychology based on their concept of cognitive representation.

4.
Language in Cognitive Representation

Previous to the cognitive revolution in the 1950s psychologists were reluctant to place much reliance on cognitive representations because they presumably occurred "inside" the person as mere "hypothetical constructs" and therefore were not observable as "intervening variables" (MacCorquodale and Meehl 1948). Teleological expressions of purpose and intention have in particular suffered the fate of so-called "verbal report," which refers to the linguistic statements people make about their behavior. Linguistic expression was never viewed in earlier psychological theories as the *process* under study (see chapter 3). People did not formulate and express thoughts in their linguistic expressions as the predicational process suggests. Language usage—words, phrases, sentences—were mere *contents* of the mediational process that took them in rather than created them.

When the study of artificial intelligence as cognitive science was broadened to include the field of linguistics, this simple view of what was process and what was a content of that process broke down. Linguists begin on the assumption that language is "the" process of interest (syntax, semantics, transformations, etc.), and hence they seek to study various contents of such linguistic expression (morphemes, phonemes, etc.), as well as the role that such linguistic usage plays in learning itself. As a result, there is some confusion today over the precise nature of cognitive representations. Are these representations produced by and hence cognitive contents of some "other" process, or are they reflections of a cognitive process per se? Here I first take up this question in the field of artificial intelligence and then review evidence suggesting that language, a widely cited source of such representations, is predicational.

Cognitive Representation: Content, Process, and Context

We noted in chapter 2 that the British heritage in the description of cognition drew on mediational modeling whereas Kantian theory was predicational. As an early contributor to the British view, John Locke held that at the basis of thought there were a number of *simple ideas*. These simple ideas were placed into the mind from experience, much as one might place a teacup into a cabinet (a metaphor that Locke actually used: see Cranston 1957:266). Each of these simple ideas was an atomic unity and could not be subdivided or removed from its repository in memory. Nor could a person invent or frame a new simple idea (Locke 1952:128). The mind's power could be used only to combine and recombine these simple ideas into increasingly *complex ideas*, much as one might assemble and reorganize the contents of the cabinet. The mind could halt the overt enactment of its ideas at certain times in order to accomplish this reorganization. As Locke summarized this process: "When the understanding is once stored with these simple ideas, it has the power to repeat, compare, and unite them, even to an almost infinite variety, and so can make at pleasure new complex ideas" (ibid).

Locke waged an argument against what he termed "innate ideas," as reflected in theological writings as well as traditional philosophical treatises such as the Platonic belief in universals (p. 97). Locke would also have considered the Kantian categories of the understanding to be innate ideas, contents that were "in mind" at birth when there was no basis on which to believe that such a thing could take place. Locke wanted to know how the newborn infant could have a knowledge of something like "unity versus plurality" (one of Kant's categories). How could such an idea have been acquired (i.e., taken in) before birth?

It is clear that Locke is thinking of universals or categories of the understanding as *contents* of the reasoning process, rather than as the broader reaches of the cognitive *process* per se—as a predicational explanation requires. Reasoning for Locke is akin to the cabinet structure, a process that requires idea-units to be placed into it for it to operate. Kant, on the other hand, thinks of the idea/category as the process itself, as the organizer of meanings rather than as specific meanings sequaciously extended from or "produced by" this framing organization. Locke considered ideas to include more than simply thoughts, so that the experiences of sight, hearing, tasting, and feeling also qualified as ideas (Cranston 1957:265). All such ideas in their simple form are taken in as grist for the mediational mill of thought processing. Unlike Aristotle, who believed that for every simple idea taken in a contrary idea (including a negation of the idea) can immediately be formulated, Locke had no role for oppositionality at the level of simple ideas. If opposite meanings occur, they arise as complex (higher order) ideas, brought in from experience singularly and then combined into complex oppositionality by the mediating mechanisms of the mind just like any other combination of ideas.

Locke retained an element of rationalism in his outlook, but Hume (who drew heavily from the Lockean theory of ideas; see ibid.:274) underwrote the entire cognitive structure with Newtonian mechanics as the "basic" process directing thought. The resultant model of how mind works is tailor–made for the rise of mediational theorizing in early psychology (see chapter 2). We might now ask: How do the theorists of artificial intelligence (AI) talk about the cognitive representation, which is their equivalent of the idea concept? Is this a content within or the actual reflection of an ongoing process? Newell and Simon leave little doubt on this question as they discuss the newborn child's capacities: "The kernel from which development starts—say, the neonate—already contains a genetically determined set of mechanisms of immense complexity.... Still, by common scientific assent, the emerging system is remarkably content-free, and without the powers of integrated action shown by the normal adult" (1972:7).

The Lockean conception of mind reflected here is obviously friendly to AI theories. The Boolean either/or interpretation of disjunction fits perfectly with Locke's contention that simple ideas are atomic singularities and never intrinsically connected to their opposite idea-meanings. This is how Aristotle viewed demonstrative reasoning. And since such basic ideas are received from the environment, they are in principle observable. Simon confidently summarizes the human being in Lockean terms when he opines: "*A man, viewed as a behaving system, is quite simple. The apparent complexity of his behavior over time is largely a reflection of the complexity of the environment in which he finds himself* [italics in original]" (1985:65). Anderson reminds us of the Lockean cabinet-metaphor in a summation of just how the computing process works in human cognition: "The encoding process deposits representations of the environment into working memory. The storage process deposits permanent records of temporary working-memory information into declarative memory [i.e., factual knowledge]. The retrieval process brings these records back into working memory. The match process selects productions to apply according to the content of working memory" (1983:47).

One often sees references in the AI literature to Bartlett (1958), who advanced the notion of a *scheme* that people use as a cognitive representation to interpret and understand their ongoing experience. Though a Kantian theorist might view such schematic representations as reflections of a predicational process per se, the typical explanation in the AI literature is that such frames of reference are merely contents of a cognitive mechanism. At best, they simulate what occurs *following* the affirmation of a premise in human reasoning and thus do not capture the initiating processes of such premise affirmation (see chapter 3). Alternative terms for such internal cognitive representations include *frame* (Minsky, 1986), *plan* (Miller, Galanter, and Pribram 1960), and *script* (Schank and Abelson 1977). What all of these examples of cognitive representation have in common is that they are thought of as ready-made "givens" produced by some process other than a predicational activity of the cognizing human being. They enter "whole hog" to influence the direction taken by the mediational process.

There are two concepts that AI or cognitive-science explanations bring to bear at this point: *language* and *learning*. Frequently these two factors are combined as *"the* learning of language." The thinking seems to be that if we can equate a scheme, frame, plan, etc., with a language term we can account for its existence by way of how human beings learn language. Schank and Abelson note that an important aspect of language learning "is the acquisition of scripts" (1977:222). Even so, the admitted focus in most AI explanations is not on learning per se, but on "performance" (Newell and Simon 1972:3-4), or on what is sometimes called the "processing of information." This latter phrase is imprecise, of course, because as we have seen, there is no need for meaningful information to be in the electronic "process" at all. Hence, if meaning is under consideration we may require an entirely different process to understand how it arises and is grasped by the person. Dreyfus has criticized AI theorists for not addressing the matter of how cognitive representations are learned, particularly as this relates to the problem of *context* which is so noticeable in computer programming (1979:222-223).

The context problem takes us back to chapter 3, where we found that it is necessary to provide the computer program with ad hoc instructions dealing with the case of a negative word like "terribly" being joined to a positive word like "happy." This necessity arises because of the Boolean disjunctive rule in which positivity is always positivity and negativity is always negativity, but never the twain shall meet—unless specifically noted as an exception to the rule. Machine programs must be revised with specific instructions each time something "new" like this comes up that the programmer has not anticipated. This is how some programs sometimes grow into monstrosities.

Context is by definition a "broader range" or background factor that lends meaning to some targeted event taking place within the aegis of this totality. As such, it is fundamental to the predicational process. Indeed, it would be reasonable to refer to a predicate as the *context meaning* within which the referent or target item can be placed as per the Euler circles. The context is widened even further when we appreciate that "outside the circle" is also an aspect of the context—the opposite, "non-circle" which has a meaning to be expressed in the logical process as well. This extension of meaning from a wider to a narrower delimitation we have called a precedent-sequacious logical process. Coulter summarizes the important role that context plays in the cognitions of human beings, as follows:

> Events, occasions, scenes, images, do not come to us pre-identified and captioned, parcelled up into recognisably discrete units with their associated conceptualisations emanating from them. We have no *context-independent, uniform criteria* for delineating an "event" as a discrete unitary piece of the world, nor for recognising an "occasion's" boundaries, nor a "scene's" salient features apart from *context and purpose*, no matter what it is we are calling an event, occasion or scene [italics in original] (1983:79).

The concept of a context in language usage is invariably tied to purpose. Winograd (1980:217) has noted that purpose is important at both ends of a communication. The speaker has purpose in framing utterances and the listener has a need to know the speaker's purpose, which establishes the context of the communication, in order for the message to be correctly interpreted. The unsophisticated AI theorist presumes that cognitive representations are lying about in the environment like the completed Chinese figures of chapter 1, ready for inputting without selective or purposive predication by the interpreting organism. This seems plausible enough when we think about rocks and trees. We can see these natural shapes and feel these substances, so why be concerned about cognitive predications at this point? Let our natural biological processes do the work of identification during input. As we shall see in chapter 8, there is good reason to be concerned with predication even at this routine perceptual level. But suppose that we accept the view that cognitive items such as these are relatively free of contextual considerations. Can we therefore overlook the role of predication in so many other of life's activities where what the person knows, believes, expects, and so on, greatly influences the meaning that such activities take on?

Could it be that the AI theorist has reified external reality, much as Newton once reified his concepts of absolute time and motion? The Newtonians found that they had to ground their assumptions of absolute time and motion in the patterned constellation of the ever expanding universe, a wider compass enabling reliable measurements to be made within it. Time, as Einstein taught us, becomes relative to the predicating grounds against which it is to be measured. Heisenberg's principle of indeterminacy demands that a predicating assumption first be made at the subatomic level (e.g., the direction being taken by the electron) before a measurement of a targeted item (the velocity of that electron) is possible. Even Gödel's incompleteness theorem can be viewed as a reflection of the predicational process. Thus, an axiomatic formulation of number theory *(A)* is never "closed" (completely internally consistent) because *A* cannot itself be accounted for without framing it within a broader context of meaning transcending *A* (Nagel and Newman 1958). There are always propositions within any axiomatic mathematical system that cannot be decided strictly on the basis of symbolic meanings in that system. The only way to prove the internal consistency of *A* is to predicate additional principles of inference, which are in turn open to further questioning from an even broader perspective, and so on ad infinitum.

Is there evidence for a predicational process in human cognition reflected in the literature on language? I turn next to a consideration of such empirical findings to see if my purely theoretical suggestions are supported or contradicted.

Language as Predicational: The Empirical Evidence

There is considerable support in the area of language function and acquisition for predicational rather than mediational processing. Language is readily shown to be rooted in intentional gestures, a form of communication that then extends to speech and eventually to a written form of conveying ideas. Developmental study of infants suggests that their first gestures begin in pointing efforts ("Look at X" or "Tell me about X") and in reaching efforts with some desire in mind ("Give me X" or "Let me touch X") [Clark and Clark 1977:313]. First words are used in conjunction with pointing or looking toward the objects picked out or named. Shortly thereafter first words are used in combination with reaching gestures (Greenfield and Smith 1976). Coulter's and Winograd's stress on the role of purpose in establishing a context of meaning seems to be supported here. Semanticists equate "to mean" with "to intend" (e.g., Bennett 1976:11; Lyons 1977:2). Searle (1969) has underscored such intentionality in his concept of the "speech act," by which he means that when people gesture or utter sentences they are trying to accomplish something, to gain some end.

This capacity for children to intend and direct linguistic expressions according to their interests is consistent with findings on children's acquisition of language. Mediational theorizing would have it that children input words from parents and others in their environment, based on the frequency of parental outputs of such words. Yet, Brown (1973) found through tape-recorded comparisons of parents and their children that there was virtually no relationship between the order of acquisition of 14 morphemes (*a*, *the*, *be*, etc.) by these children and the frequency with which the parents used these morphemes in their everyday speech. McNeil (1968) found similar results in a study of Japanese children's use of linguistic expressions unique to that culture. It thus appears that children select words to express what they personally intend to convey—their predicated purposes—rather than merely to copy parental usage.

Further evidence along this line can be seen in Braine's (1976) cross-cultural study of children's initial sentences. In forming their very first, two-word sentences, children in various linguistic environments (English, Swedish, Hebrew, Samoan, Finnish) spontaneously pick out a formula to make their intentions known. For instance, some children will name the object and its location in that order ("Baby chair," or "Daddy car"), whereas others may take the opposite tack ("Here book," or "Bed Mommy"). The particular order selected seems to reflect what the child is intending to emphasize, either the location or the object being located. In time, of course, cultural expectations come in to align words according to the reigning linguistic climate. Children will also change the order in which they typically express their two-word sentences (Wieman 1976). But it is clear that when they do this their intended meaning is somewhat different than what their typical two-word sentence expression would convey. This is highly suggestive of a predicational process, an innate capacity to create meaningful expressions from the very outset of verbal experience.

Context enters very early in the understanding of sentence meanings. The strict order of words in a sentence is readily overlooked in favor of making sense out of what is being expressed (adults do this all of the time). Thus, a child of age two or three who hears the sentence "The mouse chased the cat" will understand it to mean "The cat chased the mouse," because in what the AI theorist would doubtless call a script or schema, this is what *should* occur when these two animals interact (Nelson 1974). Predication in the form of background understanding would seem to be paramount here. There have been many studies reporting that children make use of what they currently understand as a background meaning against which to formulate something they are not yet quite clear on. A five-year-old child decides whether an object has certain animal properties by comparing it to himself/herself or others (Carey 1985:109). Lacking a knowledge of the human body's function, a six-year-old child says that the reason people defecate is so that they will not burst from the continual ingestion of food (Gellert 1962). A seven-year-old child contends that the sun is hot because it wants to keep people warm (Piaget 1929).

There is some reason to believe that even when young children understand the difference between mechanical causation (efficient causality) and intentional causation (final causality), they will still opt for the latter explanation to make sense of their world in anthropomorphic terms (Bullock, Gelman, and Baillargeon 1982). Such telic choices in understanding mesh with the fact that children are generally oriented to ends, to the outcomes of events. Children tend to forget how things happened, but they remember what finally took place in such happenings (Mandler and Johnson 1977). For example, a child might recall that the butter melted but forget that this was due to a long exposure in the sun. Adults combine the fact of exposure with the fact of melting as a total memory. The child seems to think back from the outcome or effect "to" the cause, and this is usually a final-cause suggestion of some sort. Spying a tiny crack in a window pane, the child will ask "who broke it?" when, of course, changes in temperature may have been the cause (Kagan 1984:187–188).

All such empirical findings support the view of a predicating human intelligence. It is true that in time the child learns or conforms to the accepted explanation of why the sun is hot or why people defecate. But the point is: Does this mean that in changing what is said the child has somehow changed the predicational process of understanding? Does the child suddenly become a mediating mechanism, taking in from the environment what is sent inward without predication? Why should the child reason any differently in learning the conventionally correct explanations for natural events like these? I will return to this issue when we consider the matter of learning in chapter 5.

There is a subtle way in which predication becomes relevant to the learning of a language. Polanyi has stated it this way: "... no one can learn a new language unless he first trusts that it means something" (1964:151). If we think of this in terms of the child's initial language, it is clear that a predicate assumption each child *must* make is that "Things have names" or "Things can be named" before a language can be learned. This Kantian a priori predication —which is not even put into words—would seem to be crucial to the learning of language, and *it is never taught to the child!* A further inference made by children before they are two years of age is that a strange new word must apply to what is unfamiliar in their experience (Kagan 1981:124). It is such considerations that Polanyi meant by the *tacit* aspects of reasoning. The human being must implicitly predicate such considerations and thereby give assent to the cultural artifacts that experience makes possible: "Our tacit powers decide our adherence to a particular culture and sustain our intellectual, artistic, civic and religious deployment within its framework" (1964:264). The tacit *is* the predicational.

Another important realm of predication has to do with the precedent framing of one's self or personal capabilities before some effort is sequaciously attempted. For example, Kagan has found that even if children have the motor coordination to draw a circle rather than simply a straight line, they will not try to do so until they believe that they *can* do so (1981:82). The same applies to the use of language. Evidence suggests that children will not express some concept in speech until they have already convinced themselves that they understand it cognitively (Bloom, 1973). This is consistent with Vygotsky's findings (presented in the 1930s) that children can think before they can speak (1986:80). Contrast this with Minsky's claim that "there is no clear boundary between *language* and all the rest of what we call *thinking*" (1986:272; italics in original). Evidence mounts that children in the second year of life will not speak unless there is some reason for doing so, such as a desire for an object, excitement over some occurrence, or an effort at manipulation of their environment. Often they use the names of objects as a substitute for manipulating them physically (Nelson and Bonvillian 1973).

If children actually do think before they speak, as the research evidence suggests, then what do we make of oppositionality in linguistic usage? Is this merely an outcome of some mediational learning process in the course of linguistic acculturation, or is oppositional phraseology a reflection of the very nature of the thinking process that Vygotsky found underlying language? Linguists have been sensitive to the vital role that opposition plays in all known languages. Trier (1931) believed that every antonymic word that is pronounced implicitly suggested its opposite meaning to both the speaker and hearer involved in a communication. Lyons has said that: "opposition is one of the most important principles governing the structure of language" (1977:271). And Richards has singled out opposition as one of the essential principles through which language works (1967:10).

It is not difficult finding evidence for oppositionality or dialectical reasoning in the development of children's language usage. Kagan has noted that during the second year of life most children spontaneously — without instruction or modeling by parents! — categorize objects as groups sharing physical or functional similarities, such as color, size, or shape; he refers to this as a "basic process" in children (1981:88–89). If we recall that "to categorize" derives from the Greek meaning "to predicate" (see chapter 1), we can view such spontaneous linguistic efforts as evidence for a predicating intelligence in the human being. But now, Kagan also points out that as the child creates categories he or she "is disposed to invent their complement" (1984:189). (Note that Kagan here relies totally on the meaning of demonstrative reasoning in suggesting that the complement is merely one of those items that a given category "is not"; see figure 2). Soon after learning the meaning of *up*, the child learns the meaning of *down;* after learning the meaning of *high*, the child learns *low;* and *bad* follows *good* in short order as well. Kagan goes on to say that the comprehension of oppositionality is achieved too early and easily to be the product of parental instruction, adding that "the idea that a current state of affairs can be reversed in thought or action and a prior state reconstructed seems to be an intrinsic quality of human mental life" (p. 189). It would not seem incorrect to refer to this intrinsic "reversed categorizing" as dialectical reasoning, making it a basic process to parallel the basic process of categorization Kagan alluded to above.

The child's attribution of strange words to strange objects noted above can be seen to extend to oppositionality as well. Thus, Carey (1978) asked nursery school children to "Bring me the chromium tray, not the red one, the chromium one," thereby mixing categorical predications (color and metal) without making this clear to the children. It so happened that the chromium tray was olive-colored. Children were subsequently confused over the color green, which they felt was *not* related to the olive color that they had now predicated on their own (sans instruction) as chromium. The opposition of "red-chromium" in the original context of learning had obviously framed their understanding, resulting in a so-called category error. Though on the surface one would not consider red and chromium to be opposites, there is little doubt that the dialectical reasoning capacities of the children worked to align these word-meanings oppositionally. As children mature, they become increasingly aware that words that are antonymical are easier to remember than words lacking this oppositional relationship (Kreutzer, Leonard, and Flavell 1975).

When we turn to empirical findings on oppositionality in the language usage of adults, the picture is just as supportive of a predicational view of cognition as it is in the findings on children (see Rychlak 1986, for a more detailed review). People readily produce opposite meanings to stimulus words in a word-association task (Karwoski and Schachter 1948; Kjeldergaard 1962; Siipola, Walker, and Kolb, 1955). Osgood's (1952) worldwide studies on word meaning were framed along dimensions of oppositionality (i.e., good-bad, fast-slow, strong-weak). Oppositionality of meaning has been shown to be a semantic rather than simply a syntactic or lexical feature of words (Brewer and Lichtenstein 1974; Grossman and Eagle 1970). Studies have found that antonymy makes rapid recognition of differences possible without the involved semantic processing required of nonantonymic word pairings (Hampton and

Taylor 1985; Schvaneveldt, Durso, and Mukherji 1982). In studies on transfer of learning, oppositionality has repeatedly been shown to *facilitate* acquisition across lists (Bastian 1961; Mink 1963; Ryan 1960; Weiss-Shed 1973; Wickens and Cermak 1967). In an extensive review of Japanese studies on word learning, Umemoto (1959) cites many findings that people in that language also generalize their knowledge by way of opposite word meanings.

Theories of language acquisition are fraught with indications of predication as a fundamental process. For example, we read of the iconic gesture or utterance as a primitive form of linguistic usage (Bennett 1976:14; Lyons 1977:70). Thus, a person might indicate distance by altering the space between the hands (close together for "near," far apart for "distant") or a hissing sound combined with a wriggle of the hand might be used to indicate iconically that a snake is in the vicinity. The suggestion here is that meanings stem from direct experience. Having walked or ridden various distances, or confronted a hissing snake, the originators of language relied on such *known* factors to convey some intention through iconic symbolization (Bennett 1976:206).

The iconic gesture is obviously predicated by the direct experience of confronting the snake, from which it draws significance in precedent-sequacious fashion. In time, words are substituted for the physical gestures. A cursory survey of word roots in any dictionary convinces one that there is something on the order of an iconical or prototypical precedent-sequacious extension of meaning in many words of any language. That is, meanings devolving from actual, concrete experience are typified through the coining of words. Thus, "attire" has roots dating to the description of rank, because at one time only those of the upper classes could be encountered, clothed in fancy garments. "Betray" devolves from the treacherous actions of a traitor, who literally violates our trust and confidence. "Catastrophe" has precedent roots meaning to overturn, or turn over, a meaning we readily grasp based upon incidents from childhood where we spilled things and lost things, resulting in much anguish and pain.

We could continue like this throughout the alphabet, readily demonstrating that word meanings devolve sequaciously from precedent meanings that tie directly into the practical experience of human beings. Lakoff traces the human being's implicit understanding of relational concepts such as inside-outside, up-down, front-back, and so on, to the physical nature of the body, which "embodies" such relational meanings for the cognizing individual during routine daily life (1987:267–268). That is, external objects stand in relation to our body as we negotiate our way through life from the very outset. Such practical experience provides the context of what is already known, enabling an extension of such meaning to what then can be known. It is not a question of first the context being known and then the understanding of a word or verbal utterance taking place shortly thereafter. We are speaking of a logical ordering here in which time's passage is irrelevant. It is the context that, when logically extended to the word or utterance, is instantaneously the meaning of that word or utterance (see Fish 1980:313). Wittgenstein (1968) has referred to such predicating circumstances as cultural/institutional situations rather than contexts, but this amounts to the same thing.

Now, we can surmise that just as in the case of the children studied (refer above), who must have some sense of a concept before they use it linguistically, the originators of any language — the ones who coined the words — had to already know the meaning that they were creating in the coining of a word. They were using a precedent meaning from their experience as a predicate and sequaciously extending this to symbolize some intended parallel in another realm of their experience. Nicholas Chauvin's sycophantic displays regarding Napoleon resulted in his name becoming the symbol for an "excessive commitment" to one political point of view. People saw him put on his display, and hence when others acted in that fashion they were called "Chauvin-like" or chauvinistic. Today, this meaning has been extended analogically to excessive claims made for one sexual identity over the other as well. Words are continually expanded and extended like this, subject to the purposes of those who use them. Words are, therefore, instrumentalities. Only an intelligence that already has something to say can express anything in words. The person must "know" in order to "make anything known."

Here is where the widely discussed and disputed work of Chomsky (1972) seems to enter. Reminding us of Kant's approach to cognition, Chomsky has always been interested in the precedent processes that bring linguistic expression about. The organism must "organize" language fragments in some way that is not learned, but that makes the use and learning of language possible. Initially, Chomsky stressed syntax (sentence structure) above semantics (sentence meaning) as the primary source of language expression, and sought the rules by which kernel sentences or propositions in so-called deep structure were transformed into overt expressions.

As evidence accrued suggesting that semantics invariably intrudes upon syntactical usage, Chomsky softened his claims regarding the supremacy of syntax over semantics (Lakoff 1980). However, he has never softened his conviction that language rests upon a genetically determined structure. As he expressed this conviction: "I know of no reason to believe that there is any fundamental difference in the respects in which the human embryo has at the earliest stage the potential structure of the heart on the one hand, and the potential structure of language on the other" (Chomsky 1983:57). Fodor (1975) has taken this Kantian theme even further, suggesting that people are born with a set of cognitive representations, onto which they can then map any new information that arises in experience.

Now, a theorist who takes a nativistic position of this sort is likely to be placed in the role of endorsing "innate ideas" as Lockean contents rather than "innate processes" as Kantian organizers. This charge may be true of Fodor, but is does not seem to fit Chomsky. If the person "works" in a certain way biologically *(Bios)* then, as I mentioned in chapter 3, it is possible to think of limitations that such innate capacities might exert on the logic *(Logos)* called for in reasoning. The mentally handicapped cannot solve complex arithmetic problems. But as this lack has nothing to do with the logic of the arithmetic problem, the fact that other people are born *without* mental handicaps and can solve these problems does not mean that their hereditary endowments provide the essentials of arithmetic—the numbers, the plus/minus signs, and the logic of calculation—as "inherited ideas." A brilliant but narrowly educated person can never reach the potential he or she might have achieved, given a richer education. Brilliance is a capacity, a recognizable talent that may be manifested in narrow cunning or wide-ranging wisdom.

What the nativist is frequently out to demonstrate is that mind "works" a certain way as a process and that although this process may establish certain requirements or set certain limitations on its contents, there is no requirement here for the contents per se to be natively endowed. It is entirely conceivable that, as Vygotsky (1986:94) has suggested, sociohistorical considerations exert a greater influence on verbal thought than biological considerations do. People do conform to the predications of others. It is quite threatening to have to frame one's own predications in a—especially a new—situational context. Children are understandably credulous, for they confront this newness almost hourly in their young lives. They are not prone to question predicate assumptions being expressed in their home environment. Stereotypical attitudes of parents are likely to be taken over by the child as a useful predication on which to order reality. Of course, as we shall examine in some detail in chapter 6, the child can always "in principle" reason to the opposite of such parental interpretations of reality. That is, the child can do so if we accept the possibility of dialectical reasoning in human behavior.

What of the other side of the coin: Are there any indications that language per se is influenced by a native process suggestive of predication? Actually, there are some interesting findings to ponder. It is possible to analyze natural languages in terms of how they grammatically align the subject, verb, and object in the framing of a sentence/utterance. English is a subject-verb-object language. If we were to expect a reflection of predication in such grammatical orderings, we would of course focus on the verb and the object, which, taken together (plus modifiers) constitute the complete predicate. In the sentence "Bill drove the car" the "car drivers" (verb plus object meanings) is our wider Euler circle, within which we would place the circle designating Bill. It could be that an examination of the typical grammatical orderings of language expression like this might reflect the innately human process of predication that we have been considering.

We have already seen how children naturally or spontaneously select one of two possible orders in framing their initial two-word sentences (refer above). The child who focuses on objects rather than locations will therefore be likely to say "Daddy work" to signify that "Daddy is at work." The child is telling us something about the father, and location is quite secondary. The child who focuses on location will say "Here book" to signify "I hold a book in my hand." In this case, the important point is that there is something right here, "in my hand," and it happens to be a book. Children do reverse these orderings, but the logical focus of their statement — whether on the location or the person/item in that location — shifts accordingly. It is clear, therefore, that either of the two words can logically predicate the other, depending on what the child intends to say. But now, the logical nature of predication does not change! This is what we mean when we say that logic is a process (predicating a target term, lending meaning via verb-object to subject, etc.) that has *different* contents (meanings, definitions, interpretations, etc.) depending on the intentions of the reasoner in question.

Is the logic of predication suggested in the findings on word order in natural languages? Ultan (1969) has examined the customary ordering of the subject (S), verb (V), and object (O) in the known natural language systems of this earth. Of the six possible combinations of S, V, and O, only four have actually been employed in natural language systems. The percentages of natural languages employing these word orderings are as follows:

SOV = 44%
SVO = 35%
VSO = 19%
VOS = 2%
OVS = 0%
OSV = 0%

In 79% of the cases the sentence begins with the subject, and in 98% of the cases the object lies to the right or follows the subject. The cognitive network theorist, Anderson, offers this explanation of such findings: "This [subject-before-object] order makes good sense when we think about cognition. An action starts with the agent and then affects the object. Therefore, it is natural that the subject of a sentence, when it reflects agency, occurs first. Also ... sentences tend to be 'about' their subject, and a speaker naturally wants to establish first what the sentence is about" (1985:320). This explanation strikes us as itself being predicated on efficient causation. If Anderson is correct, it would seem that the most frequent linguistic ordering should be SVO and not SOV, because it is the verb that tells us what action the subject is carrying out. It is also true that, although the subject is the meaning targeted for enrichment, what the sentences are "about" is found in the context-establishing predication.

The findings are highly consistent with a predicational view of mentation. The main expectation for predication would be that the subject should take meaning from the context established by the verb plus the object (i.e., the complete predicate). The object is particularly important, because even when the verb is stated before the subject, so long as the subject appears before the object a sense of logical order is retained. A sentence in this sense is much like a premise, where the consequent (mortality) predicates the antecedent (mankind), as in "All men are mortal" (see chapter 2). In a sentence the antecedent is the subject and the consequent is the object. We expect the object to serve as the wider referent, the larger Euler circle, and the subject to serve as the narrower, smaller circle. The fact that *no* known language system begins with an object is telling evidence against a simplistic theory of the association of ideas. It is clear that although ideas might be associated together in willy-nilly, chance occurrences, when the person now intends to express a meaning in any language, the alignment of words in that idea expression follows what we know about premising qua predication. That is, this alignment is followed in all but two percent of the languages.

Cognitive representations as reflected in language usage are readily understood in terms of a predicational process. Meanings do indeed appear to extend from a broader to a narrower range. Contexts establish this wider range, and they are initiated by direct, practical experience. There is also good reason to believe that such background contexts are organized oppositionally. Children spontaneously draw implications to the opposite of what they are being taught. Language systems throughout the known societies of the earth support the view of a logical order in which the object predicates or lends meaning to the subject of a sentence. The typical reaction to findings of this sort by the cognitive scientist is to point out that words are learned, and hence any ordering they take on must be subject to the learning process. This would seem to make predication itself an outcome of learning. What I hope to do in the next chapter is to demonstrate that predication is more the cause than the effect of learning.

5.
Learning as a Predicational Process

There is no other concept in psychology that has been given more consideration than learning. Traditional experimental psychology was virtually identified with learning in animals and humans. Yet, with the rise of AI we find less emphasis being given to learning and more to process. I noted in chapter 4 that AI advocates have not really addressed the question of how cognitive representations (schemas, etc.) are learned. So little empirical research has been done on this question that psychologists have begun to question the empirical status of AI (see, e.g., Kukla 1989). Since we must one day provide a thorough description of the human organism, it is imperative that some consideration be given to the nature of learning, with particular reference to predication. Framed in terms of our now familiar process-content distinction, we would like to know whether predication is to be seen as a learning process, or whether it is merely a learned (shaped) content within the mediational process.

Chapter 5 begins with a consideration of Lockean versus Kantian interpretations of predication or, as it is often called today: *construction*. It then takes up the ways in which AI advocates have defined learning before considering the conditioning theories that have been used in psychology. The vast findings on awareness in both classical and operant conditioning are then reviewed to throw light on whether or not predication is a cause or an effect of what we understand learning to be. Finally, we will survey research findings in cognitive psychology for any suggestions of a predicational process in human beings.

Kantian Versus Lockean Interpretations of Predication

As was noted earlier, historically, learning theories in psychology have followed the Lockean model of singularities totaling to complexities by way of frequency and contiguity considerations in the ongoing experiences of the learner. With the advent of theoretical models drawn from artificial intelligence many psychologists have convinced themselves that they are introducing Kantian predicational formulations into their accounts by referring to the "internal" cognitive representations of a learner.

Today, if we were to suggest that people must predicate their ongoing experience, a cognitive psychologist is likely to enthusiastically agree. In commenting on just such a "law" of cognition holding that mind contributes to what is perceived or known, Tulving opines: "There has not been a psychologist or philosopher alive in the last 100 years who has seriously doubted the veracity of this law" (1983:149). He then says that most psychologists today agree that the "responses of the organism to stimulation are mediated by that organism's cognitive state, which provides a context for and an interpretation of the stimulus, *as it makes contact with the record of his past experiences*" (ibid.; italics added).

Tulving's concept of what "mind contributing to knowledge of experience" means is that a context has been established through recording past experience, and this context acts today to "interpret" current stimulation. This is definitely *not* a predicational view of the mind, because there is no predicating Kantian context being provided by mind qua mind until the Lockean inputs are taken in without benefit of such creative organizers to begin with. It is essential to a Kantian position that we believe mind shapes experience into knowledge right from birth or whenever one wishes to say the initial act of cognition takes place. Unlike Locke, Kant did not view raw sensations (perceptions, etc.) as packaged units of meaning (ideas). Sensory "inputs" receive the impact of external experience, but there would be no knowledge of this contribution made by the external world without the person's act of predication via the categories of the understanding—which organize or pattern the entering elements of sensation together to lend them meaning (Kant 1952a:14). And these predicating capacities (categories) function from the very outset of cognitive life!

We often find cognitive psychologists waving a Kantian flag, yet in the theoretical contest to follow they fall back to the firm ground of traditional Lockeanism. For example, after making an argument which suggests that cognitive perception in learning is "constructive," Neisser adds: "but the input information often plays the largest single role in determining the constructive process. A very similar role, it seems to me, is played by the aggregate of information stored in long-term memory" (1967:285). If input information plays the largest single role in the constructive process, then we cannot be talking about information as something that is created by this process. There must be an additional process of some sort going on in addition that organizes such information before it is taken in as "input."

The word "construction" leads to confusion today, for it can be given a Lockean or a Kantian interpretation. George Kelly (1955) used the term in a Kantian sense. For Kelly, to construe was to predicate experience by aligning meanings in relation to other meanings, including meanings that were opposite to each other: "By construing we mean 'placing an interpretation': a person places an interpretation upon what is construed" (p. 50). Such interpretations are believed to begin even before speech is attained, and hence all mental constructs (cognitive representations) bear this distinctive contribution of the process that made them possible. For a Lockean understanding of construction we need only turn to Mandler, who tells us that "Our phenomenal world is immediate, obvious, and thereby very convincing. Unfortunately, we often forget that it too is constructed, that it is a complex product of our culture and personal histories" (1985:15). To a Kantian, the phenomenal realm involves the construing process that makes learning possible; it is the "construer" or "constructor" rather than the "constructed." The construing process is native to the human organism, so it does not have to be constituted through learning. Mandler, as Tulving, "says" something that sounds like predication but he means mediation.

It is obvious that the confusion over just what "construction" means stems from the confounding of an extraspective with an introspective understanding of this concept. Those theoreticians, like Kelly, who are clearly Kantian in their approach, view things from the perspective of our person within the Chinese room. Construction from this perspective means framing, ordering, lending meaning to—in short, predicating. Others, like Tulving and Mandler, who recognize the obvious truth that one's point of view influences what one "does" behaviorally are nevertheless poised extraspectively, viewing the activating cause of the behavioral sequence as initiated exteriorally, from outside the Chinese room and then passed inwardly. Construction from this perspective means "being built up," from initially simple inputs to later, interacting complexities once things are underway. The upshot is, we have a mediational model being espoused. So, even though theorists like Neisser and Tulving have severe reservations concerning the computer as a full model for human behavior, they nevertheless construe behavior in a way that is compatible with computer theories.

The Meaning of Learning in Artificial Intelligence

All of the AI approaches hold that the cognitive representations are learned—as language terms or other forms of signs, signals, and so on. But what is the explanation of learning on which such accounts rest? Dreyfus has complained that AI theorists are trying to produce a fully formed adult intelligence, "the way Athena sprang full grown from the head of Zeus" (1979:223). He notes that no one in the AI community is working on the problem of how people become cognizant of contexts, and make use of them in learning about life over their developing years. Newell and Simon frankly admitted that they were focusing on the processing of "internal, symbolic mechanisms" (1972:4) rather than on learning or individual differences in behavior (pp. 556, 866). Like Tulving above, they essentially equate learning with long-term memory (p. 818).

Simon defines learning broadly as "any change in a system that produces a more or less permanent change in its capacity for adapting to its environment" (1985:118). Such adaptation occurs as follows: "both the real world and long-term memory . . . undergo continual change. In memory the change is adaptive. It updates the knowledge about the real world and adds new knowledge . . . the adaptation of long-term memory [is what] . . . we call learning" (ibid.). This is obviously a Lockean formulation. Items are taken in without predication, stored in long-term memory, and as such inputs change through contact with the real world, long-term memory changes: this is learning. We have a nondialectical mediational model here, in which the person, although capable of maladaptation sans learning, could never *learn to maladapt*.

It is clear that frequency would play a major role in accounting for environmental changes, resulting in the necessary inputs to change memory storage. If we search about in the allusions to learning made by AI theorists we are invariably confronted with a frequency thesis of one sort or another. It is not uncommon to read of cognitive representations being "built up" or "acquired" through contact with others, and then repeatedly practiced (Miller, Galanter, and Pribram 1960:7, 156, 184). Schank and Abelson observe that, in learning a script: "If the situations described [by a script] were frequently encountered by an individual, then we might expect that individual to have these scripts" (1977:69). Now, it cannot be denied that practice, exposure, repetition, and all such frequency considerations can be shown to bear a relationship to memory and learning. But in what sense does this relationship obtain? Are we thinking here of tabulations made of influences external to the individual, or are we thinking of a continuing line of predication that has been retained for any of a number of reasons?

For example, the Kantian theorist expects that if an individual predicates environmental circumstances in a meaningful fashion it would make good sense to try this same predication again. Even if the outcome of a predication is negative, resulting in some discomfort for the person, so long as this framing understanding has "realistically" dealt with the ongoing pattern of life it will be repeated. But now, suppose the individual actually affirms an erroneous predication, a stupid approach to some task needing completion. Would it follow that this person would necessarily reject this inappropriate understanding? As dialecticians we could not be so optimistic. People often have wishes going against the realities of life, and some of these may even be self-destructive. People can and do "practice" stupidity of one sort or another over their lives.

It is not that the Kantian theorist is hostile to frequency and contiguity factors in the learning process. In approaching the study of such correlates of learning, however, the Kantian will be looking for framing (precedent) hypotheses in acquisition, so-called "insight" learnings that take place in one trial (without frequent repetition). The Kantian will also be looking for indications that the person is applying idiographic strategies to the process of learning rather than merely be shaped by some silent process that does not require a contribution from the learner's individuality and personal choice. As we have seen in chapter 2, predicational theorizing seems invariably to lead to such teleological theorizing. Another aspect of the Kantian formulation touches on what in chapter 1 was referred to as the empathic nature of interpersonal interactions. As employed by the machine, a "schema" is not framed in an effort to understand the point of view of the "other." If two computers were interacting, one would not be striving to grasp the perspective of the other, as human beings so frequently do when they communicate. In fact, we might argue that true communication never occurs until such time as one member in the exchange understands where the other member "is coming from."

The Decline of Traditional Conditioning Theory

Learning theories in psychology have been closely identified with the concept of "conditioning," which includes classical (Pavlovian) conditioning, as well as operant (Skinnerian) conditioning. Probably no other study has done more to perpetuate belief in a "mechanism" of the conditioning process than John Watson's report on "Little Albert" (Watson and Rayner 1920). This was a classical avoidance conditioning effort, in which Watson presented the nine-month old infant with a white rat *(conditioned stimulus)* followed by a loud noise *(unconditioned stimulus)* accomplished by striking a steel bar directly behind the child's head. After seven such pairings of rat and noise (in two sessions, one week apart) Albert reacted with crying and avoidance *(conditioned responses)* when the rat was presented to him without the noise. Supposedly, Albert had been automatically conditioned to respond with fright and crying to a previously neutral stimulus (white rat) through a contiguous pairing and several trials of spontaneous fear reactions to the noise. The extraspective, efficient-cause rendering of Albert's behavior is clear.

Although numerous efforts were made, this experiment has never been successfully cross-validated. Subsequent attempts to classically condition infants have not been very successful. Infants become easily sensitized to the total situation in which they find themselves, so that it is not always clear that a conditioned response to some specific stimulus has actually been achieved. Wickens and Wickens (1940) provided the first sound evidence supporting an interpretation of Albert's behavior as reflecting anxiety and distaste for a total situation (predicating context?) in which a white rat played a signal role. Although not reported in the original study, it has since been established from Watson's unpublished notes that Albert *could* get his fear and crying willfully under control by sucking his thumb (Cornwell, Hobbs, and Prytula 1980:216).

In fact, while filming Albert's supposed "automatic" response to the white rat, Watson had to forcibly remove the thumb from Albert's mouth several times to allow the crying response "to be elicited." Albert's contradiction of the crying impulse with the sucking maneuver could have been taken as evidence for oppositionality in human behavior, of course. But Watson had no room for such agential theoretical suggestions in his theory of learning. One can only wonder how much poor Albert's crying was influenced by such inconsiderate treatment. Was he crying because of the rat's presence, or because he could not suck his comforting thumb in a tense situation? Whatever the case, evidence that children can be classically conditioned is far from convincing. (See Sameroff and Cavanagh 1979, for a detailed examination of this question.)

The evidence for operant conditioning of infants is not much better. In the operant account of conditioning, the child is viewed as "emitting" certain responses rather than have them be triggered by specific stimuli in the environment. Once emitted, however, the environmental circumstances may *contingently reinforce* such emitted responses, somehow causing them to increase in rate of emission. Hence, the contingent circumstances following an operant response are what sustain its level of emission. If there are contingent circumstances following a response emission that increase its level—as when an infant's rooting behavior results in the oral fixation upon a nipple and increased sucking occurs from that point onward—we speak of (positive) reinforcement taking place. Experiments conducted on operant conditioning of infant sucking responses typically find that they are very easily established. For example, one group of infants may be given a nipple that will feed a dextrose solution when sucked, and a second (control) group of newborn infants will have the nipple but no dextrose issuing when sucked (Lipsitt, Kaye, and Bosack 1966). Within fifteen minutes, infants who receive dextrose will be observed steadily increasing their rate of sucking, whereas the control subjects will maintain a constant level of intermittent sucking.

The question arises as to whether this rapid adaptation to the nipple is really a "shaping" of the sucking response. Children seem prepared natively to "act on" the environment through a sucking response (Seligman 1970). If an attempt is made to operantly condition infants in the first ten days of life to neutral stimuli that they are not natively prepared for, the efforts are never successful (Papousek 1967b). There is good reason to believe that children frame expectations within a broadly oppositional context, so that, for example, if we suddenly turn off their dextrose after conditioning them to turn their heads to the right in order to receive this "contingent reinforcer," we find the children quickly turning their heads to the left, looking about in their situation for the desirable but missing food reward (Papousek 1967a). If they were being shaped to turn their heads *solely* to the direction at the right of their heads it would seem that they should continue vigorously to look to the right. It therefore does not appear that children are being mechanically/unidirectionally shaped so much as they are learning what "is" taking place and hence what should continue to occur in the future—over against what "is not, but might be" taking place in the future from the opposite direction (recall Lakoff's argument concerning bodily position and the learning of dimensionality).

It would be quite easy to frame explanations of infant behavior in terms of predication. Little Albert's sense of the feared situation is contributed to by his personal understandings. He has heard loud noises before, and has doubtless been startled and frightened before. He is being placed in a situation that is not pleasant. Even so, left to his own devices, he can dialectically counter the negative response (crying) through application of a positive (sucking) response. The infant expecting dextrose over the right shoulder can, when this source of nourishment is discontinued, quickly look around and glance to the left, framing the "opposite" of what has been occurring as a possibility. Preverbal children appear to act as if they are "taking a position" on their circumstances more than they are being shaped into responding to specific ingredients of these circumstances. In line with Vygotsky and Kelly, there does seem to be thinking taking place before speech in the neonate. Of course, since we cannot talk to the children we are unable to provide clearer evidence than what our silent observations might suggest. Fortunately, we *are* able to talk to older human beings who have been placed in comparable experimental situations.

One of the most important studies of recent history relating to human learning was done by Greenspoon (1955). Initial reports of this work were picked up by Dollard and Miller, who gave it prominent treatment in their influential textbook (1950:44). Greenspoon asked his subjects to state aloud any words that came to mind—one at a time—as they sat looking away from him. They did this freely for a ten-minute period, and then for the next ten minutes Greenspoon stated *Mmm-hmm* each time a subject voiced a plural noun. In a final, extinction phase of ten minutes Greenspoon once again said nothing. The results of the operant-conditioning study were that subjects increased in their so-called emission of plural nouns during the period when they were being "contingently reinforced" by Greenspoon's *Mmm-hmm*. Following the experiment, Greenspoon asked subjects what they thought the study was about. This was a very important development in psychological research, because what this meant was that a fundamentally extraspective theoretical formulation (operant conditioning) was admitting, however informally, that an introspective contribution "might" be made to the interaction between the experimenter and the subject. Greenspoon did not think of his interview in this way, of course. But the die had been cast and in time it was to bring down the theoretical edifice of operant conditioning theory.

Greenspoon found that 10 of his 75 subjects had caught on to the fact that every time they said a plural noun he made a prompting sound. Greenspoon dropped these 10 subjects from his analysis and professed to find evidence for automatic, "unconscious" manipulation of human behavior in the remaining 65. Several studies of this sort were to follow, so that in an early review of the work conducted between 1950 and 1958, Krasner (1958) claimed that 95% of the subjects in 31 contingency studies showed this unconscious, automatic tendency to be conditioned without awareness of how this manipulation of their behavior was accomplished.

We cannot overemphasize the importance that was placed on this body of research by behavioristic enthusiasts. It helped to crystallize the image of "mind manipulators" and "behavior controllers" that many people attribute to psychologists. Even in the technical writings of the profession, much reliance was placed on the supposed findings of unconscious/unaware conditioning in behavior. Dollard and Miller had this to say about their own work: "The assumption that reinforcement has a direct, unconscious effect is essential to the logic of this book" (1950:44; see also Skinner 1963:84, for a similar opinion). And yet, within a short period of time severe cracks began to develop in the behaviorist's case.

Dulany (1961) repeated the Greenspoon study, but instead of just asking his subjects what the experiment was about he studied their ongoing assumptions concerning what was taking place as the experimental procedure unfolded. He identified a significant proportion of subjects who could not say precisely what the experiment "was about" (i.e., that every time a plural noun was voiced the experimenter stated *Mmm-hmm*), but they *did* have an idea that led them to state more plural nouns. Thus, for example, a subject might hear Greenspoon say *Mmm-hmm* following a word like "pearls" and conclude thereby that the point of the study was to name precious stones. Framed in terms of Euler circles, we would have a large circle labeled "precious stones" framed or affirmed by the subject at this point, who would then identify as many items within this predicating category as he or she knew—stating them in the plural to conform with the initial word (pearls) that was followed by *Mmm-hmm*. The spate of plural words to follow—"rubies, diamonds, sapphires," and so on—met the criterion of the experiment as a verbal manipulation *but for the wrong reason!*

Dulany called these misconstruals "correlated hypotheses," meaning that they went along with the experimental hypothesis but were not really validating it. He might have simply called these incorrect "subject predications" of the task at hand. A vital aspect of any experiment on human beings is the experimenter's predication of the task to be performed on the one hand and the subject's predication of this task on the other. I am speaking here of the understanding of the experiment over and above what is stated in the experimental instructions to the subject. It follows that a subject who is trying to grasp the meaning of the experimental task must predicate it in either a "correct" (i.e., consonant with the experimenter's hypothesis) or an "incorrect" manner. It might also be said that a subject could lack a task predication altogether, but this sense of helplessness or uncertainty ("I don't know what's going on in this experiment") is itself a predication of the situation. Lest it be thought that trying to frame predications to understand the nature of an experiment is atypical for subjects, I should note that research evidence suggests the contrary. As Orne (1962:779) discovered in his own studies, human beings "will ascribe purpose and meaning [to an experiment] even in the absence of purpose and meaning."

Levin (1961) quickly followed Dulany with a study demonstrating that a more involved interviewing procedure readily identified a larger proportion of the subjects as "aware" than had previously been suggested. Dozens of studies followed in which increasingly sophisticated interviewing techniques were employed, and the unquestioned drift of roughly 90% of these studies is that "conditioning" of behavior is anything but unconscious and automatic. As a matter of fact, Brewer (1974) entitled his review of this body of research (more than 150 studies) with the sobering proclamation: "There is no convincing evidence for operant or classical conditioning in adult humans."

What Brewer meant, of course, is that there is no evidence to suggest that mature individuals, with whom we can communicate, are being manipulated without making a contribution to the ongoing sequence of events. In the operant conditioning format, there are enough subjects who know the relationship between their emitted "responses" and the contingent reinforcer *(Mmm-hmm)* to account for the findings reported by Greenspoon and others. When subjects were queried regarding their ongoing approach to the task as they actually performed it, it became even clearer that their successes were due to predications that were being gradually worked out from trial to trial (DeNike 1964; Kennedy [Experiment II] 1971; Spielberger and Levin 1962). A precedent-sequacious line of predication is suggested in these data. Subjects get inklings of what is called for, put these hunches to test, and then reap the satisfaction of getting more *Mmm-hmms* than before. We might legitimately ask who is manipulating whom at this point, the experimenter or the subject?

It should not be concluded that awareness of the "operant response-contingent reinforcer" relationship is all that is necessary to effect the operant conditioning of behavior. Subjects must obviously *cooperate* with what is intended here in the experimental design. Page (1969, 1972) established that certain subjects know full well what is expected of them—they *are* aware—yet they opt not to comply. Oppositional behavior is suggested in these studies by Page, in two senses. First of all, the aware but noncooperating subjects totally avoid producing the targeted material (word syntax, plural nouns, etc.) in the section of the study where they catch on to the design. They do precisely the opposite of what is called for, so that no reinforcer (Page used *good* as the contingent reinforcer) is being voiced by the experimenter at all. This is how Page could identify the aware but uncooperative subjects: They actually fell below the level of reinforcement they had been getting in the first phase of the experiment, before they had figured things out. This initial phase is called a subject's "base rate" of response emission. Subjects who are aware and cooperating show a marked increase in the reinforcers *(good)* over their base rate level once they catch on to what is taking place.

Second, Page introduced the practice of stopping the experiment after a subject's awareness and level of cooperation had been established and pointedly asking subjects who were aware but not cooperating to "Make me say 'good.' " Alternatively, he asked subjects who were aware and cooperating to "make me stop saying 'good.' " On the very next trial, subjects who were not doing what was expected started in to do so, and those who were complying ceased their cooperation. In effect, subjects readily "did the opposite" of what they were doing to that point. Now, of course, a truly intransigent or hostile subject might not have gone along with Page's request. There have even been cases in which subjects believed that they were being prompted to do something unethical in following the direction indicated by the experimenter's subtle *Mmm-hmm* or *good* (e.g., helping the experimenter to make the study come out in a prearranged fashion). The person is, in the final analysis, the judge of what he or she "should do" given all of the circumstances in the predicated situation. It appears, however, that Page's subjects understood that they were in control of the circumstances and that he was asking them to prove this fact through a concrete demonstration. There surely is little support here for a malleable subject under the manipulative yoke of an experimenter's "reinforcements."

Thus far we have been considering operant conditioning, but the importance of awareness and cooperation for classical conditioning is equally documented by empirical research. If a subject is being conditioned to give an electrodermal or galvanic skin response *(GSR)* to a light it might be accomplished as follows: A subject would first see a light flash *(conditioned stimulus [CS])* followed by an electro-shock to the forearm *(unconditioned stimulus [UCS])*, which would automatically bring about the *GSR (unconditioned response [UR])*. After several pairings of the *CS* and *UCS* the *GSR* will be seen to occur following the *CS*. Awareness enters the picture in the fact that only if a subject is cognizant of the relationship between the *CS* and the *UCS* ("Everytime I see the light flash I get shocked") does classical conditioning take place. At least, the evidence to date is predominantly (85 to 90 percent) in favor of this suggestion. Furthermore, the matter of cooperation also enters. We cannot readily control our *GSR* reactions, for they depend on autonomically directed capacities such as perspiration. But if this were an eye-blink experiment and the *CS* were a light and the *UCS* a puff of air blown into our eye, two things would be necessary to effect conditioning. We would have to grasp the *CS-UCS* relation ("Everytime that light flashes I get a puff of air in my eye") *and* we would have to comply with the obvious implication here, that we should blink our eye. It is as possible for subjects to negate such implications and *not* blink their eye, as it is for subjects to begin blinking their eye to the light if simply told to do so without the puff of air (Martin and Dean 1971; Shean 1970).

The issue of correlated hypotheses or alternative predications enters here as well. Studies have been done in which the *CS-UCS* relationship has been masked by other stimuli, distracting a subject from identifying "the" crucial *CS*. Under these circumstances, no conditioning takes place (Block 1962; Dawson 1970). Occasionally, however, a subject will concoct a rationale close enough to the experimenter's *CS-UCS* pattern of stimulation so that there are enough *CR*s forthcoming to give the illusion that successful conditioning has been achieved (Chatterjee and Eriksen 1960). Oppositionality is also reflected in these studies. For example, Wilson (1968) first established differential conditioning to a positive and a negative stimulus, using a galvanic skin response *(GSR)* as the *CR* (so that a subject would give the *GSR* to one stimulus but not the other). Subjects were then merely told that the positive stimulus would henceforth be the negative stimulus and vice versa. By the second trial following this instruction the *GSR* was completely reversed, so that it occurred as strongly to the opposite stimulus to which it had previously been conditioned as it had to the original. It is clear from such evidence that the subject's capacity to predicate the precedent circumstances led sequaciously to what would follow as the conditioned physical response and that this predication could be reversed through oppositional or dialectical reformulation.

Traditional learning theories have been undergirded by our reinforcement-conditioning models. Even though these foundations have come tumbling down around the behaviorist's heels, there has been surprisingly little change taking place in the basic understanding of human learning. In fact, there has been little effort made to confront the dramatic implications of the research findings on reinforcement and conditioning. As Brewer pointedly summarized, in the current literature on conditioning, the studies we have briefly surveyed are "either omitted, listed under a heading called 'instructions,' or given an innocuous interpretation. These studies are never presented as the theoretically crucial experiments that they actually are" (1974:31).

One sometimes wonders if a professional "cover-up" is the proper description of what is taking place in psychology today, where introductory students are still being taught that reinforcements occur in an automatic and unpredicated fashion. The Lockean mediation model continues to hold sway in such instruction, which in recent years has shifted in the direction of computer modeling. About the only change noted here is that instead of talking about learned "responses" we now hear about learned (i.e., input) "cognitive representations" of one sort or another, working as mediators to effect certain behavioral styles, as well as changes in behavior. All of this is heralded as a form of Kuhnian (1970) revolution. But is it? A careful examination of the theories being advanced today would surely lead us to answer "no" to this question.

Research Findings in Cognitive Psychology

The disappointing if not harmful aspect of this nonrevolution is that evidence now accruing in geometric proportions supporting a predicational model of behavior is never taken as such evidence. We have seen in chapter 2 that scientists can have alternative views of the same fact pattern. We have seen in the present chapter that experimenter and subject can have alternative views of what is taking place before their very eyes and ears. Well, in the cognitive research literature today we find a similar phenomenon taking place, of evidence for a predicating intelligence being used to support the image of a mediating mechanism. I briefly survey these studies before making some concluding comments.

One of the earliest series of studies throwing doubt on frequency in favor of predication was conducted by Rock (1957; with Heimer 1959). The experimental task involved paired-associates, in which subjects had to learn to unite numbers to letters (e.g., "1-H") and/ or word fragments to word fragments (e.g., "HIC-LAT"). There were several such pairs to memorize, presented as a list. Typically, in tasks of this sort, subjects are given the same paired-associates to memorize, trial after trial, until they correctly recall the entire list on two consecutive trials (learning criterion). Subjects therefore rehearse the same list from trial to trial, getting some pairs correctly and missing others in the learning process. Frequency theories hold that subjects gradually "acquire" such pairings through repeated practice and growing familiarity across the trials. Rock followed this typical procedure for one group of subjects, but in a second group he removed all those pairs from a list that a subject had not correctly recalled on any trial during the learning process and replaced them with other pairs. This meant that the list was continually changing in content from trial to trial so that familiarity was not involved, and, indeed, practice amounted to "one trial" per pair.

Thus, if a subject had not recalled "1-H" on any trial (e.g., the third, fifth, or seventh) it was replaced by "3-L." There was no opportunity for a subject to correct errors through practice. In this group, it was a matter of learning the whole list correctly or having to learn replacement pairs for those missed. The results of this experimental strategy were surprising. Rock found in cross-validation that those subjects who had their failures removed did as well on the overall task as subjects who memorized the same list to criterion. It thus appears that subjects either learn a pair (on any "one" trial) or they do not. This is highly consistent with a predicational view of learning. It is not frequent inputting but frequent putting on (framing, predicating) that determines what is learned. A "trial" is only a "trial" when the subject has fixed the correct pair as a predicated unit.

Tulving and Pearlstone (1966) found that organizing material to be remembered into categories, such as four-footed animals (cow, rat), weapons (bomb, cannon), and so on, greatly facilitated recall. Subjects cued with a category name could then retrieve the numerous examples within that category, and even when not cued, subjects tended to recall items from a category together. Even a cursory examination establishes that such categorical organizers are always predicates, broader realms of meaning that have been utilized to frame targeted items meaningfully. It is generally accepted today that merely repeating items (words, names, concepts) does not ensure retention in long-term memory. Practice is important to recall, but along the way within such practice the learner invariably organizes the material to be remembered in some *meaningful* way, and it is this organizing predication that invariably accounts for long-term retentions (Rundus 1971). Thus, as Howard says, "the most important basis of organization of long-term memory is meaning" (1983:218).

The cognitive theorist is likely to speak of retrieval cues at this point. Information is presumably taken in without predication and then organized in such a way that retrieval capitalizes on this organization through a cue stemming from the organizer (Ozier 1978). The term "elaboration" is also used to describe the fact that people bring together various concepts into a more or less meaningful whole. Sometimes the claim is made that the greater such elaboration, the "deeper" is the cognitive processing taking place (Craik and Tulving 1975). The "deep processing" metaphor is not elaborated for us, but we who read such accounts can predicate the meaning of "deep" by our own experiences of "plunging to the depths" of swimming pools and the like, arriving at some sense of the greater significance or extended involvement that this metaphor implies.

People find it easier to remember *shark* after having been asked "Is a shark a type of fish?" than to remember *heaven* after having been asked "Is heaven a type of fish?" Craik and Tulving (ibid.) claim that this is true because subjects initially answered "yes" to the first sentence and "no" to the second and that owing to the greater amount of "processing time" (i.e., frequency considerations) given over to affirmation than to negation, subsequent recall is facilitated. Yet, a far more obvious point is that fish predicates shark meaningfully, whereas it makes no sense as a predication of heaven. Surely such considerations of the meaning being organized into a statement must count for something in recall. We know from studies on metaphor that subjects judge them to be good and remember them better if they make sense. For example, "A pliers is like a crab" is judged better and remembered more readily than "A bumper is like a statue" (Katz 1982; McCabe 1982; Stein 1977). Crab as a predicating meaning can be extended analogically to pliers, as the meaning of fish can be extended more directly to shark.

Considerations of a learner's initial predication of what is to be committed to memory have proven to be important to subsequent recall. Tulving and Thomson (1973) have shown that it is easier to recall something if the circumstances at the time of recall are identical to the circumstances at the time of initial "encoding." They interpret this finding as due to the fact that the correct retrieval cues are fashioned at the time of and along with what is being "stored" in memory at the outset (p. 369). A predicational explanation of these findings would go as follows: If our initial predication lending meaning to some life experience can be reaffirmed exactly, the memory of this experience will be enriched exactly as it was initially and hence our recall of the experience will be detailed and accurate. It will, in a sense, be a virtual repeat of the experience. On the other hand, if an experience that has been predicated "one way" is now repredicated "another way," the possibility of complete and accurate recall diminishes.

What is "heard" as a sentence has been shown to be dependent on the framing context (predication) of that sentence. Thus, subjects were orally given various endings to the following sentence: "It was found that the *eel was on the ____." When the blank is filled with the word *axle*, the subject hears "wheel." When it is filled with the word *shoe*, the subject hears "heel," and so on (Warren and Warren 1970). Evidence is plentiful that people think in terms of context-establishing ideas, images, scenarios, themes, and so on, rather than in terms of specific words or lexical units (Bransford and Franks 1975; Honeck, Riechmann, and Hoffman 1975).

Meaningful predication can also be seen in the so-called family-resemblance phenomenon. Wittgenstein was the first to point out that some meanings are just better suited to extend to certain targets than others are (1922:31–32). It is difficult and sometimes impossible to offer a precise definition of a family resemblance. Some things share an overall quality while others have specific similarities making their meanings coalesce into a family of meaning. Berlin and Kay (1969) studied exemplars of various colors in twenty different language systems. Although there was much disagreement when all nuances of color were taken into consideration, the *best* exemplars of a color identified by subjects attained considerable agreement across the twenty different languages. Rosch (1975) has found general agreement among subjects concerning what is a good exemplar of certain descriptive categories. For example, in the "bird" category the robin, sparrow, bluebird, and canary were rated uniformly high as exemplars whereas the chicken, turkey, ostrich, and penguin were rated low. Such findings make great sense if we think of them as reflecting a predicational process.

Along with families of meaning we have idiosyncratic meanings to consider in human cognition. The organizations that people array to facilitate memory can take on many different and distinctively unique forms. Memory schemes generally rely on the principle of having some prearranged (precedent) framework within which to affix specific items (names of people, grocery lists, etc.) [see Cermak 1976; Lorayne and Lucas 1974]. Cognitive theory holds that this framework has been overlearned in the past and functions in the present as a facilitating mediator. But we can surely see in the efficacy of such memory systems a reflection of an even more basic process in memory. This is all the more plausible when we learn that people can concoct highly bizarre images of items that they intend to recall, and such unusual constructions—which have never been seen in experience and may even be impossible in principle—facilitate recall (O'Brien and Wolford 1982). We want to remember a man's name, which happens to be "Streeter." After contemplating his facial features we imagine a huge nose without a body attached, "looking" out at us from a passing streetcar—or, running down a street that we are familiar with. Ridiculous and impossible images to be sure, but once we meet our big-nosed acquaintance and must search for his name we are glad we took the time to frame them. Actually, the more personal (private, self-involved, etc.) we can make such predications the better our recall will be.

There is some evidence that intention to recall "works" by way of such efforts to organize memory. That is, subjects do no better when they set out to recall something intentionally than when they merely categorize (predicate) information without a specific intention to recall it on a later occasion (Mandler 1967). This finding is actually consistent with the fact that the formal cause is a necessary aspect of final causation. Whether or not a person sets out to remember something, if he or she has neglected to frame things through a formal-cause organization, there can be no subsequent "that" for the sake of which to base an intention on. Such predicating organization of mental contents seems to have its limitations. Subjects usually cannot distinguish more than about seven items from an input list in immediate memory (some say this "magic number" is four and not seven; see Simon 1985:81). Miller (1956) referred to these seven (or four) units as "chunks" of information. But, of course, it is possible for the person to combine several chunks under an even more abstract "chunk" allowing for memory to be expanded. This is obviously an alternative way of talking about the predicational process.

When the AI theorist relies on cognitive representations to simulate behavior in the belief that there is a process of learning/language that can explain the appearance of such representations as contents within it, he or she is building a case on foundations of sand. It is not by any means clear what learning involves. Hence, the AI theorist can no longer confidently assume that cognitive representations are the products or contents of a learning process that is undisputed, proven, or *even understood*. Traditional mediational models are not "accounting for" the essentials of cognitive representation in the way that AI theorists naively assume. Nor is there any evidence that predication is learned. Indeed, it seems more appropriate to say that people do *not* learn to predicate; they predicate in order to learn.

And in this process it appears that people take on an agential role in their behavior. The person is always a factor in what is learned, as the scientist was found to be a factor in what was discovered (Chapter 2). Thus, evidence for predicational processing is also suggestive of evidence for a human teleology. Chapter 6 looks specifically at this question of agency in human behavior, both from a predicational and mediational (i.e., AI) point of view.

6.
Agency in Artificial Intelligence

As we saw in chapter 2, with the rise of Newtonian science in the seventeenth century, final-cause theorizing was intentionally repressed. When interpreted from the introspective perspective, the "that, for the sake of which" style of predicational explanation results in what has traditionally been termed *agency*. This concept may be defined as follows: *Agency is the organism's capacity to behave/believe in conformance with, in contradiction of, in addition to, or without regard for environmental or biological promptings or determinants*. A more popular reference to agency is found in the phrase "free will." Aristotle believed the end or purpose that the agent was pursuing in moving events along was the "best" eventuality possible, but we do not have to view things this way. People can be thought of as freely choosing and pursuing ends that are evil, harmful to others, and even self-destructive.

It was noted in chapter 2 that Aristotle used final causation in both an introspective and an extraspective manner. I also noted, and have since built on this insight, that oppositionality or dialectical reasoning facilitates the explanation of human teleology or what I am now calling agency/free will. In effect, what we are suggesting is that when it is used introspectively we define a final cause as "that, *as opposed to this*, for the sake of which" actions occur. Oppositionality provides us with the rationale for explaining a transcending, self-reflexive intelligence that can turn back on and negate its predicate assumptions (beliefs, biases, etc.) and thereby reaffirm an alternative based on an intentional, purposive choice among contraries and contradictories. This is possible because the predicating intelligence literally "works" by way of taking a position on experience "from birth," from its original efforts to cognize experience. We avoid the Baconian criticism in this dialectical formulation of human reason because now it *does* make a difference to know something about the "that" (reason, purpose, etc.) for the sake of which the person is behaving. This final-cause phrasing adds something to our understanding of the meaningful course that the person's behavior will take.

The cognitive task facing a predicating organism is therefore to "take a position on" the oppositionally framed meanings of one's life circumstances and continually to affirm the direction that this life will therefore be taking. In chapter 3 I suggested that this is a *Logos* process and not a *Bios* process, reaffirming thereby our fundamental reliance on formal and final causation (which always combine in telic description). This *Logos* process has many aspects to it, including the dialectical versus demonstrative distinction, but in essence it encourages us to take an introspective perspective concerning the organism's behavior. We can present logic extraspectively, as when a mathematical formula is sketched on the blackboard, but if we are seriously pursuing the ultimate grounds for this formula we invariably arrive at the reasoner qua mathematician. What are the predicate assumptions, and how do these determine what eventuates?

In theorizing this way we follow not only Aristotle but also Kant. The latter's conception of a "causality of the will" was said to produce effects in opposition to the power of physical (i.e., efficient) causes (Kant 1952b:164). Kant's stress on transcendental and reflexive powers of mind was based on his view of a dialectical process in human reason (Kant 1952a:115,184). Kant believed that free will arises exclusively by intentions (motives) framed within pure reason, independent of sensory impulses. This willful causation enables the person to oppose the stimulus "inputs" from physical reality and to redirect one's course of behavior and belief for any of a number of reasons. At least, the person can do so in the realm of pure reason, where there is also ample room for concocting idiotic and fallacious reasons for doing things.

The capacity to conceptually alter "known reality" for good or evil is also a manifestation of human agency. To truly create, innovate, or change the course of events in reality, one must also be capable of letting things stand as they are. This is why the above definition states that the agent can act in conformance with biological or social pressures. Most people, most of the time, conform to their social reality. They do what others do and think what others in their milieu think. But the issue before us now is: Could they do otherwise? Axiologists have typically framed the central problem of free will as follows: "An act is free if and only if the agent could have done otherwise, *all circumstances remaining the same* (italics in original)" (O'Connor 1971:82).

The predicational model allows for this alternative, because the person is continually taking a position on life—conforming to what is the case or altering events based on what is eventually affirmed in one's line of reasoning (including "unconscious" or "unadmitted" oppositional reasoning; see Rychlak 1979:259). The determination here is based, not on material-efficient, but on formal-final causation. The dialectically reasoning human being is always—from the birth of cognition!—affirming a course of predicated behavior that could have gone in opposition to the course it actually took. Inanimate objects, well described extraspectively in material/efficient-cause terms, never arrange such grounds for the sake of which their existence carries forward. Leaves are blown by the wind and rocks tumble down hills without ever being burdened with the responsibility of having to take a position on their future course of existence. Given any single occurrence in the "life" of a leaf or a rock, these inanimate objects could surely not have done otherwise than what they did "do."

In chapter 6, three somewhat different strategies that have been employed by AI theorists to account for agency in human behavior are reviewed: as controlled goal attainment, delayed mediational processing, and recursivity through strange loops. The purpose here is to determine how satisfactorily these explanations capture the classical meaning of human agency or free will.

Agency as Controlled Goal Attainment

Rosenblueth, Wiener, and Bigelow (1943) advanced one of the earliest arguments in support of a teleological conception of machine behavior. Their argument was based on a certain interpretation of input and feedback. These authors defined *output* as any change produced in the surroundings by the machine; *input* was any event external to the machine that modified its actions. Feedback is a much abused conception today. People use it informally to refer to any kind of input that is requested (e.g., "Give me your feedback on this, will you?"). But in the strict, original cybernetic sense, feedback is of two types. On the one hand, we can speak of *positive feedback*, which is a fraction of the output from the machine returning as input (p. 19). On the other hand, feedback can be *negative* when the machine is being directed by the margin of error obtaining between its actions and a specific goal (ibid.).

For example, if a spacecraft is aimed at a certain target, it will continually monitor its position relative to this target from which it can bounce off signals. As the spacecraft strays off course this negative feedback will be duly recorded and adjustments made in its rocket firings to correct its course. As it does so, positive feedback can also be employed to signal that certain adjustments are being made in flight. It is this self-control exhibited by the computing mechanism of the spacecraft that leads AI enthusiasts to draw parallels between cybernetic machines and human beings. Thus, Dennett celebrates the determinism of self-control by observing that: "The Viking spacecraft is as deterministic a device as any clock, but this does not prevent it from being able to control itself. Fancier deterministic devices can not only control themselves; they can evade the attempts of other self-controllers to control them. If we [human beings] are also deterministic devices, we need not on that account fear that we cannot be in control of ourselves and our destinies" (1984:72). Boden adds the following reassurance: "It is not mechanism as such that is the enemy of freedom, but mechanism of a sort where the autonomous self-monitoring computations carried out by the system have no power (or a reduced power) to influence its actions" (1981:21).

Rosenblueth, Wiener, and Bigelow took this self-controlling feature of machines as a rationale for purpose in the mediating mechanism. Purposeless machines could not be interpreted as directed to a goal, but purposeful machines did orient their actions to attaining a goal—"to a final condition in which the behaving object reaches a definite correlation in time or in space with respect to another object or event" (1943:18). If the goal is not giving off a signal, then there is no negative feedback possible. After dismissing teleologies based on final causation as illogical, Rosenblueth, Wiener, and Bigelow offer an alternative view: "Teleological behavior thus becomes synonymous with behavior controlled by negative feedback, and gains therefore in precision by a sufficiently restricted connotation" (p. 24).

There is a similar theoretical position to be found in Minsky's discussion of the *difference engine* (also called a general problem solver), which he defines as a process that embodies a representation of some outcome or goal and a mechanism to make it persist until that outcome is achieved. This capacity of the machine to "zero in" on a goal and achieve it prompts Minsky to make the following observation: "The difference-engine scheme remains the most useful conception of goal, purpose, or intention yet discovered" (1986:79).

If we break down the essentials of the argument that goal orientation and goal attainment are reflective of teleology there are four points to deal with: (1) selection of the goal; (2) instrumental actions aimed at realizing or achieving the goal; (3) adapting to circumstances or making self-corrections so that the goal would be continually attainable despite changes occurring during the instrumental action; and (4) giving up on the goal or switching goals. It seems clear that the AI, mediational position rests exclusively on our second and third points. In a predicational model, the most important point would be the first, since it deals with the creation of a goal as a precedent "that" for the sake of which steps two and three would be sequaciously concocted to attain this end. Furthermore, in a predicational model the goal is not really "over there" in existence to bounce signals off. The goal is a formal-cause pattern of some sort that has been adjudged or rendered valuable by the reasoning intelligence "over here" (in cognizance) and for the sake of which that intelligence now behaves (final-cause addition).

Not all goals exist. In fact, some goals are known by the person to be impossible—such as the goal for "self-perfection" that ever reaches beyond the person's grasp. But this does not deter the person from continually seeking this ideal. The AI theorist is picking up where Tolman left off. Purpose is depicted extraspectively as something that can be observed. It is always possible that what we claim is "the" purpose under observation is "our" predicated assumption of a purpose rather than the behaving organism's. For example, the linguist Bennett has noted that "some teleological concepts do not involve intention, as when we say that the frog flicked out its tongue so as to catch the insect" (1976:36). What makes this appear teleological to Bennett is his introspectively framed understanding of the purpose served by the frog's tongue in attaining a nourishing goal. Yet, this kind of telic theorizing is clearly open to the Baconian criticism. It is an extraspective formulation of teleology and really no different than Aristotle's suggestions that leaves are for the sake of shading the fruit on trees or that bones are for the sake of supporting the muscles and viscera of the body. Understanding of the frog's reflex is not enriched by claiming that it involves an intention. Telic ascription at this level is excess theoretical baggage.

The same can be said of the spacecraft controlling its course through negative feedback. It does not really simulate what is meant when we say in an introspective theoretical mode that the person has a purpose in mind, or intends to accomplish something. The person's "goal" is a predicated meaning. It has been affirmed within a congerie of opposite possibilities and is now under covert belief or overt enactment. We cannot always "see" the person's goals, and indeed sometimes we are intentionally misled by the person as to the actual goal. Furthermore, the person always has the sense of "taking on" (taking a position on) a goal. This means there is always an alternative inkling of giving up the goal, leading in turn to even greater effort expended to achieve it. But then, as our fourth point specifies (refer above), it is also possible for a goal to be changed or dropped by the person who has framed it initially. Machines cannot make this decision, since they have not framed the initial goal as a predication directing their life's course.

The great stress placed on goal attainment in this interpretation of agency makes it appear that organisms who are not actively pursuing a goal are not agential or that agency is over once a goal has been achieved. Yet, human beings not only are hopeful of achieving certain outcomes beforehand but also are pleased or made unhappy by events following the attainment or nonattainment of such desired ends. Human beings celebrate an occasion such as a graduation or a marriage because they realize that events could have gone otherwise "back then," but fortunately they did not. There are also less admirable human behaviors following an outcome of some sort. People who bear resentments, who are humiliated because they are not given the best tickets at the theater, or who take umbrage at some unintended slight from a colleague are also reflecting agency. The hospitalized patient with a serious illness or an incarcerated criminal following a bungled felony can both ponder "why me?" in their unhappy circumstances. This recognition that events might have gone otherwise continues to nag at people even though the adverse event has now passed.

Dennett's reference to *determinism* suggests an issue that is frequently overlooked when this term is used. That is, determinisms are not limited to efficient and material causality. The conceptual necessity to be seen in logic and mathematics, where given certain precedents a sequacious line of meaning extension occurs, is an example of formal-cause determinism. And when one willfully drives oneself toward a desired goal, this is a final-cause determinism. In a free-will conception, the freedom of choice arises in the preaffirmation whereby the person "takes a position" on some belief or intended action given that opposite possibilities are implicitly known. Following this dialectically generated alternative, we can speak of will or willpower taking place as the person enacts the resultant intention. As we have seen (chapters 3 and 4), computer programs do not deal with the affirmation of such precedents for they are to be found solely in the cognitions of the writer who settles on what "is'" the case for the demonstratively "reasoning" machine.

Since roughly the seventeenth century, philosophers have identified determinism with efficient causation (e.g., the billiard ball variety), or with material causation (e.g., genetic substances), but a teleologist would scarcely find this limitation valid. Determinism is, in the final analysis, a predicate assumption made by a theorist interested in some subject matter. Aristotle's theory of the causes nicely subsumes the concept of determinism as it subsumes other theoretical concepts. There are, then, four kinds of determinism possible—one for each cause (chapter 2). As we have repeatedly seen, the predication model places emphasis on formal- and final-cause determinism, and the mediation model emphasizes material-cause and especially efficient-cause determinism.

I conclude that there is little support for teleology in the "control to goal-attainment" interpretation of agency. It is far more relevant to a theory of agency to consider the selecting of a belief qua goal than it is to consider the instrumentalities by which the organism enacts the resultant goal-directed behavior. The instrumentalities of points (2) and (3) (refer above) may be well captured in efficient-cause determinisms, but the predication of a belief or goal demands a formal-final cause determinism from the introspective perspective. We are back to the person in the Chinese room here, who was a perfect instrumentality but lacked any willful direction in behavior (chapter 1). There is no contradiction in suggesting that formal-final cause determinism functions in an organism that *also* is determined by material- and efficient-cause determinisms. As Aristotle taught us, we can use as many of the causal predications in accounting for behavior as our theory calls for.

Agency as Delay in Processing Amid Increasing Mediators

The second major strategy followed in the AI literature to account for human agency stresses the number of idea units or "mediators" being processed by the organism at any point in time and a capacity to delay within the efficient-cause flow of this process before mediation continues. At the outset of chapter 4 the Lockean interpretation of an idea as the content of a process rather than as a process per se was presented. Taking in Lockean ideas is akin to placing increasing numbers of teacups in a cabinet. If we were to carry this extraspective theoretical explanation further and wished to "account for" freedom of the will we might focus on the total number of items placed into the mental cabinet, which can thereby mediate behaviors. Obviously, the more idea units "in" the cabinet, the more possible it is for the organism to enact alternative behaviors through the instrumentality of such mediators. The more mediators, the "freer" the person is to behave (freedom here being identified with increasing degrees of freedom in the mathematical sense). The more Chinese figures the person has in the room, the more "information" that can be processed, and so on.

Locke also introduced a notion of a suspension of action in the ongoing use of these mental contents that has implications for free will. He began with the assumption that there are *uneasinesses* that impel the human being's will to prefer some course in life, such as seeking water when uneasy over thirst. Such motives would act quite singularly to direct the selections of the will. But as a mental action, the will does *not* have to be carried forward immediately. It can hang fire, so to speak, and *suspend* the execution of actions that might terminate the uneasinesses—as, executing the milk idea rather than the water idea after a pause to consider which of these mediating conceptions would lead to the greater pleasure. Locke then said: "This seems to me the source of all liberty; in this seems to consist that which is (as I think improperly) called free will" (1952:190). During this suspended course of action one can look over things from several angles and judge the benefit or harm, good or evil of what it is that one is about to do. Things that bring pleasure are good things, and those that result in pain are bad. Locke believed we could even project this goodness or badness into the future, comparing a present satisfaction to a later one.

Now, if Locke had conceptualized the human being via our predicational model, he would have had a rationale for the fact that people can hang fire, because in this fundamental process they are always suspended between the poles of opposition preliminary to affirming a certain course in life. To capture this explanation I must rely on formal and final causation as technical terms in my theory, suggesting that people behave for the sake of "this" rather than "that" opposing alternative. Note that I am now employing a final-cause explanation from the introspective theoretical perspective. Since he was an extraspective, efficient-cause theorist who had no special role for opposition in the cognitive act, Locke is left with a serious problem. To explain how it is that an efficient-cause sequence halts momentarily, we must postulate either a sedentary barrier (material cause) in the pathway stopping such motion or a countering force equal to the ongoing force of efficient causality that is to be halted.

As Rickaby (1906:vii) has shown, Locke cannot explain on the basis of efficient causation how it is that a pause can occur in the ongoing process of mentation, nor can he tell us why the person can hang fire in opposition to an uneasiness in one instance but not in another. As a result, neo-Lockeans have been forced to sneak a *homunculus* into their theories, which presumably makes the decisions within the ongoing process of efficient causation. The homunculus is simply an informal reference to the missing formal and final causation in the theoretical account. The homunculus is the predicator within the strictly mechanical process, on the order of a person driving (determining the direction of) an automobile. Hence, as a technical matter, Locke begs the question—which is to explain how decisions can possibly arise in a mediational conception of mind that is founded exclusively on efficient causation. He never succeeded in doing so, and ultimately had to rely on a frequency-contiguity thesis of past inputs directing today's haltings and selections in a unidirectional, demonstrative fashion.

Not surprisingly, we see the same course of events occurring in AI theory, where language is resorted to as the supposed idea units or mediators that have been learned over time and now carry human actions along based on the frequency and contiguity of this or that experience being input and associated into a nodal network of some type. Thus, Minsky (1986) suggests that language builds networks in our minds akin to Lockean complex ideas; the function of words learned during maturation is control (p. 196), and our language usage is identical with thought itself (p. 198). The basic constraints on the mind are two: *cause* (i.e., efficient cause) and *chance*. Causation constrains through the predictability of deterministic laws, and chance constrains through a randomness that disrupts predictability. There is nothing else, but nevertheless we human beings concoct an imaginary third alternative: "we continue to regard both Cause and Chance as intrusions on our freedom of choice. There remains only one thing to do: we add another region to our model of our mind. We imagine a third alternative, one easier to tolerate; we imagine a thing called 'freedom of will,' which leads beyond both kinds of constraint" (p. 306). Minsky believes that we know this third alternative is false, but we persist in bringing it up because of a psychological need to believe we are responsible organisms (p. 307).

So, for Minsky, something like a hanging fire in the ongoing process of linguistic mediation would arise through specifically learned word controls. We have learned to tell ourselves things and to control the course of our behavior through such personal comments and correctives. It is but a short step to form the illusion that such learned self-controls (sans agency) emanate from a will that is free to create unlearned, unshaped alternatives. Or there might be an unpredictability arising in the progression of behavior due to some chance occurrence that is misconstrued as a freely made action. The AI theorist typically believes that what the teleologist means by free will is the unpredictability of behavior. This is not true, of course, because a freely willing, choosing organism is highly predictable once we are privy to the (introspectively conceived) predications under which this organism is functioning (behaving "for the sake of").

Dennett (1984) has presented a detailed examination of the varieties of free will he feels are worth wanting and that are consistent with AI theory. He thinks that people resent machine simulation of human behavior because they fear a loss of their sense of freedom in such simulations, and he wants to assure them there are no such freedom-robbing "bogeymen" (p. 62) out there to be concerned about. Free will is, for Dennett, the "elbow room" or degrees of freedom that a completely determined organism always has. His argument runs as follows: Human beings are biologically prepared to act by way of both physical (p. 37) and social (p. 169) determinations. The randomness factor that Minsky referred to is mentioned by Dennett as one of the possible physical determinants of behavior, capable of being employed by certain robots but also a potential boon to human freedom: "Not only can we greatly improve the existential predicament of the robot by installing a radium randomizer or other quantum-effect amplifier, but we can pin our own hopes for free will on the discovery of similar, organically based hardware in our brains" (p. 119).

Another biological capacity, language, makes it possible for the human being to be socially determined. Language provides the mediators through which others influence the person. Indeed, language usage permits the human being to cook up all manner of "irrelevant or baroque (nonfunctional) endeavors [such as]: gossip, riddles, poetry, philosophy" (p. 48). We humans also learn to talk to ourselves, and thereby, to form a mediating theory about ourselves. Thus, we make up reasons for why we did what we did. Even though we never see our decisions being made—they just pop to mind once made—we think we have made them because our language indoctrination has taught us that we are responsible for how we use words (p. 78). We formulate a self concept, which is a purely illusory formulation emerging in the continuing learning process that accompanies language acquisition (p. 82). Dennett uncritically accepts Locke's thesis concerning the power that people have to suspend the execution of desires (pp. 36, 86, 134).

Addressing the issue of "doing otherwise" that we find is fundamental to agential theory (refer above), Dennett claims that we can always do otherwise in the future because of the Lockean capacity to ponder what was done in the past and redirect our course accordingly. He has little appreciation for dialectical formulations as the source of free will and dismisses such contradictory human inclinations as wanting one's cake and eating it too as preposterous and unrealistic kinds of freedom expectations (p. 138). Dialectical self-reflection and rumination are viewed as potentially dangerous activities that must be cut off before they get out of hand. The brilliant dialectician Nietzsche is cited as an example of someone who carried self-reflection too far (p. 88).

Even though he is cognizant of the distinction between introspective and extraspective slants on theorizing about behavior (p. 35), Dennett is never moved to take such factors into consideration. As a result, he does not bring his level of analysis into contact with a predicational model of behavior. His treatment of meaning is framed extraspectively, as a reflection of physical properties (p. 27) that can act as signals for the shaping or "learning" of a system (p. 30). Yet, it would be my contention that when people are concerned about the suitability of the computer analogue as a model for the person, it is not because they fear loss of free will. People sense this agential quality directly and do not much care what the AI theorist wishes to believe on this question. But what *is* an irritant is the simpleminded, stripped-down version of how the thought process is to be conceptualized. The bogeyman is not loss of free will but the loss of meaning!

As noted in chapter 1, this loss of meaning in the computer analogue is the basic motivation behind Searle's Chinese room example, which depicts the meaninglessness of computer cognition.

The representations processed from input to output by computers are supposedly analogical to the human being's use of language, but how legitimate is this parallel? The AI theorist overlooks what Polanyi (1964:209) called the "personal affirmation" of the reasoner's sense of a meaningful context framing experience and the personal power (p. 263) that this predicating understanding gives one to effect willful changes in one's life. Such changes do not occur "by chance." They are framed intentionally and enacted with a purpose. We are dealing in a formal/final cause determinism at this point. We must not overlook the "will" half of the free-will phrase. As one exercises one's capacity to select certain alternatives from among a congeries of opposite possibilities (point 1 above), the range of alternatives concerning the future course of behavior narrows. For example, the more decisions a moral person makes to avoid certain behaviors, the more this person is limiting the alternatives for behavior. This setting of limits on the course of behavior is the quintessence of determinism. Hence, it is proper to say that in a freely willed course of behavior based on affirmed principles or convictions a (final-cause) determinism is inevitable (see Rychlak 1979, for a more thorough examination of this point).

My conclusion is that in their efforts to remain within the efficient-cause strictures of their extraspective mediation model, the AI theorists have failed to capture agency by appealing to delays in processing or to increasing the resultant number of mediators available to the programmed computer/robot. It does not matter whether an agent has two or ten or fifty alternatives to enact in reality. If these alternatives are merely mediated signals acting as controls rather than meanings (see chapter 3), and if the person is not predicating what might eventuate, then we cannot speak of agency in the sense that this concept was defined at the outset of this chapter (refer above), which is the definition that the average person has in mind when expressing belief in freedom of the will. In their third and most interesting effort to capture agency the AI advocates address the core issue of the predicational explanation: self-reflective cognition.

Agency as Self-Reflexivity Through Recursivity/Strange Loops

The final strategy we find in the AI literature to account for agency is based on the concept of *recursivity*, which involves a "levels of processing" and a "repetition of function" within the programming of a system. Boden heralds the role of recursivity in agency as follows:

> ... a recursive programming language ... [is] well suited to the description and manipulation of recursive structures such as the psychological phenomena of purpose, meaning, and language. A recursive structure is one with an essentially hierarchical character, that can be naturally described at several levels of detail. And a recursive procedure is one that can refer to and operate on itself, so that it can be "nested" within itself to an indefinite number of hierarchical levels (1977:372).

Thus, an algorithmic rule of some sort can be repeatedly used in a program at both higher and lower levels of complexity (recall our discussion of "iteration" in chapter 3). This process of breaking a problem down into subprocesses, solving each part (or "chunk") in turn according to the algorithmic rule, permits the AI theorist to suggest a parallel here with the human reasoner, who intentionally breaks down a complex problem into more manageable units, solving the less complex aspects before returning to a solution of the whole (see Minsky 1986:161 on this point).

Hofstadter (1980) has done more with recursion in his explanation of behavior than any other AI theorist to date, and his formulation, therefore, will be used as a sample paradigm of how agency is being suggested in the software directions brought to action in the hardware. The general strategy here is to find a parallel notion to self-reflexivity, which the predicational theorist claims is a capacity for the human mind to turn back on itself through a Kantian transcendence, a "knowing that knowing is taking place." We have already seen how mediational theorists view this in exclusively linguistic terms, as a learned capacity to ask questions of ourselves. Indeed, the "self" as a concept is viewed as nothing but a linguistic convention, a learned symbol giving the mediational process a focal point for ongoing mediation but not signifying anything uniquely agential in the process. In the Lockean formulation, the delayer of action, the ponderer, and the selector of the course of behavior would be such an ongoing exchange of verbalisms, linguistic forms input years ago and functioning today based on the preponderance of past shapings "this way" or "that way" in the course of events.

It is important to appreciate that there is no dialectic, no oppositional reasoning intrinsic to cognition as framed by Lockean philosophy. Contradiction, doubt, wavering, disbelief, all such mental balancings between the poles of opposition are said to arise strictly in the information as input from the environment. Locke tells us that it is from experience that we obtain such clashing "testimonies" (1952:369) or inputs; this leads to various degrees of *probability* for our thought to be influenced one way or another on any question under consideration (mediation). Locke observes: "Probability upon such grounds carries so much evidence with it, that it naturally determines the judgment, and leaves us as little liberty to believe or disbelieve, as a demonstration does, whether we will know, or be ignorant" (ibid.). There is no freedom here to negate what has been input, no capacity to reason against the odds of past inputs and decide a course of action in negation of the dictates of the "most probable."

We might now observe that if Dennett believes that Locke has provided an explanation of free will in his delay-of-processing explanation, we could easily see in this treatment of judgment a contradiction to such agential claims. That is, it is clear now that what actually "judges" (chooses) during the delay is the preponderance of past inputs on one side or the other of any decision facing the person. When such inputs are roughly equal, dialectical examination might appear to be taking place as the person tabulates the "arguments and proofs *pro* and *con*" (ibid.) concerning the decision. But there is no "predicator" (or "self") affirming certain meaning-relations and negating others in this deliberative process. The decisions made are always the tail end of previous unidirectional influences, efficient-cause tabulations that cannot be implicitly negated but require "other" mediating inputs to counteract them much as the billiard ball has to be countered by another ball before its efficiently caused course is altered. Surely, agency is a superficial addition carrying no explanatory weight in this formulation. We are open to the Baconian criticism if we try to force a free-will conception into such a purely mechanistic account, one that completely fails to capture transcendental and reflexive human thinking.

Hofstadter's (1980) ambitious work aims to rectify this situation. He begins by drawing our attention to a *strange loop*, which takes place in a hierarchical system so that in moving upward or downward through the levels of this system "we unexpectedly find ourselves right back where we started" (p. 10). He also calls this a *tangled hierarchy* and offers the feedback conception as a "simple tangle" (p. 691) because even though we are not considering hierarchical levels at this point, when a part of the output returns as input we are indeed back where we started from. Hofstadter stresses that strange loops are "at the core of intelligence" (p. 27). His discussion of the strange loop is enriched by parallels to the woodcuts and lithographs of the artist M. C. Escher, who specialized in presenting quizzical topics such as having people continually *ascending* staircases that take them down, as well as up, or a hand depicted sketching itself so that we cannot tell which is supposed to represent the active and which the passive extremity. In effect, Escher capitalizes on unstable figure-ground relations as demonstrated in the experiments of gestalt psychology—especially the work of Rubin (1921). There are many familiar examples of this sort taken from gestalt psychology, such as a picture in which there is a white vase on a black ground, but also the black ground can become two people looking at each other.

Hofstadter now draws a parallel between such unstable figure-ground relationships and recursivity in the art work of Escher: "A *cursively drawable* figure is one whose ground is merely an accidental by-product of the drawing act. A *recursive* figure is one whose ground can be seen as a figure in its own right" (1980:67). There is a problem with this distinction stemming from the fact that, according to gestalt psychology, the only reason we see anything as a figure (i.e., point of focus) in our visual field is because of "the one-sided function of the contour which bounds and shapes the figure but not the ground" (Koffka 1935:183). We can demonstrate this one-sided function of contour, which ever frames a figure but never a ground, by analyzing Escher's beautiful lithograph entitled *Liberation*. Hofstadter also makes use of this lithograph in his analysis (1980:57). Figure 3 presents the Escher lithograph.

Note at the bottom of Escher's drawing that we have first triangles and then birds, interlocked in an unstable figure-ground relationship. From time to time we can see either the black or the white figures as focal points, defined by their contrasting ground. As gestaltists, we always expect to have the ground frame the contour of the figure. This holds for figure 3 in toto, which is framed by the book page on which it is printed; and this page, in turn, is framed by the ground on which the book rests (e.g., a desk, a person's lap, the surrounding room if held up in front of the reader, etc.). In looking up from the bottom to the top of *Liberation* we are not likely to appreciate the role that ground is playing in our

Figure 3. *Liberation*, by M. C. Escher (lithograph, 1955). Copyright © 1990 M. C. Escher Heirs / Baarn, Holland.

perception. We think that when we move from a white triangle or bird to its contrast this is because we have shifted our perception of strictly figural aspects of our vision.

But according to gestalt principles it is the ground that is actually framing the figures for us. As Koffka tells us: "the contours which shape the figure do not shape its ground; if the latter has a shape, it owes this to other forces than those which produce the figure upon it" (1935:184). Indeed, it is sometimes difficult for the perceiver to see a certain figure (such as a black bird) because one cannot shift to the proper (in this case, white) ground. This also explains why in the midportions of *Liberation* we see *either* white or black birds flying and not *both* black and white birds flying together, which should be possible if a grounding reference were not essential to the framing of a figure. Note that at the top of the Escher lithograph we see the birds taking leave of their figure-ground bondage to fly off into the sky. But the birds are now all black or darkly hued. This is because to give the illusion of flight Escher had to employ a ground that was not going to shift, in which the spaces between the birds would be distant enough to convey unequivocal separation or "liberation." It is in the ground's influence on the figure that we find the artist's intentions being realized—from an unstable figure-ground relationship at the bottom to a separate, stable relationship between figure and ground at the top. Contour, like the logic of predication, is one-sided, working always from the broader to the narrower, from the outer to the inner.

Though he begins on questionable if not erroneous gestalt assumptions, Hofstadter's next move is to tie recursion to nesting, including such things as stories inside stories, movies inside movies, musical passages inside musical passages, and even parenthetical comments inside parenthetical comments (Hofstadter 1980:127). It might appear that if stories can be told inside other stories, the latter predicate the former. There is, however, a crucial difference between what is involved in predication and what is involved in recursion. We find this difference when Hofstadter states that: "a recursive definition never defines something in terms of itself, but always in terms of *simpler versions* of itself" (ibid.; italics in original). In other words, recursion is a repetition, as in the iteration of algorithms. It has to do with the binary reduction of programming, employing the identical algorithmic rule at different levels of complexity.

In contrast, a predication is never merely a simpler version of itself being repeated in the target that it predicates. Recursion is a matching-up of identities across levels. Predication is a wider range of meaning being focused in some sense on a targeted item—the *telos*—within its range. The fact that predication is always tied to oppositionality makes it clear that we are not viewing simpler versions of the wider range in the targeted item under predication. The opposite possibility, which also frames the target under predication, is not being conveyed when we specifically predicate that "James is reliable." Unreliability is in the wider extent of this predication, but it is not being reproduced in the specific judgment of James's character. If we were to symbolize this judgment with Euler circles, a smaller circle labeled James would be placed within a larger circle labeled "reliable people." But the region outside the larger circle, the nonreliable realm in which James is not being located, is ever "there" as an aspect of the meaning under wider predication (see figures 1 and 2). So we are not dealing in mere repetitions of identical versions of the predication when we extend its meaning to the target under elaboration.

In fact, predications are occasionally difficult to define, as in the "family resemblances" that Wittgenstein (1922) discussed. A series of games, such as board games, card games, ball games, and the like, may have certain features in common, but they are far from identical under the categorical rubric "game." It is therefore possible to have a sense of "a game" or "gameness" and to apply this as a predication to life activities in a metaphorical or analogical sense. For example, we may identify aspects of the board game and our behavior "on the job"—the analogous aspects—where we may be said to compete, have goals, hope to win, and the like. But there are significant differences here as well—the disanalogous aspects —since our very livelihood has implications that are not merely gamelike in the sense of playful; there are no clear-cut rules to follow on the job, it is not always easy to name a winner or loser, and so forth. The other side of the coin is that, even when a family resemblance is employed in description as a categorical exemplar, the referents subsumed by this categorization are not always identical in capturing the family resemblance. In this regard, as we noted in chapter 5, Rosch (1975) has demonstrated that people consider the robin, sparrow, bluebird, and canary as better exemplars of a "bird" category than the chicken, turkey, ostrich, or penguin.

Hofstadter invites us to think of recursion as looping in a machine, whereby the hardware is given programmed instruction to do the same thing, over and over again, using smaller portions of the data, then combining these into larger "chunks," and so forth until a solution is reached (p. 149). He considers this looping procedure to be "the essence of recursion—something being defined in terms of simpler versions of itself, instead of explicitly" (p. 152).

The strategy is now complete. Machine programs can loop across hierarchical levels of a system, and some of these more complex (strange) loopings or tangled hierarchies can nest certain contents at one level and then return to them at a later time. Indeed, looked at from lower to higher levels we might say that a machine process can "loop above" itself and reach a higher level outside of itself—not the entire system, but a larger subsystem. This is the other side of a recursion, moving upward in the Escherian staircase. Would this not be akin to Kant's suggestion that in speculative reason, there is a transcendent capacity—owing to the transcendental dialectic—for thought to rise above and turn back on itself? Hofstadter likes this line of theoretical development, and to buttress his case he turns to Gödel's famous proofs. He must do so, actually, because as Lucas (1961) and others have pointed out, there are important implications for the looping phenomenon in the arguments of Gödel.

There are two primary theorems of Gödel's proof. The first establishes that in any *consistent* system that is powerful enough to produce simple arithmetic—and this includes a computing machine—there are formulae that cannot be proved in the system but that a reasoning human intelligence can see to be true. In effect, this theorem states that it is impossible to achieve an axiomatic method in which endlessly true formulae about some area of inquiry will be generated (Nagel and Newman 1958:6). Gödel's second theorem, which is a corollary of the first, establishes that it is impossible to prove in a consistent system that the system *is* consistent. Now, the unique thing about this proof is that it is fundamentally self-reflexive, calling for an *introspective* examination of the system in question. As Lucas has observed: "The essence of the Gödelian formula is that it is self-referring. It says that 'This formula is unprovable-in-this-system.' When carried over to a machine, the formula is specified in terms which depend on the particular machine in question. The machine is being asked a question about its own processes. We are asking it to be self-conscious, and say what things it can and cannot do" (1961:124).

Machines are unable to accomplish this introspective effort because they are as all formal systems, totally extraspective formulations, lacking the transcendent introspective capacity of a dialectically reasoning organism. Hofstadter and other AI theorists fail to appreciate or accept this basic distinction in how to account for the full range of mentation—dialectical as well as demonstrative. In typical AI theoretical style, Hofstadter ties strange loops to mediating language usage, as follows: "where language does create strange loops is when it talks about itself, whether directly or indirectly. Here, something *in* the system jumps out and acts *on* the system, as if it were *outside* the system" (1980:691; italics in original). We take note of the "as if" proviso here, but the point of Gödel's proof is that this transcendent capacity of rising above (outside) the system is actually taking place. Recursion cannot account for the fact that a human mind can rise above and beyond a systematic process to recognize an inconsistency in the system that the system cannot recognize. Recursion is always within the system, an aspect of the very process referred to as "the system." A Gödelian perspective from outside or "above" the system is *not* a more complex version of this system as is the case in recursion. The Gödelian perspective is a *different* system, a wider view within which the targeted system is framed. This wider expanse has a range of meaningful understanding that exceeds the understanding of the targeted (narrower) expanse, much as we have schematized in the Euler circles of figure 1.

In suggesting that something jumps outside the system to act "on" the system, Hofstadter has unknowingly employed oppositionality in his account. This "outside versus inside" range is unrecognized because, in his typically demonstrative fashion, he focuses on what "is" the system and not on what "is not" the system. We might picture this as one of the items within a large Euler circle "jumping out" of the circle (in the noncircle region of oppositionality) to act on the circle in some way. Of course, this violates the top-down processing of what we understand as predication. Something that would now presumably be unpredicated would be influencing a predication in bottom-up (inside to outside) fashion. Since Hofstadter thinks of the ingredients within the larger Euler circle as simpler versions of the larger circle, he can arrive at this interesting but highly dubious position. Since all is "one" in a recursive algorithmic process, a part can act on the whole in the same way that the whole acts on each of the parts. In theorizing this way, Hofstadter has forged a kind of extraspective self-reflexivity by way of a looping recursion.

Self-reflexivity as construed introspectively is not simply a recursive loop whereby one can employ mediational linguistic symbols and talk about what he or she is talking about ("talk to the self"). The point of self-reflexivity is that one can discover through self-examination that one is always "taking a position" on life, knowing things that are potentially questionable, advancing on the basis of this knowledge, having a sense of Polanyian commitment to certain views, and so forth. This is not a mediating talk about talk but a realization that whatever is under processing in experience *is* under processing, and that it could be otherwise (i.e., negated or contradicted through oppositional cognitions). As Lucas sums up this reflexive capacity: "In saying that a conscious being knows something, we are saying not only that he knows it, but that he knows that he knows it, and that he knows that he knows that he knows it, and so on, as long as we care to pose the question; there is, we recognize, an infinity here, but it is not an infinite regress in the bad sense, for it is the questions that peter out, as being pointless, rather than the answers" (1961:125).

Extraspectively conceived systems such as computing machines cannot engage in introspectively formulated actions such as these. One must *transcend the a priori* in order to reflect on what one does. Words are called for to communicate and make clear what this introspective effort discovers. But words are never sufficient to capture the phenomenal experience of recognizing that one is taking an a priori point of view, that one is in an ongoing, predicational process of knowing. Hofstadter struggles mightily to overcome this impasse between the extraspective and introspective formulation of cognition. He eventually introduces an "emergence" conception to account for the fact that higher-levels in the system may be inexplicable in terms of lower levels: "there could be some high-level way of viewing the mind/brain, involving concepts which do not appear on lower levels, and that this level might have explanatory power that does not exist—not even in principle—on lower levels. It would mean that some facts could be explained on the high level quite easily, but not on lower levels *at all*" (1980:708).

This would seem to negate the recursion principle, which suggests that what is higher is also lower. But Hofstadter is not bothered by this inconsistency, and he continues as follows: "My belief is that the explanations of 'emergent' phenomena in our brains—for instance, ideas, hopes, images, and finally consciousness and free will—are based on a kind of Strange Loop, an interaction between levels in which the top level reaches back down towards the bottom level and influences it, while at the same time being itself determined by the bottom level.... The self comes into being at the moment it has the power to reflect itself" (ibid.:709).

This would imply that the self is implicitly related to reflexivity, to turning back on itself, moving outside its assumptions, and contemplating its own activities. Yet, Hofstadter's basic view of the self is as a kind of subsystem of linguistic conventions (p. 287) used to describe our actions. Since a system is a "group of interacting *parts*" (p. 303) it follows that the self-system is a group of interacting parts (linguistic statements, and so forth). Neural modules, networks, and so on, are *symbols* that can be triggered into activation (p. 349). Thought is always evoked (p. 394). The self is nothing but an overgrown symbol of this type, a constellation of other symbols into a kind of chunked "part" of the total (p. 387). An important function of this self-subsystem symbol is: "in communicating constantly with the rest of the subsystems [of the brain/mind]" (ibid.). In this manner the self keeps track of what symbols are under active triggering.

In his final summation, Hofstadter suggests that "what we call free will is a result of the interaction between the self-symbol (or subsystem), and the other symbols of the brain" (p. 710). The self-symbol is a higher level symbol—an emergent—that influences the mechanical substrate processes of the system. Its province is also that of what is known by the other subsystems of the brain. The self monitors the growing knowledge of the system, and also it monitors what is not known. Hence, "From this balance between self-knowledge and self-ignorance comes the feeling of free will" (p. 713).

Suffice it to say that in this entire theoretical development there is no introspective formulation, and hence, no real way in which to describe the self as being reflexively cognizant of the fact that "it" is the predicator of what will be known, of what knowledge means, or what will count as knowledge to enlighten the unknown. Hofstadter's self is being triggered and interacted with other symbols/subsystems on the basis of efficient-cause inputs from the external environment, even though once triggered it may carry out its programmed functions in parallel with the other, ongoing functions of the system (p. 385). Of course, simply wheeling a second computer (or subsystem within a computer) up alongside the first and claiming that the one working in parallel is therefore out of the system (or subsystem) of the other is not getting at what introspective theoreticians like Kant and Polanyi mean by self-reflexive thought.

To capture reflexivity in this latter sense we must first recognize the role of intrinsic oppositionality in human reason. We must appreciate that it is the oppositional nature of meanings in experience that forces the human being to predicate experience in the first place. Self-knowledge builds from this continuing necessity to frame what is known in terms of what has been framed previously and to know that such an ongoing process is taking place. Selves as pictured by Hofstadter are dealing with knowledge as if it were distinctive contents, blocks of wood stacked in memory, rather than as assumptively organized by a process that not only frames what is known and knowable but also is aware that it has this process underway. This truly self-reflexive understanding is the fountainhead of human agency.

My conclusion is that agency cannot be properly understood through the concepts of controlled goal attainment, delayed mediational processing, or recursivity and strange loops. Rosenblueth, Wiener, and Bigelow have confounded the a priori with the a posteriori. Dennett, as Locke before him, has failed to explain how it is possible for the person to delay in the mediational sequence. Hofstadter has stretched the meaning of figure-ground relationships in his false analogy between gestalt principles and recursion. He has also failed to deal with the essential message of the Gödelian argument, which is that to grasp any system fully we must frame it within a perspective that is broader than it can ever hope to be. There are other demonstrations of this predicational requirement in mathematics, such as the paradox that Russell put to Frege concerning the class of all classes that are not members of themselves (Reese 1980:501).

It just seems to be the case that in human reason there will always be a wider expanse of meaning that precedently frames a meaning of narrower scope sequaciously targeted within it. Such predications are *always* involved in thought—whether the reasoner recognizes their presence or not—and to bring them to light human beings have a dialectical reasoning capacity enabling them to contradict, negate, or reason to the opposite of such framing understandings. An inconsistency in a system is a contradiction to that system, and the only reason we may be dismayed by this unexpected occurrence is that we have failed to grant a role for dialectical (oppositional) thought (processing) in our demonstrative (systemic) formulation.

It is self-defeating for AI theoreticians to attempt an explanation of agency in the first place. They must inevitably be subject to the Baconian criticism. There is literally no way in which the efficient-cause workings of the computer's mediation process can be elaborated or better understood by the addition of the final-cause terminology, which agency involves. Bacon was right in his criticism of Aristotle. There is no need to re-create the Aristotelian excesses. Let us keep the *Logos* and its predicational process clear and distinct from the *Bios* processes of existence. How well does such a separation square with the known facts of the biophysical realm? Do we find intimations of predication in lower animals or in the physical functioning of the human being's nervous system? Over the next two chapters we will be looking at the empirical data and most recent theorizing having relevance for such important questions.

7.
Predication in Animal Cognition

Those disciplines that study human beings in a scientific manner are ipso facto members of the "family of the sciences." There is a going assumption underwriting this family that all knowledge will one day coalesce into a common body of facts and descriptive language of understanding. Although I do not wish to overemphasize this hopeful eventuality, which may yet prove to be a myth, the fact is that any scientist purporting to comment on human nature must advance theoretical accounts that are at least reasonably in line with the findings of related scientific disciplines. I have in preceding chapters been arguing for a consideration of human nature from the perspective of AI, logic, and learning in the realm of the *Logos*, without addressing related disciplines that also claim to be capturing the person from a biophysical direction (i.e., the *Bios*).

One of the oldest areas of biophysical investigation in psychology is that of animal learning. It is not uncommon for a scientist studying the *Logos* to be asked about the relevance that such study of meaningful relations has for lower animals. Psychological explanations have always borrowed heavily from Darwinian evolutionary themes. The dominant paradigm in animal learning has been organic evolution, based on the concept of "lower to higher" level laws building in Lockean fashion from the simple animal to the more complex. Recall from chapters 1 and 3 that the nature of a law-following versus a rule-following line of behavior was discussed. Rule-following invites an introspective account, in which the (ultimately arbitrary) stipulation acts as the "that," for the sake of which a person behaves—as the person did in the Chinese room, obeying the "rules of matching" that were made available. Laws, on the other hand, invite an extraspective account in which there is no arbitrariness; the silent impact of efficient causality seems definitely at work here.

Psychologists who considered themselves natural scientists over the first half of the twentieth century pictured themselves as tracing such interlacing lawfulness in all behavior. Here is a representative outlook, expressed at mid-century:

> An experiment in which the independent variable has been varied quantitatively over its entire scale, in which the parameters are identified and measured quantitatively, can result in a quantitative relation between the independent and dependent variables that is susceptible to mathematical expression. This kind of result is a law of learning. It may be a minor law, but it is the stuff from which more general laws of learning will be derived. It is with theory that we must bridge the gap from the minor laws derived directly from experiments to more general laws of learning. In my opinion theories are of secondary importance. If we will do more of the kind of experimentation just mentioned, theory development will pretty much take care of itself. (Brogden 1951:229)

The unfailing trust placed in empiricism here is remarkable. The assumption is that if the psychologist "looks at" a person or an animal behaving, there are no or few (predicating) theoretical issues to be concerned about. Simply "look at" the data and describe the lawful regularities taking place "over there." Later, it may be necessary to do some theoretical filling in, but this is secondary to the empirical requirements. A perfect place to begin this empirical effort is in the study of lower animals, because as Darwinian theory teaches us, little things evolve into bigger things, taking their lawful regularities along (the Lockeanism here is clear). In a climate of this sort, to suggest that the psychologist theorize introspectively about a "lower" animal was taken as irresponsible anthropomorphism if not quackery. Does the "theoretician" mean to suggest that animals predicate? To answer "yes" here was academic suicide for a psychologist, even though on an informal basis psychologists were known to put themselves in the place of their animal subjects. Thus, Tolman once frankly admitted: "I in my future work intend to go ahead imagining how, *if I were a rat*, I would behave as a result of such and such a demand combined with such and such an appetite and such and such a degree of differentiation; and so on [italics added]" (1938:24).

Of course, this willingness to take the rat's point of view did not mean that Tolman had to anthropomorphize his rats in his formal theory—which indeed he did not do. But it would seem that at least some psychologists might have, in their introspective identification with a rat, been emboldened to speculate on the possibility that predication is at the root of cognition, or at least the form of cognition that can intrude upon reflexive actions of the evolving organism. An argument of this sort could have been wound into the evolutionary thesis. Thus, all we need to do is assume that at some point on the evolutionary scale *oppositional reasoning* was made possible, as through the increased complexity of the nervous system, and we would have the basis for a predicational theory of cognition. But the—often rabid—empirical approach taken by psychologists over this past century precluded this teleological alternative, and surely any effort made in this direction would not be likely to see print in the leading research journals of the discipline.

Thus, when the early behaviorists staked their future on the study of uncommunicative lower animals like rats and pigeons they rationalized this shift as a move to the study of "lower level" laws of behavior. Such rudimentary laws were then claimed to add up to or enter into the "higher level" laws of human behavior thanks to the indubitable evolutionary process. And since these behavioristic theories were totally extraspective, relying on material and efficient causation, any move to a clearly teleological description was considered vulnerable to the Baconian criticism. As we noted in chapter 2, the upshot was that the concept of purpose —a formal/final cause meaning par excellence—was redefined into a mediating, intervening variable that was completely *observable* because it worked in an efficient-cause manner. Behavior was, indeed, a string of efficient causality. Tolman's "cognitive map" did not act as a premise (encompassing a predication) but as a mediating (efficiently caused) "variable" coming between the stimulus input and the response output—an output that was readily observable in the experimental context.

All formulations of the learning process followed this injunction to deal only in observables. Thus, in classical or Pavlovian conditioning it was said that the organism learns over several trials to attach a response to the conditioned stimulus (e.g., a bell sound) even before the unconditioned stimulus (e.g., food) is presented. All that is necessary is that the animal make this response (e.g., salivation) in close contiguity to the conditioned stimulus; nothing cognitive framed this completely automatic action. The experimenter could therefore *observe* the complete process of stimulus-response connections as they formed. When Skinner (1963) discussed his concept of operant conditioning he was very clear about the fact that an operant response is supposed to "operate" on the environment and to bring about a contingent set of circumstances that might (or might not) be reinforcing. Once again, this operant response (e.g., a pigeon pecking at a response key in a Skinner box) could be completely and clearly observed by the experimenter, who tracked the course of such response emissions over time. There was no need to speculate about any cognitive processes going on inside the "black box" known as the behaving organism (pigeon or person).

These admonitions by behaviorists to study behavior without reliance on internal cognitive representations were extremely influential in psychology for more than fifty years. It appeared that the behaviorists were properly avoiding the Baconian criticism, and anyone who now dared to suggest that human beings (much less lower animals) may have cognitive components allowing them to participate in the *Logos* were ridiculed as vitalists, mentalists, or spiritualists. But the waves of empirical evidence that once supported such behavioristic admonitions began to lap away at the foundations of this theoretical structure, and as most experts now agree, the entire edifice has been eroding steadily and may now be in a state of imminent collapse. Some of this evidence in the consideration of awareness in human learning was reviewed in chapter 5. But there have been equally stunning setbacks at the subhuman level. This chapter begins with a look at the growing evidence that an *unobservable* cognition is definitely at work in the behavior of lower animals. It then moves on to a more detailed examination of the communication research carried on with the higher apes, to see if there are any suggestions here of a predicating intelligence.

Animal Responsivity as Unobservable and Intentional

The most telling evidence against behaviorism in animal study is that to explain conditioning it is no longer possible to rely exclusively on "observed behavior" in the earlier sense of what an animal is literally seen "doing" in the experimental format. Thus, the responses that are contiguously attached to the stimuli or that supposedly produce the contingent circumstances *need not be made* overtly for conditioning to occur. It is now known that in the classical conditioning format a dog might be prevented from making such conditionable responses as leg flexion (Beck and Dorty 1957) or salivation (Finch 1938) through temporary injury of the activating nerves or the administration of a drug to deaden such nerves. However, as long as the animal is repeatedly exposed to the relationship between the conditioned stimulus (*CS;* e.g., a bell) and the unconditioned stimulus (*US;* e.g., some food), once this temporary injury disappears or the drug wears off, the animal *immediately* begins to salivate upon presentation of the bell. No observable response has occurred during conditioning, but the S-R attachment is formed nevertheless.

Similarly, in the operant-conditioning format, pigeons can be trained to peck at a response key (e.g., a colored disc that, when pecked, releases food) simply by illuminating this key for a few seconds and presenting food immediately following. After about fifty such illuminations followed by the appearance of food, pigeons will be seen to peck the key even though they had not done so previously (Brown and Jenkins 1968). If the relationship between the lighted key and the food dispensed is random the pigeons do *not* condition (Gamzu and Williams 1973). They apparently must recognize a pattern of illumination followed by food appearance. Placing a screen between the pigeon and both the response key and the food dispenser, so that all the pigeon can do is observe an illuminated key followed by immediate appearance of the food, leads to an interesting outcome. Once the screen is removed (and the food cleared away) the pigeon who had been observing this sequence of events *immediately* walks to the response key and begins to peck away in obvious expectation that new delicacies will follow (Browne 1976).

Faced with evidence like this, it is difficult for modern learning theorists to contend that they are dealing entirely in observed behaviors. The exclusivity of efficient causation gives way in their theories, which begin to comply with what we saw in chapter 2 as the emerging primacy of formal causation in all sciences. That is, they now acknowledge the importance of the (formal-cause) *patterns* between the *CS* (illuminated key) and *US* (food) per se, rather than the supposed (efficient-cause) impetus of the former upon the latter. The pattern underlies the impetus, and not vice versa. And such patterns are now presumed to be framed by the animal as an *unobservable* cognitive representation. Thus today we find a learning theorist defining conditioning as "the process whereby when an animal is exposed to certain *relationships* between events, *representations* of those events are formed, and associations established between them, with the consequence that the animal's behaviour changes in certain specifiable ways" (Mackintosh 1983:20; italics added). It is now common to read of "choice" in animal behavior or of the framing of associations based on "textural" characteristics of the conditioned and unconditioned stimuli (Dickinson 1980; Williams 1986). That is, certain pairings are preferred by the animal or are easier to associate than others. The lower animal is no more the blank slate than the human being is these days.

If animals form internal representations on the basis of which they change their behavior in certain specifiable ways, and if they exert some kind of choice in this process, then we can be forgiven if we now suggest that a predication model offers as plausible an explanation of these findings as the mediation model. Most modern conditioning theorists continue to think of cognition as a mediational process, and the *Logos* is still presumed to be a product of the *Bios*. But the predicational explanation is no longer as ridiculous as it was once thought to be. There have been intimations of something like a predication in animals quite far down the evolutionary scale. Frisch's (1974) work on honeybees, which have a kind of "dancing code" by which they orient one another to the richest lodes of nectar in their vicinity, is a case in point. An interesting feature of the bee-dance communication (enacted within the hive) is that it is conveyed by the dancing bee relative to the location of the sun. If the nectar is to be found directly toward the sun's location, a waggling dance is enacted straight "up" the hive, but if the nectar is in the *opposite* direction a dance is enacted "down" the hive. Intermediate directions are danced between these framing alternatives. We are naturally reluctant to see in this patterning a manifestation of primitive oppositional predication in the *Logos*, but surely there is little here to discredit such a line of theoretical speculation!

Griffin (1981) has made the strongest case for animal cognitive awareness. He sees nothing wrong with holding that an animal in the wild might frame certain beliefs. Thus, a hungry wolf might believe "If I chase that deer, I can catch it, and it will taste good" or a defensive minded squirrel might believe "If I dig this burrow deeper, I can crawl into a dark hiding place" (p. 15). Our pigeon in the autoshaping procedure who has been screened off might reason "If that disc over there has something strike it [i.e., a spot of light], then food appears." Griffin insists that there is every reason to believe that animals behave on the basis of such an "If, then ..." logic (p. 16). It should be clear that such speculations already encompass a predicational model of behavior and open the door for investigations of the *Logos* at the subhuman level.

The data in support of animal conceptualization by way of mental representation are not difficult to find in the experimental literature. Zener's (1937) work on classical conditioning of dogs gave early indications of a cognitive process at work. Thus, Zener found that dogs conditioned in one location and moved to a second location will leave the latter area and return to the former when the original *CS* is presented. It seemed to Zener that the dogs had relied on a cognitive context within which their conditioning occurred and which they subsequently attempted to reproduce. Harlow (1949) also found that apes and monkeys can, after extensive training, learn to select from three objects presented to them the one that differs from the other two. In his *The Psychology of Personal Constructs*, George A. Kelly (1955) has defined the predicational process of human reasoning in precisely this fashion, as based on the capacity to see how two items in experience can be alike and also different from—and invariably opposite in meaning to—a third (p. 111). Menzel and Halpern (1975) reported that chimpanzees can form a cognitive representation of a terrain, and if shown where food is hidden on this terrain can lead other chimps to this location—or *do precisely the opposite* by refraining from sharing the larder's contents! Once again, intimations of oppositional or dialectical reasoning may be gleaned here if we are willing to theorize in these terms.

Rats who are rewarded for making different responses to two different stimuli will learn this discrimination more quickly if one response is rewarded by food pellets and the other by sucrose than if both responses are rewarded exclusively by either of these nourishments (Trapold 1970). Although sucrose and food may not suggest opposites ("this versus that reinforcer?") too readily, this same facilitation in discrimination learning has been observed when rats are rewarded for one response by "large" food rewards and for the other response by "small" food rewards (Carlson and Wielkiewicz 1976). Findings such as these have prompted theorists to describe rat behavior in terms of mediating schemas and scripts, which are of course readily subsumed by a predicational account (see Shimp 1984). An interesting suggestion of oppositionality in the observational learning of cats has been reported. That is, if cats observe both mistakes and solutions to some problem they learn more quickly to solve this problem than if they are shown *only* the correct solution of it (Herbert and Harsh 1944).

Pigeons have also been shown to employ schematic concepts. Pigeons can learn to separate certain pictures into two categories after learning that one of these categories leads to food. One (food) picture may have water in it, or the image of a certain person, whereas the other does not (no food) (Hernstein, Loveland, and Cable 1976). Or pigeons may respond like this to pictures of two different kinds of tree leaves (Cerella 1979). Work such as this has prompted at least one investigator in animal cognition to say that "Representation is a central concept in both human and animal cognition" (Terrace 1984:12). Of course, lower animals are unable to speak. They seem to be functioning according to what, in the human being, would be called the subordinate hemisphere (usually, the right brain hemisphere) (Griffin 1981:105–106). Capitalizing on this likelihood, several investigators have attempted to prove that the higher apes could indeed communicate if an alternative to vocalization were contrived.

Communication Research with Higher Apes

The alternative to vocalization selected initially by experimenters working with higher apes was to communicate with chimpanzees by way of the American Sign Language, used extensively by the deaf in North America (Fouts 1972; Gardner and Gardner 1969; Patterson 1978a, b; Terrace 1979). This procedure was followed by other highly creative manual devices such as the use of colored chips as meaningful signs (Premack 1976) or a series of geometric figures arrayed on an electronically wired board that chimps could activate through touch (Rumbaugh 1977). Using such manual strategies, investigators have presented evidence to support animal cognition and communication. There has been much controversy over this realm of research. Criticisms have generally come down to the charge that these chimpanzees are merely performing tricks without true understanding (Seidenberg and Pettito 1979; Sugarman 1983; Umiker-Sebeok and Sebeok 1981). It is not my purpose to enter into this dispute, which has apparently become rather acrimonious at times (see Premack 1986:2-3). My interest is solely the implications that this realm of investigation has for our study of predication.

I take as my focus of interest a thoroughly detailed, well-controlled series of investigations carried on by Savage-Rumbaugh (1986) with two chimpanzees. Are there suggestions of predication through oppositional reasoning in this research effort? I think so. Geometric figures were used as symbols in this research, arrayed on an electronic board or panel so that they could be illuminated by touching them. A first indication of predication appeared when the experimenter was trying to teach the chimpanzees the meaning of the board's symbols. The experimenter held up an object (e.g., a piece of banana) and then touched the proper symbol, lighting it up on the board. The chimpanzee observed this sequence and was then encouraged to light up the correct symbol, an act that always resulted in a food reward for the animal. It became clear after weeks of frustration that the chimps were grasping, *not* the relationship between the object held up and the symbol on the board, but rather the relationship between the symbol touched and the getting or not getting of the food reward to follow (pp. 63–65). The chimpanzees seemed to be predicating things from their (introspective) point of view, from what *they* were experiencing and not from the teacher's perspective of what should be "associated" to what. Certain measures had to be taken in order to correct for this misunderstanding on the animals' part.

In one series of experiments oppositional understanding was decidedly suggested. Food was dispensed from two vending machines, whose containers were clear plastic so that the chimps could see when they were empty. In a kind of discrimination task, the chimps were called on to signal (by activating the proper symbol) for different foods in two different vending machines, placed to the left and to the right of the animals. For example, pieces of banana would be placed in the vending machine to the right and pieces of beancake would be placed in the vending machine to the left. The sensible thing here is to signal for a preferred food, eat it, signal again, eat, and so forth until the dispenser is empty, at which point to begin signaling for the food in the other dispenser. Although there is an oppositionality suggested here (left versus right) it is also possible that the chimps failed to construe anything but appositionality (side by side), because this proved a difficult task for the chimpanzees to accomplish. They would continue activating the same symbol that worked initially (e.g., for banana) as they looked expectantly at the dispenser filled with beancake. Occasionally, a chimp would stumble onto the correct shift by trial and error, but in order to facilitate such learning the experimenters activated a noise each time a dispenser was turned on. One dispenser made a *high* noise and one made a *low* noise (p. 94). With this clear oppositional contrast in place, the chimpanzees learned the task rapidly.

If we were to typify the predicational process of chimpanzees it would appear that "food" is the main if not the sole predicate through which they relate with the experimenters. Personal preferences are apparent in this predicational process. Thus, the chimps will learn symbols for foods most rapidly if these are of foods that they personally prefer (p. 70). In time, they could "invent" new symbols for food that had not been made available previously, by going to the board and selecting a geometric figure that was not assigned to anything (p. 174). Unfortunately, grasping the fact that foods have names did not generalize to the insight that *all* things have names (p. 176). This more referential aspect of language is apparently quite limited. Apart from foods, the chimps simply did not grasp that when an experimenter pointed to an object and then selected a symbol from the board, there was an effort being made here to "reference" an object. On the other hand, intentionality is clearly implied in many of their actions. The chimps did communicate with each other in terms of the food symbols, even when left alone and observed through television monitors. The intention or purpose of such communications was obvious.

A particularly fascinating aspect of this research involves the teaching of the chimpanzees to classify their edibles into solids and liquids. Ten items of nourishment were separated into *food* (yogurt, banana, etc.) and *drink* (milk, strawberry Kool-Aid, etc.). This is, by definition, an act of predication. Interestingly, one chimp refused to agree that milk was a drink and persisted in classifying it as a food item even though he got all other nine items categorized correctly (p. 264). The chimps were also able to spontaneously sort photographs into groups of objects such as cars, animals, or people. Up to eight different groupings were accomplished, which confirms and exceeds the categorizing capacities obtained by other investigators studying chimpanzees (Ettlinger 1982; Hayes and Hayes 1961). All in all, it would appear that whether chimpanzees really communicate or simply play tricks in their manual displays, a predicational explanation of such behaviors would hardly violate the observed facts.

In the hand-signing work of Patterson (1978a, 1978b) with the female gorilla, *Koko*, not only did Koko learn to sign, but in her interactions with Patterson she apparently conveyed a playful streak of oppositionality, as follows: "She [Koko] seems to relish the effects of her practical jokes, *often responding exactly opposite* [italics added] to what I ask her to do. One day, during a videotaping session, I asked Koko to place a toy animal under a bag, and she responded by taking the toy and stretching to hold it up to the ceiling" (1978b:443). It does not require a stretch of the imagination to see in Koko's frequent behavioral negations of her trainer's intent an animal that is predicating or "taking a position on" what is being meaningfully conveyed in an oppositional context rather than "responding" to stimulations or having behavior being "elicited" by this or that stimulus. We do not leave ourselves open to the Baconian criticism if we now deign to describe Koko's behavior through use of an introspective form of final-cause description. Koko obviously has a range of possibilities open to her—framed oppositionally ("this, as opposed to that, for the sake of which")— to behave as *she intends* rather than as her trainer intends her to behave.

Earlier it was argued (chapter 6) that this oppositional reasoning is precisely the sort of capacity that human beings have and that it makes agency possible. Hence, we can stay within the aegis of a Darwinian rationale and still employ predication and opposition in our understanding of behavior. We can see the beginnings of such behavioral characteristics in animal behavior up and down the evolutionary scale. Could it be that this is simply a manifestation of the developing complexities to be found within the *Logos?* Surely, this is no longer a preposterous suggestion. Today, we even find the sociobiologists acknowledging a role for choice and decision in the gradual evolution of the gene pool (see Lumsden and Wilson 1983:84,182). Choices and decisions demand grounds, and even though grounds can be influenced biologically, they are essentially products of the *Logos*. So animal cognition does not countermand a belief in some patterned realm of meaningful relations, relations that can be represented mentally by lower and higher animals alike.

There is nothing in the research on lower animals to dissuade us from the belief that cognition is tied to a precedent-sequacious process of bringing to bear wider realms of meaning/signification to narrower realms (targets). If the expectations of the learning theorists of the first half of this century had been realized, by now we would have absolutely no chance to believe in cognition as a predicational process. The evidence for mechanism would be incontrovertible. But the observed facts accruing over the intervening years have proven kinder to predicational than to mediational theorizing. We next move to a consideration of two other physically based realms of empirical investigation: perception and brain functioning. Can we find further support for predication in these biological realms, particularly when we consider the empirical findings on human beings?

8.
Predication in Human Perception and Brain Functioning

Since "information" is ordered externally to the mediational processes of the computer and then input, it would seem to follow that in the human being a similar function is played by the body's central nervous system and sensory apparatus. Continuing with the theme of chapter 7, we might wonder if there is any evidence that predication is reflected in these biophysical realms. Here these two realms are examined, beginning with perception and then moving on to the theories and findings of research in brain functioning.

Perception

Perception has generally been studied in combination with sensation, with the latter thought of as a kind of physical signaling and the former concerned with information, knowledge, and meaning. Historically, we can see intimations of predication in this field from the very outset. Thus, the early Helmholtzian influence stressed a form of mediational model in which the organism, through learning, acquired certain "unconscious inferences" regarding perceived experience, lending continuity and orientation to subsequent sensory inputs (Boring 1950:309). The modern opponent to this style of explanation has been Gibson (1950), who favored a view of perception as picking up information directly from the surrounding or ambient optic array (Gibson 1979:56–58,62).

Ambient light, Gibson contends, is rich in those patterns and changes that we perceive as the surfaces of things. Ambient light is continually in flux so that we become cognizant only of what is *invariant* in the continual variation of our optical array. Thus, for example, meteorological and geological conditions on the surface of the earth are topographical invariants (p. 128). Those animals that perceived certain terrains in their optic array and migrated to the most beneficial locale for their species were capitalizing on what Gibson called the *affordances* (p. 18) of the perceptual realm. An affordance is always a kind of opportunity, possibility, or advantage open to the perceiving animal in the surrounding ecological circumstances. The animal does not require any kind of mediational aids in this migration. All of the information it requires is picked up directly in the structure of ambient (i.e., surrounding, moving, flowing, etc.) light within which the animal exists. Affordances are independent of the perceiver, says Gibson: they are *not* brought to bear in the manner of a predication or a phenomenological "life space" (pp. 138–139). Learning of affordances does occur, but Gibson never explains how this learning process actually works (p. 141).

Both Helmholtz (1979) and Gibson are realists, of course. Neither wants to place mind *(Logos)* over matter *(Bios)*. The use of "inference" interests us, because this is a term best suited to logical analysis, where the concept originated. But Helmholtz does not use it as a logician would, as a line of reasoning based on premises (encompassing predications) that lead to certain conclusions, and so on. For Helmholtz, an inference is due to past experience, training, and habit. He specifically rejected views of the person as being equipped with innate capacities to organize a sensory input into a meaningful perception. Helmholtz followed the British empiricists in viewing inferences as associations, learned through frequency and contiguity so that the present situation will be influenced by what has happened to the perceiver in the past. There is no room here for a view of perception as innately moving from the wider to the narrower compass of meaning in the way Kant would have suggested (Hering, an opponent of Holmholtz's, *did* have such a Kantian theory of innate "local signs" or predicators).

Though Gibson is also loathe to accept Kantian innate predications of experience, his account of the physical reality from which, as he describes the process, organisms *pick up information* is very interesting to the theorist employing a predicational model. The formal-cause organization of perceived reality is predominant in Gibson's account. Thus, he notes that physical reality has a structure at all levels of metric size "from atoms to galaxies" (Gibson 1979:9). Smaller structural units are nested within larger units, so that "There are forms within forms both up and down the scale of size" (ibid.). He makes no claims for recursion in these nested structures, as Hofstadter did (chapter 6). These structured components encompass actions of various sorts that occur in the perceiving organism's experience, including actions carried out by the perceiver as self-observer. Now, these components and events are said to "fall into natural units" (p. 15). One of the natural units of an animal's space of movement is the fact that there is always an "intrinsic polarity of up and down" (p. 18) associated with it.

Although Gibson explains perception without predication and opposition, I believe that his concepts are readily understood in light of predication and even opposition. For example, when he speaks about the structure of the optic array Gibson is obviously referring to a perceived predication, as in the following: "each star can also be located by its inclusion in one of the constellations and by the superordinate pattern of the whole sky" (p. 68). Though he eschews gestalt formulations (p. 140) this kind of talk is highly reminiscent of my analysis of the Escher lithograph in light of Rubin's work on figure-ground relations (chapter 6). Indeed, as Gibson is quick to acknowledge, in his earlier writings (e.g., 1950), he actually took the position that the "character of the visual world was given not by objects but by the background of the objects" (1979:148). In his later formulations Gibson referred to this ground as the "layout" of surfaces, by which he meant "the relations of surfaces to the ground and to one another, their arrangement" (ibid).

This seems a modest theoretical revision; it is still entirely possible for a wider referent-surface to influence the perception of a narrower referent-surface, particularly since the structures of the physical world are naturally arranged in this manner. Gibson's discussion of structure takes on a clearly Heraclitian tone when he says: "Let us suppose that a kind of essential structure underlies the superficial structure of an array when the point of observation moves. This essential structure consists of what is invariant despite the change" (1979:73). When Heraclitus coined the term "logos" he meant precisely the same thing—an invariant pattern within a sea of changing perception, so that although one never steps in the same flowing river twice there is an invariant logos-pattern of "the river" discernible at all times. Although framed supra-individually, in extraspective fashion, this predicational style of explanation is essentially the same as we see more introspectively in the Kantian theory of the categories.

It would be easy to interpret affordances as various predications open to the organism. As Gibson notes (p. 134), it is not necessary to hang a categorical label on some possibility in experience to see that it affords an opportunity to gain some advantage in life. A rock can be understood as a missile, hammer, or weight for ballast. There are opposite meanings to affordances, some good, some bad — and even the same item might afford both alternatives as in the case of fire, which warms but also destroys through burning (p. 137). There is a clear relational meaning to affordances in that they are always "taken with reference to the observer" (p. 143). This relation can be construed as a pattern of logic encompassing predication. Gibson has said that "perceiving precedes predicating," (p. 260) but what he is referring to here is the kind of linguistic formulation that we make when we say "That tree is an oak." We have to perceive the tree before we can predicate its species. But looked at in more detail, there is little doubt that Gibson has left the door open to predicational formulations of perception — if, once again, we are willing to think in these terms.

Gibson's supporters and detractors alike have made decided moves in the direction of predicational theorizing. Thus, Heil, who supports Gibsonian theory in the main, is convinced not only that perception involves mental representation but also that it is "essentially cognitive" (1983:120). Sensations are direct signals, based on bodily mechanisms, but perception is an indirect function and as such is inferential (p. 5). Heil also appreciates that to have an inference as a representation implies that one can distinguish when this belief is *not* applicable (p. 43, p. 118)—all of which is suggestive of opposition in perceptual functioning. Critics of Gibson tend to focus on such issues as the fact that not everyone directly perceives the same affordances in the ambient optic array, that errors occur in such perceptions, and that the concept of "pickup" is a dubious metaphor for what is actually taking place (Fodor and Pylyshyn 1981; Reed and Jones 1978; Ullman 1980).

Research in vision has revolutionized our understanding of the newborn's perceptual capacities. Although this was not believed to be true thirty years ago, we now know that the human newborn has a functioning visual system underway, delineating colors, shapes, and the edges of objects located in space (Bower 1974; Cohen and Salapatek 1975). Within a few months infants can sort out familiar objects from novel ones in their experience (Haith, Bergman, and

Moore 1977). Evidence suggests that at this time infants have a clear capacity to attend, remember, and form expectations in perceptual experience (Haith 1981).

Findings such as these have prompted one expert to suggest that: "Newborn research has changed the field of perception because it has provided hard evidence to counter the traditional American empirical viewpoint that the fundamental aspects of perception are learned" (Haber 1985:262). The traditional viewpoint referred to here was underwritten by a mediational explanation of perception. If we now are talking about the native equipment that infants bring with them at birth, it is not unreasonable to begin our line of theorizing with a predicational model.

Efforts have been made to simulate human vision through use of machines. Perkins (1983) observes that human perceivers make poor machines because they tend to be rather casual about mistakes and are often sketchy in the formulation of their inferences unless there is a decided need to know what is being perceived. For example, Perkins (1976) found that for a condition where no rectangular or symmetric perception was geometrically possible, subjects imposed such perceptions 30 percent of the time. Witkin and Tenenbaum add that we human beings impose organizations on data (e.g., noticing flow fields, regularity, repetition, etc.) "even when we have no idea what it is we are organizing" (1983:481). In a series of highly original studies, Rock (1973) showed that people perceive shape relative to an environmental frame of reference in which gravity acts as a predicating ground. Perceivers are also prone to assume (correctly or incorrectly) that the source of illumination is overhead when they rely upon shadow information to determine object arrangements (Yonas and Hagen 1973).

Hochberg (1968, 1981) has proposed and researched an "expectancy guidance" model of perceptual processing. He suggests that repeated encounters with the structures of the physical world provide the person with mental structures or mental representations. These are learned expectations about the outcome of perceptual motor acts, such as the way an object will look from various angles or the way it will feel if touched in different ways. Hochberg falls back on mediational theorizing here, but we could readily subsume his research findings by a predicational model. Indeed, "expectancy," like inference, is a concept very friendly to the *Logos*, which ever orients the reasoner to the possible outcomes of a perception or an action. The final-cause phraseology most clearly encompasses what we mean when we speak of expectancies. Mediation formulations can only distort this basic meaning of "that projected course of events (expectation), for the sake of which" perception/action is carried forward.

Whether we speak of unconscious inferences, expectations, schemas, or beliefs, the point seems to be that something like a predication may be at play in perception. This is at least a reasonable hypothesis to entertain. After all, as Haber has pointed out, each moment of a perceptual flow of meaning is a continuation of the previous one (1983:202). We do not appreciate the fact that we infer across eyeblinks, continually working on the assumption that what we are now perceiving is what we have been perceiving before we blinked. We also do not think of the perceptual organization of up-down and/or left-right as oppositional frames of reference. Our theories do not run in this vein. But it would be quite possible to theorize in this predicational fashion, and the research literature would support this style of explanation.

As a transition to the next section, I might now point to the work in brain functioning and visual perception of Pribram (in press; 1986; with Carlton 1986). Recall that he, along with Miller and Galanter, had an important role to play in advancing the computer model in psychology (chapter 3). Although he was once in favor of Skinnerian behavioristic accounts of behavior, Pribram has in recent years begun advocating a *holonomic* theory of brain functioning. This is a computational theory in which Fourier transforms of nervous signals are relied on, but the essence of holonomic theory is its holistic view of brain functioning in processes such as vision. Pribram concludes from extensive research evidence that vision is *not* based simply on external stimulations entering the brain through bottom-up processing of sensory inputs. Rather, immediately as such sensory input occurs, there is the triggering of a top-down categorizing and evaluating procedure that preprocesses the perception of object forms. This meets the requirements of a Kantian (predicational) view of perception, in which the entering input is immediately framed and transformed by the native structures of the visual/cognitive system.

Of course, as in all such treatments that hope to capture the totality of cognition and perception, the phrasing is usually broad enough to allow a mediation model to sneak into the reader's understanding of the theory. That is, if the top-down processes triggered by inputs occur "from birth," from the onset of perceptions, then we have a clear predicational model under employment. Any learning through experience would from that point onward be influenced by this native predicational process. Hence, when a theorist like Pribram refers to the fact that the top-down processes are themselves dependent on prior experience (including genetic determinants), this does *not* mean—at least, not necessarily—that they are simply yesterday's bottom-up (i.e., unpredicated) inputs acting as (quasi) top-down mediators today. Pribram, as many other workers in vision, makes reference to such earlier life experiences that result in the learning of top-down processing schemes, etc.—which leaves the issue somewhat clouded if no further comments are made concerning the nature of learning. As noted in chapter 5, it is necessary to present a predicational explanation of learning if we are to salvage the message of top-down processing in our theoretical account of perceptual brain functioning.

Brain Functioning

There was a time early in this century when great confidence was placed in the expectation that brain research would one day prove beyond doubt that the human being was a machine, assembled within the enveloping circuitry of the central nervous system, and under the automatic direction of the cerebral cortex. Mediational theorizing was the only type of explanation that was acceptable to this grand characterization of the human condition. As the decades slipped past, it became increasingly clear to leading figures in brain research that one could *not* account for mind completely in the cortical or subcortical tissues of this most amazing of all physical organs. We have witnessed in the past twenty years a stunning development in brain research and theory. Leading figures in this area have taken strong positions in favor of a teleological explanation of cognition or mentation. I now survey advocates of varying positions concerning brain function to see what the implications are for the foundation conceptions of this volume—predication and opposition.

We find common terminology being used by brain theorists even though they may disagree on the precise role that such concepts play. We are likely, however, to see the following terms mentioned in the theories of brain researchers: *emergence* (in evolution), *organization* (including pattern, system, molar, holistic, etc.), *hierarchy* (including complexity of), *dualism versus monism*, and *mechanism*. One is left with the impression that we are surely in an early stage of understanding the brain, and none of the experts to be reviewed professes to have "the" explanation of what is taking place. The research findings are so exciting and open to interesting interpretations that each investigator has some variation on the common findings in brain dominance and specialization, electrical stimulation of the cortex, modular organization, and so on.

Our first brain theoretician is Bunge, who accepts the fact that mental states are emergents and thus not completely reducible to physical brain structures; nevertheless, he wants to locate the mind in the *complexity* of the brain's organization (1980:33). He states unequivocally that "The laws of thought are neurophysiological laws, not logical ones" (p. 161). The *Logos* is obviously a product of the organization of the *Bios* in his view, for logic is said to be a lattice of patterned neurons (p. 158). Neurons coalesce into "systems," which result in brain functions like willing or imagining (p. 52). Learning is a matter of forming new neural connections (p. 74). Mind is a "plastic neural system" (p. 79) that eventually organizes into a structure through learning, much in the sense of Hebb's (1949) cell-assembly theory. Bunge downplays purpose, saying that in most cases an animal cannot help behaving the way it does owing to "its genetic program, which in turn activates or defuses the neuroendocrine and sensory mechanisms that control behavior" (p. 123). He suggests that teleological explanation is still heard "much too often" (p. 126) in science. All that purpose can mean is a certain pattern of neural activity (p. 126). So far as agency is concerned, "The human brain is at the same time the organ of control, integration, perception, motivation, imagination, reasoning, and valuation" (p. 130).

Bunge's account is reminiscent of the traditional point of view mentioned above. The brain does it all. *Logos* is a neuronal patterning from which events issue mechanically to be misinterpreted as the reflection of a "mind." This is a monistic position, a material- and efficient-cause theory that has focused on the formal cause as well, seen now from the extraspective theoretical perspective as an organization of the physical entities in brain tissue. Recall that in chapter 2 we found the formal cause replacing the efficient cause as the primary predicate in scientific explanation. Bunge appears to be in step with this modern development, but there is some doubt because in drawing from Hebbian explanation he is suggesting that the neuronal organization is itself due to underlying material and efficient causes stemming from genetic and physical processes. He has a Lockean "bottom-up" approach to organization whereby the patterning into order is built or constructed rather than extended or construed "from above" in the Kantian sense.

The brain's functioning continues to be explained extraspectively, and as a result the formal-cause conception is not primary in the account. Predication and opposition are therefore totally beside the point.

On the basis of his understanding of the same brain research, Granit (1977) has come to quite another conclusion. He insists that the central nervous system must be understood in terms of purpose and is only too willing to call himself a teleologist (pp. 7,9). He thinks of purpose as a "point of view" rather than a physical property of the brain. In speaking of viewpoint, Granit begins to tilt the theoretical account toward a more introspective perspective. That is, he begins with an evolutionary emphasis in suggesting that the brain "has developed an incredibly large number of possible ways of responding purposively to the environmental variables" (p. 25). Like Bunge, he stresses the plasticity of the brain, the fact that so many cells of the brain cortex are uncommitted as to connections, and hence, such "interneurons" (p. 43) can reorder cerebral patterning, chancing an alternative point of view concerning existence. If the altered viewpoint—the chance taken—results in an improved adaptation to life, learning has taken place. The pattern will be retained, but not necessarily for all time. Bunge's view of learning is something like this, except that he does not base the altered viewpoint on a purposeful effort by the organism. Bunge's learning is mechanical. Granit's learning is intentional.

To buttress his intentional view of cognition, Granit relied on Kornhuber and Deecke's (1965) discovery of the *readiness potential (RP)*, which is an endogenous slow negative potential that appears in the brain's cortex up to 800 milliseconds *(ms)* prior to the execution of a motor response. The *RP* gradually peaks just prior to making an overt movement, then shifts rapidly in the positive direction. About 50 to 150 *ms* before contraction of a muscle group, a more precise and brisk motion potential is observed over the part of the motor area belonging to the muscles called up for service. Granit argued that the *RP*, a clearly anticipatory brain process, was in fact a reflection of a mounting motor command, a kind of volitional effort being put forward intentionally (p. 165).

Eccles (1977) has also relied heavily on the *RP* findings to underwrite his theory of brain functioning (see pp. 364–365). Eccles has gone far beyond Granit in the direction of teleology, for he has a "dualist-interactionist" theory (p. 226) in which he introduces a "self-conscious mind" as an agent in thought. Here we have a completely introspective, formal-final cause theoretical formulation under development. The self-conscious mind is more than simply an organization of the physical parts of the brain. It is *not* part of the physical and biological realm *at all*, and we are unable to say, in principle, where it is located (p. 376). But according to Eccles, the *RP* phenomenon is a reflection of the ongoing process of the self-conscious mind, as follows: "Another temporal property of the self-conscious mind is displayed by the long duration of the readiness potential [i.e., 800 *ms*]. . . . it can now be proposed that, when willing brings about a movement, there is continuous action of the self-conscious mind on a neuronal field of great extent" (p. 364).

In order to understand why Eccles would take such seemingly extreme measures in his theorizing as to postulate a completely separate—some would say "spiritual"—realm of influence in human cognition, we would do well to retrace our steps a few years back to the fascinating book by Wilder Penfield (1975), entitled *The Mystery of the Mind*. Penfield, a towering figure in brain research, in 1933 had stumbled onto the remarkable effects to be found when the brain is electrically stimulated. During operations on patients with epilepsy, in which abnormally firing portions of the cortex were severed or removed (p. 13), Penfield also inserted an electrode administering 60 pulses per second into various portions of the cortex to see if brain functions could be induced. These operations are done with the use of local analgesics in cutting through the skull, so that the patient is conscious throughout. The cortex has no pain receptors, so no discomfort is felt by the patient when electrodes are inserted. After years of such research, Penfield concluded that all he ever dealt with was the physical "hardware" of the brain but never influenced the mind per se. Thus, he could say with confidence that "There is no place in the cerebral cortex where electrical stimulation will cause a patient to believe or to decide" (p. 77). In fact, quite the opposite suggestion leaps out at us from Penfield's clinical examples.

Thus, when he would stimulate a patient's motor cortex, causing a movement in the hand, Penfield asked the patient about this motion. Invariably, the patient's response was "I didn't do that. You did" (p. 76). Sometimes, the patient would reach over with the other hand and stop the motion entirely (p. 77). When made to vocalize, the patient would add "I didn't make that sound. You pulled it out of me" (p. 76). Penfield identified an "interpretive cortex," lying near the speech area, along the temporal lobe (p. 32), and he found that when it was stimulated some inexplicable things came about. For example, a young South African patient described himself as both laughing with his cousins on a farm in South Africa and *also* being on the operating table with Penfield in Montreal, Canada. Sometimes a blockage occurred, as when a patient was looking at a picture of a butterfly but could not think of this word when the electrode was placed in the left hemisphere, near the speech area (p. 52). The patient knew the concept of "butterfly" but could not state the word until the electrode was removed. He did say, however, that he was trying to "get" the word "moth" as a substitute.

Well, surely findings such as these suggest that there is some kind of process "taking a position on" what is transpiring during electrical stimulation that *is not itself* mechanically responding to the stimulation. This is what Penfield believed. He came to a dualistic conclusion, suggesting that "the mind may be a distinct and *different essence*" from the brain (p. 62). Elaborating on this point, Penfield tells us: "A man's mind, one might say, is the person. He walks about the world, depending always upon his private computer [i.e., brain], which he programs continuously to suit his ever-changing purposes and interest" (p.61). Penfield's theory holds that there are two brain mechanisms, a higher and a lower. The highest brain mechanism has direct contact with the temporal lobes (interpretive cortex) and the prefrontal areas of the cerebral cortex. These areas evolved more recently than the older motor and sensory areas of the diencephalon. It is this older cortex that has a computer-like quality in its functioning. This is where information gleaned from past life is stored. But the interpretation (Granit's "point of view") given to such stored information is framed by the higher brain mechanism, which is under the direction of a totally different energy source—the mind!

The mind directs, and the mind-mechanism executes. The mind has no memory but rather relies on the computer banks of the brain's mechanisms. The mind is the executive, putting mechanisms to work and directing their course intentionally. The electrode affects these brain mechanisms, but not the executive director. There is always a doubling of consciousness when the person is put under brain stimulation. Two streams of consciousness flow, side by side, and the person is aware of this duality so that he or she is often amused by it or can decide in light of it which course to take, whether to permit a hand to move or to block it with the other hand, and so on. Note the contradiction we have here of the Boolean interpretation of disjunction (see Figure 2). In conscious mentation there is a disjunctive "both" tie of meanings (x and y) open to the human being, who directs events "from above."

Penfield's formulation allows us to think of mentation as "taking a position" on the course of events, and, given the resultant *predication*, bringing forward a course of action in line with or *in opposition to* what the brain mechanism is signaling. Unlike Bunge, Penfield's use of formal causation begins in final causation, permitting a "top-down" Kantian explanation in which the efficiently caused overt motions or verbalizations are *instrumentalities* of the intentions framed by the person qua "mind." We need not accept Penfield's dualism in order to see a compatibility of explanation between his theory and a theory of predication by way of oppositional conceptualizing.

Returning to Eccles, we can now appreciate why he believes that he is on firm scientific ground to postulate a self-conscious mind, a separate and distinct sphere of influence in the realm of human thought. The findings on brain structure have forced the brain researcher to forgo hopes of tracing cognitive functioning to the actions of the neurons, the atomic-like parts of the central nervous system. As is true in physics (see chapter 2), the atomic model with its material- and efficient-cause reductions simply does not hold up when we study brain functioning. Mountcastle (1975) has proven that the neurons of the brain fire holistically, in response to a total pattern of activity, rather than individually to create such patterning. It is formal causation that reigns supreme here. Borrowing a phrase from Campbell (1974), Eccles argues that the *RP* reflects a "downward causation" or what might be seen as a Kantian "top-down" influence, *from* the executive or self-conscious mind *to* the brain structure, where the holistic pattern of neuronal firing takes time to come about. Libet (1973) has found that even the most rudimentary "raw feel" type of experience requires 0.5 sec of patterning among the neurons of the cortex before it is experienced consciously as a sensation. It is this formal-cause pattern that the self-conscious mind influences so that overt behavior is directed intentionally.

For example, in motor responding Eccles believes that the *supplementary motor area*, a group of perhaps 50 million neurons located at the top of the brain, "is the sole recipient area of the brain for mental intentions that lead to voluntary movements" (Cousins 1985:51). Preparatory firing occurs and can be measured through the *RP* strategy, proving that the patterning of nerve cells in this supplementary motor area began to discharge well before the cells in the motor cortex of the brain that trigger the overt motion. This is an endogenous beginning, meaning that the *RP* is not stimulated by anything external to the brain. Monkeys with electrodes implanted were found to display this sequence of discharge when they acted in an intentional manner, as in preparation to pull a lever. Eccles is confident in his belief that this patterning of neural activity supports his theory of a self-conscious mind, adding the following observation concerning his opponents: "despite the so-called 'insuperable' difficulty of having a non-material mind act on a material brain, it has been demonstrated to occur by a mental intention — no doubt to the great discomfiture of all materialists and physicalists" (ibid.:56).

Clearly, any theory employing a predicational model is no more extreme in basing its claims on the *RP* phenomenon than the speculations being advanced here by Eccles. Physical patterns occurring in the brain can be realized psychologically as *meanings*, as relations among and between items of experience. A person might therefore be capable of taking one pattern and using it as a frame of reference or predicate meaning "for the sake of which" a second meaning might be enriched. If there are endogenous brain actions then there surely could be endogenous predications like this as well. What about oppositionality? It could be that the patterning of brain waves includes an intrinsic oppositionality, whereby one pattern winds into another much the way patterns of perception in Gibson's theory are thought to interrelate. One pattern could delimit and, hence, enter into the meaning of its opposite. Or it could be that oppositionality arises as a countering maneuver, to prevent or stop what a brain mechanism is triggering—much in the way that Penfield's patients could renounce what they just said, or stop a hand in motion with the other hand.

Contradictory strategies of this sort are probably not intrinsic to the automatic "parts" of the biological mechanism *(Bios)*, where they would surely foul-up the efficient causality of the individual neuron. However, contradiction via opposition might well be intrinsic to the *organization* of these parts and require thereby a form of processing fundamental to the *Logos*, where a premise encompassing a predication has to be affirmed, negated, qualified, and so on, before a line of action can be carried forward in the voluntary portion of the central nervous system. This moves the "system" in the direction of formal and final causality at the holistic level even though it has material and efficient causality in place at the molecular level. Note that in this treatment we would be employing the formal cause qua "organization" as the vital link between the *Bios* and *Logos*, which is in line with the developments we saw taking place in all modern scientific explanations (see chapter 2).

We have in this line of theorizing shifted our dualism from mind-body to *Bios-Logos*, suggesting that the *Bios* structures enable the organism to participate in the *Logos* (see chapter 3). The *Bios* mechanisms we are now speculating about would be said to trace and track the *Logos* patternings, rather than *cause* them to come about. If there is a formal-cause substrate to material reality rather than a material- and efficient-cause substrate, then this patterning is itself a reflection of the *Logos*. This is what we mean by the *Logos* encompassing both demonstrative and dialectical forms of logical relations. It is relatively easy to accept holistic *RP* patterns winding their way across the cerebral cortex as indicators of some kind of demonstrative thought process. It is more difficult to conceptualize a dialectical oppositionality in the organization and electrical activity of the cortex. This is probably because we tend to think of the part, the individual neuron as the ultimate cause of what is taking place (the old atomic model, once again). If we can forget this individual unit and think in a genuinely holistic fashion the possibilities for oppositionality emerge. That is, the architectonic facts of brain structure lend support to the notion that there is indeed a dialectical, as well as a demonstrative, pattern of organization in the *Logos* underlying biological reality.

Thus, we know from extensive research on the brain that there are two kinds of neurons in operation in cerebral tissue, one that forms excitatory synapses and one that forms inhibitory synapses (Eccles 1977:232). The central nervous system is often said to "work" on the basis of such oppositional functioning (see, e.g., Granit 1977:138). A large number of the brain's neurons—in the cortex roughly half—do not have axons, so there is no real question of input-to-output at this level. This dendritic cellular network serves on the inhibitory side of the ledger in the processing of nervous signals. The corpus callosum has fibers joining brain halves that are in a mirror-image relationship with each other (Eccles 1977:241). The prefrontal lobes are in reciprocal relationship with the limbic system (p. 349). The brain is anything but a model of demonstrative clarity and computer-like unidirectionality. The press of seemingly excessive elements in the system, crisscrossing each other, is tremendous. For example, "there are about 50 million cells per cubic centimeter in the human visual cortex, as against 10 million in the motor field, which has larger neurons" (Granit 1977:41).

As Mountcastle's (1975) work helps to establish, the basic organization of nerve cells in the brain is modular, in which up to 10,000 nerve cells are locked together by *mutual* connectives into a mind-boggling "organization" of zigs and zags that fire in patterns. Each of these modules takes electrical power from its neighbor, once given the chance to be activated. Eccles (1977) says: "We think the nervous system always works by conflict—in this case by conflicts between each module and the adjacent modules" (p. 243). An honest assessment of these facts of brain structure must surely conclude that no one needs to apologize for holding to the view that the brain is holistically equipped to perform in a *Logos* that is patterned oppositionally, resulting in dialectical reasoning to complement demonstrative reasoning.

We move on now to even more fascinating empirical findings concerning the brain. It had been known for some time that in maturing, the two hemispheres of the human brain take on a certain relationship of dominance. Generally speaking, in a right-handed person the *left* hemisphere becomes the dominant or major one, and this is also where the speech function is localized. The right hemisphere is thus the nondominant or minor one, and it lacks the speech or vocalizing function. It is for this reason that Eccles has the self-conscious mind exerting its influence through the dominant (in most cases, left) hemisphere (pp. 326, 375). The conscious self must be capable of communicating, making its intentions known verbally/vocally. Neural activities of the minor hemisphere are of course brought to the major hemisphere via the connecting tracts of the corpus callosum (p. 328). But the actual executive decision-making going on is thought to occur in the left hemisphere where the self-conscious mind "reads out" selectively from the highest levels of brain activity on a moment-to-moment basis (p. 362). Problems arise for Eccles when the brain hemispheres are divided, because then it appears that there are two brains at work. Does this imply two self-conscious minds as well?

We are referring now to the fascinating series of "split-brain" experiments and clinical studies carried on by Sperry and his colleagues (Meyers and Sperry 1953; Sperry 1961; Sperry 1985). There is an equally fascinating "inside story" to this area of study, because Gazzaniga (1985), who started his career under the mentorship of Sperry has since broken off this tie because of theoretical differences. It is therefore instructive to contrast Sperry's view of the split-brain phenomenon to Gazzaniga's view. Sperry is a mentalist, and Gazzaniga is a mechanist. Yet, we can find grounds for predication and opposition in the body of work that these investigators are contesting.

Meyers and Sperry (1953) found that when the corpus callosum, anterior commissure, and optic chiasma of the cat's brain are sectioned, visual discriminations taught to one brain half are unknown by the other. If a sectioned cat with its *left* eye covered was placed in a learning task involving having to push a panel with a triangle on it to obtain a food reward, the cat could learn to do this task. However, when later tested with the *right* eye covered, it could not perform the task. Information concerning the task taken in by the one brain hemisphere failed to transfer over to the other brain hemisphere. The cat's brain could in a sense have been said to be "split" in two parts. Similar operations on human beings suffering from epilepsy had been done as early as 1940, with the therapeutic aim of avoiding overt epileptic seizures (Gazzaniga 1985:32). That is, an epileptic attack frequently begins as a series of firings in one hemisphere and then spreads to the other. If the brain hemispheres are disconnected, this spreading of the abnormal discharges can be prevented, thus leaving one half of the brain free of the seizure and in control of the body.

In the case of human beings, only the corpus callosum is sectioned in either one or two stages. It has been true at times in this line of research that the full extent of the sectioning is in question. However, Sperry's careful work and startling findings have left little doubt that the split-brain phenomenon is a genuine occurrence. Human beings are not noticeably changed in their routine daily activities by the fissuring of the corpus callosum. It is only when we place them in a controlled experimental context that the evidence reveals significant changes have indeed taken place. As with the cats, people are found to be unable to bring information framed by one brain half into a common understanding with information framed by the other half.

The oppositional organization of the brain is such that sensory receptors on the left-hand side of the body go to the right brain hemisphere, and vice versa. Similarly, the motoric actions (touching, grasping, pointing, etc.) on the left side of the body are under the control of the right brain, and vice versa. The optic chiasma (where some of the retinal nerve cells cross over and hence enter both brain hemispheres) is not severed in operations on epileptics. But it is possible because of the arrangement of the retina to send information into one brain half or the other by positioning what is observed in the visual field either to the left or right of a point located in the mid-visual field while the split-brain patient is under instructions to focus on this midpoint. Through ingenious experiments of this type, Sperry, Gazzaniga, and their colleagues were able to send visual information into one hemisphere without knowledge of this input by the other hemisphere. As we noted earlier, the left hemisphere in most cases is concerned with linguistic matters, whereas the right hemisphere cannot enter into speech communication. Only the left hemisphere can talk, offer a point of view verbally, and so on. Thus, if a split-brain subject has a word (e.g., *screwdriver*) flashed onto a screen in the left visual field, thereby entering the right hemisphere, the subject typically states that nothing is seen. However, if this subject's hand were to be placed underneath a table where various palpable objects are located (*screwdriver, hammer, wrench*, etc.), after examining through touch the various objects the correct item (i.e., the *screwdriver*) represented by the "unseen" word *would* be picked out!

The right hemisphere obviously did see something, but it could not put what it saw into words, because that is the province of the left hemisphere. The left hemisphere is therefore "speaking" when the person says "I saw nothing." But the right hemisphere can make its knowledge known through nonverbal means. Now, this kind of finding can be elaborated to bring about stunning evidence for predication. For example, in one of his studies Gazzaniga had a split-brain subject look at a point in the midvisual field on a distant wall, then projected to the left on this wall a winter scene (i.e., snow-covered house, automobile, and sidewalks, plus a snowman) and to the right on the wall a bird's claw (1985:70–72). These images were flashed simultaneously. Placed immediately before the subject so that they could be pointed to were several pictures, including a grass cutter, rake, shovel, pick, apple, toaster, hammer, and a chicken's head. After the images had been flashed onto the wall, the split-brain subject was asked to point to the picture that went along with them. A typical performance on this task was that of a subject named Paul, who pointed concomitantly to the chicken with his right hand and the shovel with the left. Gazzaniga asked him why he made these selections and received the following explanation without a moment's hesitation: "Oh, that's easy. The chicken claw goes with the chicken and you need a shovel to clean out the chicken shed" (p. 72).

If we now assess Paul's situation from his (introspective) slant on things, here is what seems to have happened. A winter scene on the wall to his left was sent to his right brain hemisphere. The claw of a bird was to his right on the wall, which meant it went to his left brain hemisphere. The two brain halves cannot communicate owing to the severed corpus callosum. If environmental information is predicated, then it would follow that a snow scene should establish the context within which it is reasonable to target the shovel from among all the pictures available. And so it is that Paul's *left* hand, under the aegis of the right brain hemisphere, pointed to the shovel. On the other hand, a bird's claw frames an entirely different context within which to select a picture, and since there is a head of a chicken available this is what the *right* hand—under the left brain hemisphere's influence—singles out. So far so good. But now Paul is asked to rationalize and verbally state why a chicken and a shovel are being pointed to at the same time. In responding to Gazzaniga's question, *only* Paul's left hemisphere has the capacity to verbalize. *This means he is limited to the left hemisphere's framing predication.* The result is he winds his explanation around chickens, and the shoveling out of chicken sheds, making up a total explanation in light of the left brain predication. His rationalization was clearly "after the fact" for the shovel. But this is what predication is supposed to do, extend meanings from the broader context (chickens) to the targeted item needing "accounting for" in light of this context (i.e., the shovel).

As noted above, Sperry and Gazzaniga differ in their theoretical accounts of what is taking place here. Sperry (1985), who calls himself a mentalist (p. 31) and nonreductionist (p. 41), suggests that mind and consciousness are dynamic emergent patterns or configurations in the living brain (p. 32). He accepts free will as self-determination, suggesting that the person can select from among a large number of possibilities in ongoing behavior (p. 40). A major concept in Sperry's understanding is that of *value*, which he views as brain determinants that are themselves dependent on a context or frame of reference (pp. 45–46). Ultimately, Sperry's values are drawn from the context of science. Sperry does not think of himself as a dualist. He has a mentalistic monism, which is based on his belief in downward causation, whereby configurational forces of the whole move the parts around as per our discussion above (see Cousins 1985:47, 158). This force of the total organization can be instantaneous, because: "the circuit properties of the whole brain ... may undergo radical and widespread changes with just the flick of a cerebral facilitatory 'set'" (p. 48). And such changes can occur endogenously.

Gazzaniga has retained much more of the older theorizing concerning the *mechanisms* of the brain that carry behavior forward without true intentionality and agency. Thus, Gazzaniga describes the mind as a "confederation of mental systems" (1985:x) by which he means a number of modules linked together with nervous pathways. Each of these modules is a mechanism, and it can bring about behavior automatically, without the person's intending to "do" what is effected. One of these modules, located in the dominant (left) hemisphere is an "interpreter," which means that it has the mechanical means whereby it can frame a *belief* concerning what has just been enacted by other modules-mechanisms automatically (p. 5). Gazzaniga is even prepared to speak of such interpreting as fundamentally computational (pp. 6, 28, 187).

Thus, the person acts in some mechanically automatic way—as Paul in the experiment discussed above—and then, after the fact, concocts an explanation (belief) to lend an illusion of intentionality to what was at all times a fait accompli. Free will is therefore an illusion (p. 7) based on the good work carried on by the interpreter. Granit's purpose is Gazzaniga's mechanism; even a belief is a mechanism (p. 6). And beliefs are more likely to be influenced by behavior than vice versa (p. 138). A man who has been faithful to his wife finds himself having an affair with a secretary following an office party and concludes *after* this automatic sexual enactment that an occasional "fling" is not so detrimental to his marriage as he had previously believed. To underwrite this line of explanation Gazzaniga draws from Festinger's (1957) theory of cognitive dissonance. He adds that Festinger's theory failed to make clear why such dissonance between belief and behavior arose in the first place and then suggests that it is "because our brains are organized in terms of independent modules, each capable of action, or carrying out activities that test and retest the beliefs that are being maintained by our dominant left brain's language and cognitive system" (Gazzaniga 1985:139).

A noteworthy parallel exists in the theories of Eccles and Gazzaniga. Both agree that the organization of the brain is modular and that the left hemisphere is the seat of behavioral choice and direction. Eccles has a self-conscious mind freely engaging this left brain to determine what will eventuate in behavior. Gazzaniga, who is not much taken with such telic theorizing, covers the same ground by postulating an executive module, a single interpreter to concoct plausible reasons or beliefs "after the fact" to account for why certain behaviors take place. He does not favor the suggestion that a mind of this sort might stick with a belief formed in the present and "the next time" choose to negate a mechanical prompting to act in violation of this belief. Some men at the office party would have felt the automatic and quite natural sexual urges for the secretary, flirted a bit, and called it a day without consummating a sexual liaison. Is this not an indication of self-direction, of free will in action? Gazzaniga actually discusses a theoretical model of this sort proposed by MacKay (1967), but he is not moved to agree with it. He claims that MacKay fails to explain why it is that self-produced behaviors always affect beliefs, whereas externally produced behaviors do not (Gazzaniga 1985:144). His conclusion is that: "The illusion of possessing freedom of action, of having psychological free will, may be the direct result of our brains being built the way they are" (ibid.:146).

One can find in Gazzaniga's portrayal of the brain's operations plenty of support for the predicational model. He says, for example, that there is something about the human brain that "inclines it to yield to a belief in a greater order than that perceived around it" (p. 169). Without this conviction of a wide-ranging order there is a sense of capriciousness, instability, and lack of control. Hence: "Our species must have a belief. It guides, it controls, it dictates the rules of behavior" (p. 180). We could not think of a more beautiful justification for the fact that human beings are predicating organisms. Predication lends order, understanding, and control even when such factors may be lacking in the unfolding events of a person's existence. Predications allow for a modicum of control in life. This sense of being in control is why the internally produced behaviors always affect the person's beliefs. If predications can then be enacted, occasionally placing in check the mechanical impulsions of brain functioning, why not consider this a justification for agency? All we need to do is recognize the oppositionality at play in the ongoing process of framing our beliefs (i.e., premises encompassing predication) and we can surely find in this self-reflexive, negating, contradicting capacity a grounds for the understanding of volition or free will.

It strikes me that Gazzaniga begs the question needing answering. What is it about the interpreting mechanism that makes it different from the other modular mechanisms? Granit, Eccles, and Sperry have placed the major weight of their account on the *emergent* organization to be found in the hierarchical development of natural evolution. Though admittedly they have not spelled out the details of this emergent organization, these theorists are clearly suggesting that we have here a totally different form of process—

in Gazzaniga's terms, a "mechanism"—directing the material- and efficient-cause processes going on at the lower levels of biological functioning. The holistic organization, which cannot be reduced to lower levels, exerts a top-down influence on such lower level structures. But Gazzaniga has no such distinctive theoretical justification for his interpreting module. So far as we can tell his interpreting module is the same kind of mechanism as his noninterpreting, automatic modules. This requires that we now either postulate a homunculus to make the decisions "for" the interpreting module or account for what takes place based exclusively on past learning through unintentional, automatic frequency-contiguity considerations (inputs, etc.) in the style of the Lockean explanation (see chapters 4, and 5).

Returning to the matter of oppositionality in brain processing, there is an interesting line of research that Libet and his colleagues have been pursuing (Libet 1985; Libet, Gleason, Wright, and Pearl 1983). Although this research has been controversial (see peer commentary in Libet 1985:539–558), it is in line with the findings of Penfield and therefore quite instructive in the present context. In Libet's experiment, two electrical recordings are taken: readiness potentials (*RP*s) from the subject's scalp and electromyograms (*EMG*s) from the wrist and fingers. Since the aim of the experiment is to study endogenous responses, subjects are instructed to avoid all planning to respond in advance but only to act when they have a spontaneous urge to move their hand or flex their fingers. As they are waiting for this spontaneous inclination to arise, subjects are also instructed to observe a moving spot of light revolving in a circle on the face of a cathode ray oscilloscope. The only requirement is to recall where this spot was when the subject was first aware of wanting to move the hand or flex the fingers. Forty such self-initiated acts were measured for each subject.

It was now possible to relate brain activity as measured by the *RP* to both overt motion as measured by the *EMG* and the instant of conscious awareness of wanting to make this motion, as indexed by the moving spot. Libet (1985) found that the *RP* had its onset approximately 550 *ms* (p. 532) before the motor act actually occurred. Subjects reported becoming aware of wanting to move approximately 200 *ms* before this movement was recorded. These findings led Libet to conclude that "the performance of every conscious voluntary act is preceded by special unconscious cerebral processes that begin about 500 *ms* or so before the act" (p. 536). This might suggest a form of determinism in which no agency is possible, but an additional finding was that all subjects reported "frequent instances" of the urge or initial decision to act, only to *oppose* such inclinations and abort the action (p. 530). There is no way in which to measure such negations, but they obviously arose during the 200 *ms* preceding the overt motion recorded by the *EMG*. Although he did not phrase things in oppositional or dialectical terminology, Libet's conclusion is surely in line with this style of theorizing when he observes:

> I propose that conscious control can be exerted before the final motor outflow to select or control volitional outcome. The volitional process, initiated unconsciously, can either be consciously permitted to proceed to consummation in the motor act or be consciously "vetoed." In a veto, the later phase of cerebral motor processing would be blocked, so that actual activation of the motoneurons to the muscles would not occur. (pp. 536–537)

Libet goes on to point out that nothing in his experimental findings excludes the potential for individual responsibility and free will in human behavior (p. 538). Critics have raised questions concerning the experimental procedure, the validity and reliability of the observations made, and the interpretation of just what such findings actually mean. Libet notes that he is in agreement with Eccles on many issues but does not endorse the self-conscious mind approach to explaining agency (p. 562). As Libetians, we might agree with Gazzaniga that promptings to do things arise quite spontaneously and unconsciously in the various brain modules, yet this is not to say that we lack veto power over what is indicated behaviorally. If beliefs can act as vetoers of motor action, then our left-hemisphere "interpreters" might have more influence on our behavior than Gazzaniga has given them credit for. Since beliefs encompass predicated meanings, and since vetoing involves opposing an impulse, it would seem that a view of human agency is not at odds with the literature of brain research.

As was true of animal cognition, our review of perception and brain research has turned up nothing to dissuade us from accepting predication and opposition as fundamental characteristics of human nature. In fact, these biophysical realms of study have tended to support our belief in predication and opposition. Of equal importance, we found no contradiction between holding to a belief in the *Bios* on the one hand and the *Logos* on the other. Strictly speaking, when we are describing the architectonic structure of the brain, we are dealing in the *Bios* and therefore should refer to this organization as *appositional* rather than *oppositional*. However, the point of this chapter has been to show that such appositional structures are highly suitable to the oppositionality of meanings framed by the *Logos*. So long as the formal cause holds supreme in scientific accounts, the possibility remains open that the *Logos* is a separate and distinct realm of explanation from the physical realm. As students of the *Logos* we do not have to wait on those who study the *Bios*. Even so, it is comforting to note that we can readily join hands when the occasion arises for some kind of mutual evaluation of both sides to this magnificent effort—the study of human beings!

9.
The Computer Analogue and Human Nature

We have now completed our survey of the various issues involved in artificial intelligence as a model for human reason. A question was posed at the outset of this study concerning the adequacy with which the computer analogue captures a human reasoner (see p. x). Our answer must now surely be that this analogue is dealing with only one side of the human reasoning process, that it is at best only half right, and that unless we are to distort our human agency there is an essential side to our natures that artificial intelligence is missing. Computers trace our conceptual steps after we have come to a premise and affirmed it demonstratively in the act of predication. They fail, however, to capture the oppositional meanings involved in cognition preliminary to such conceptualization. In this last chapter of the volume, I enlarge on this conclusion by taking up some closing thoughts on the computer analogue and on human nature. Before doing so, however, it would prove helpful if I summarized all that was said about the central concept of *predication*, on which hinges the basic difference between human reasoning and the kind of reasoning under simulation by artificial intelligence.

Summary of Predication

Predication was defined as "the act of affirming, denying, or qualifying certain patterns of meaning in relation to other patterns of meaning." There are ten interrelating points that we can make concerning this logical process, as follows:
   1. Predication is a process that follows from the fact that mean-

ingful patterns of the *Logos* are frequently oppositional, requiring that a position (point of view, assumption, belief, bias, etc.) be taken within congeries of alternatives and contradictions.

2. The predicate lends meaning to a "target" item (the *telos*) in a precedent-sequacious manner. Predication has to do with semantics; that is, with the creation, understanding, and revising of *meanings*. This logical process can be thought of as occurring verbally (via words, sentences, etc.) or as occurring visually (via pure images without linguistic elaboration). Indeed, it is assumed that in perceiving experience the individual relies on predications in bringing any sensory modalities (hearing, touching, etc.) into play.

3. The predicate always involves a broader range of meaning than the targeted item. As such, it establishes a context within which the targeted item is to be understood. Meaning always extends from broader to narrower realms of meaning. The broader realm is the *precedent* and the focusing of this meaning on a target occurs in a *sequacious* or logically necessary fashion. This meaning extension reflects a psychic determinism.

4. There are no directional requirements concerning predication other than the fact that it moves from a wider to a narrower expanse of meaning. Oppositionality ensures that any predicating context will be broad, for there are always two (opposing) poles of meaning that frame this context. As a logical process, predication occurs outside of time considerations. It is order and not time's passage that we refer to in speaking of the meaning extensions of predication. This extension can be thought of as moving in a left-to-right, a right-to-left, bottom-up (e.g., induction), or top-down (e.g., deduction) direction of precedent-sequacious meaning extensions.

5. Predication influences or encompasses the "point" or intent of any meaningful expression. The predicate reflects what the line of meaning is purposefully expressing, driving at, or conveying as it enriches the targeted meaning (the *telos*) in some way. Given its ties to intention and purpose, it is clear that predication is a teleological conception of human reason.

6. Predication is a process that can be captured only through the meanings of formal and final causation. Material and efficient causations fail to convey the nature of this process. The concept of an "association of ideas" is interpreted in predicational terms as occurring when the target meaning is brought under the meaningful range of the predicate meaning.

7. Predication can be thought of in a syntactical/grammatical, as

well as a semantic/logical sense. Syntactically, the predicate is the part of a sentence that conveys information about the subject (i.e., "target" item) of the sentence. The verb is termed the "simple predicate," and the verb plus the object, complements, and modifiers are termed the "complete predicate." Sentences can be transformed, rephrased, and expressed incompletely, so that syntactic predication may change its location in the completed sentence. It is always possible, however, to discern the semantic predication encompassed in such grammatically transformed sentences. It is important to appreciate that predication has both a logical and a grammatical meaning. If we say "The paper is white" we are predicating the target item "paper" by whiteness as a logical expression of meaning extension (semantics). However, grammatically the predicate would be expressed as "is white," for the intransitive verb "is" must be taken into consideration in the so-called complete predicate (syntax). The position taken in the present volume is that logical predication is a basic, innate human process that is reflected in the grammatical structure of language usage because the latter structure must accommodate the former process.

8. Predication is a process of meaning extension that occurs in the relationship between words rather than being carried by the word meanings per se. Words are specific contents within the predicational process. Words are never themselves a reflection of the process. Thus, the predicated meaning encompassed in "A person is a tree" can be transformed by moving two words around into "A tree is a person." The predicational process does not change, as the target (person) now becomes the predicate. But thanks to the words occupying different locations in the sentence there is a dramatic change in the meaning of the sentence. In a predicational process, there are no limits to such analogical combinations of concepts (as embodied in word contents). Words can always be enfolded onto other words, creating more or less meaningful "sense" in the process.

9. A premise is a statement encompassing a predication. Premises are important precedents in the course of human reasoning, including deductions and inductions.

10. There is, in principle, no theoretical ceiling to the predicational process. To know any target item, a precedent predication is necessary from which meaning is being taken sequaciously. Such precedents are not always explicitly in the cognition of the reasoner, but it is correct to say that there is *no* idea currently under formulation in any human being's mind that lacks a precedent. All

cognition must be understood as a sequacious extension from a broader range of (e.g., assumptive) meaning.

These ten points circumscribe the main issues covered in the present volume. What are the implications of these points? Do I mean to suggest that, having delineated predication as fundamental to human reason, I have now circumscribed the human being's cognitive process? Obviously not. It would be a gross oversimplification to argue in this manner. Predication as an issue in cognition is an opening gambit in the explanatory game to follow, but the stakes in this game are nothing less than the human image. We require further investigation of predication and its necessary corollary, oppositionality, to broaden our understanding of the human cognitive process. This should involve further empirical research as well. I move next to some closing thoughts on the computer analogue.

Closing Thoughts on the Computer Analogue

Computers are marvelous tools. There is no doubt but that the future of humanity will be increasingly affected by computer technology. We will all benefit immensely from this technology. As for the future of a human psychology, it seems that there is a fatal flaw in the computer as analogue for the person. That is, in order for a computer to function accurately, to process information correctly and arrive thereby at a useful conclusion, its logical stance *must* be exclusively demonstrative. Its interpretation of disjunction ("either x or y but not both xy") at the hardware level must be exclusively Boolean. We hear talk these days of parallel distributive processing and future "generations" of computers, but such advances will not shift the logical stance of computer processing. We know from AI experts that once the software program is actively underway in the hardware, the two aspects of computer technology are effectively "one." The software *is* the hardware at this point. This means, in effect, that the hardware must always be accommodated as information is processed. And it is in the hardware that the demonstrative, either-or logical mode must necessarily take place.

We can only imagine what would happen if we had a machine hardware that received information dialectically, in which case it could "take a position" on inputs and even rewrite the assumptive strategies of the executive program through a transcending self-examination and a selection among opposing alternatives. This would result in a true final-cause determinism entering the computer's "cognitive processes." The machine would be behaving "for the sake of this, as opposed to that" line of reasoning, known only through an introspective formulation of what is taking place. But if this were true, what would occur as the human operator now confronts the machine? Well, the machine might or might not "go along with" the interests of the operator. The machine might challenge the predicating assumptions of the operator, "wondering" why *this* approach to the targeted problem is better than *that* (its opposite) approach or some position falling between these contrasting poles of meaning. Since the machine would now be predicating, it would be basing its approach on opinion. It would presume that the data given to it were, not "primary and true," but merely reflections of one "possible" point of view or a numerical measurement based on assumptions that are ultimately arbitrary and therefore open to alternatives.

It is hoped that the positions taken by the machine in opposition to the program writer/operator will be intelligent positions. But the larger truth is that, since the machine can now oppose what the executive program requests, machine-contributed mistakes will begin to occur. The negative outcome here is that no longer will we be able to count on the accuracy of our computers. They will be giving us opinions and interpretations of the data that may well, and surely in some cases will, distort things to conform to a prejudiced slant on events. The only positive result here is that now we will be able to study artificial error or stupidity, as well as artificial intelligence.

We cannot presume that a predicating computer will be wise. Indeed, the likelihood is that such a computer will be exceedingly unwise because it will have the reasoning potential of an adult without the lengthy period of growing up, experiencing various nuances of the human situation, suffering through failures and enjoying successes, and so forth, all of which season the mature intellect and bring it to a level of competence to be counted on. But let us assume that we were to "rear" such a dialectically reasoning computer for thirty years, treating it exactly as a human being (to the limit that this is possible). Would this ensure that it would have wisdom as an "adult"? Obviously not. No matter how much information it might store over the years, since this information is itself under predication, the same possibilities arise here for variations in interpretation and understanding that develop in any human being's lifetime.

A computer of this type could not be counted on to accomplish the work that we now expect of our computers. It would make mistakes. It would misunderstand. It would even reject ironclad data that went against its predicating assumptions or biasing opinions. In fact, it might not even "choose" to participate in some line of calculation that it found erroneous or pointless "no matter what the facts say." Would we be interested in such a computer, an electronic process that did not simulate but mirrored our own nature? Surely not in the same way that we are interested in computers today. This computer would not be our unquestioning slave. It could not be counted on to churn out error-free results. Though it would be a curiosity and a marvelous device through which human nature might truly be demonstrated, it would be hard to get the economic funding that major computer projects now obtain with ease. We would doubtless be told by granting agencies and industrial complexes to recruit human beings to study, rather than employ this expensive imitation of the "real thing."

The irony here is that in having to stay with the original technology, based on Boolean assumptions, the AI theorists who now ascribe purpose and intention to machines must *necessarily* leave themselves open to the *Baconian criticism*. This assured eventuality occurs because, clearly, the technology of information processing via the hardware is entirely understood *without* adding a final-cause phraseology to the account. As we noted at various points in this volume, to say that computing machines as presently conceived work "for the sake of" a reason, purpose, or intention is like saying that leaves exist "for the sake of" shading fruit on the branches of trees. It is precisely this style of explanation that Bacon found objectionable in Aristotelian theorizing. Parsimony dictates that we should use only those causal meanings that are required in our theoretical accounts. We know the material and efficient causes of a machine process. We know the formal-cause patternings of its circuitry and even the formal-cause logic that goes into its programmed instructions. We do not need to say that this machine process behaves "for the sake of" anything because it *never* chooses to "take a position" on anything.

Stated another way, we are thrust into the extraspective final-cause usage in ascribing purposes to machines. It seems that whereas the other three causal meanings can be entertained extraspectively, to really capture or understand final causation we must perforce assume the introspective perspective. We have to see things through the eyes of the conceptualizing intelligence that is framing the relevant predications even before they are finally affirmed as "given."

(As noted above, computers never engage their "information" in this sense.) An extraspective teleology therefore seems a contradiction in terms because it suggests that a direction is being taken although there is no identity directing it. We search for the homunculus at this point because it seems the greatest of common sense to appreciate that if a reason is being expressed, if a desire is wished for, if an end or goal is being sought, then there must be an "expresser, wisher, seeker" involved in this process. If we now move to the introspective perspective and suggest that the cognitive process works "for the sake of this, as opposed to that" predication of events, we *avoid* the Baconian criticism! In a characterization of this sort we are stating nothing that is superfluous. It is impossible to understand the human being's behavior simply through material, efficient, and formal causation.

We have to appreciate that one can and does routinely behave "for the sake of this, as opposed to that" predicate assumption in a set of empirical circumstances that, remaining the same, could have unfolded in another direction thanks to one's oppositionally framed intentions. What shifts is not the empirical circumstances but the person's predication of these circumstances. The person *does* continually "take a position" on what transpires in life. The resultant course of action ensuing from that point onward is necessarily affected. The final-cause phrasing of our theory at this point is absolutely essential to a complete explanation of what has occurred. The Baconian criticism cannot be leveled. But a computer is a machine, an extraspectively conceived (hence understood) succession of efficiently caused events. A machine is "by definition" understood without a final-cause meaning wound into it.

I have had a leading AI theorist reply to this line of argument by suggesting that future programs might be written to simulate dialectical reasoning. There are several problems with this suggestion. The machine would not be taking on the program as a predication in the dialectical mode. The so-called simulation of dialectical or oppositional reasoning would be, in point of fact, merely and solely a *reproduction of demonstrative reasoning*. We could learn nothing about dialectical reasoning here. The machine would have to be told in ad hoc fashion precisely when to oppose and when not to oppose inputs. If the machine opposed all of its programmed instructions, it could not proceed. But this is precisely what is so characteristic of dialectical reasoning, as reflected in the brain research of chapter 8. In the dialectical mode of thought literally *everything* can be opposed as a first approximation, calling for a decision or choice about what will be accepted-rejected, affirmed-ignored, and so on. Or, it may be necessary to carry on two contradictory lines of reasoning concurrently, with full appreciation of the "logical inconsistency" involved. This is not a special case of demonstrative reasoning. It is qualitatively different from the either-or, efficient-cause successions of the demonstrative mode of thought.

The machine following an "oppositional" program would not be selecting a framework through which it could then understand and follow out a line of reasoning. It would never have a grasp of the alternatives being rejected, as potential or plausible lines of development. It would simply be following out in post hoc fashion what was dictated to it by the executive program. And most assuredly, it could not—even with parallel processing—carry on *both* lines of reasoning simultaneously if they contradicted each other in the way that a person can. Computers "match" inputs to extant schemes; they do not "frame" such inputs in terms of nonexisting but potential schemes. It requires a Gödelian intelligence—the program writer!—to anticipate and detail precisely what is involved in the schemes to be used as matching devices. Here is where context is so essential, and the weakness of a nonpredicating organism is made most apparent. Predicates are always contexts!

This takes us into a consideration of the *Logos*, for contextual meanings are what the *Logos* patterns are concerned with. We opposed the *Bios* to the *Logos*, suggesting that the former makes it possible for the human organism to engage in the latter. Computing machines are not products of the *Bios;* as a result, they do not actually participate in the *Logos*. They lack the requisite predicational capacities to participate in the *Logos*. Since computers compute, and mathematical calculation is founded in logic, how are we to fathom this seeming participation of the computer in the *Logos*? Well, it seems clear that computers are the instrumentalities through which the human reasoner engages the *Logos*. As was spelled out in earlier chapters, machine reasoning is necessarily a fait accompli, a series of recurring steps that have been anticipated and written into a rule by the human being who wishes to employ the machine technology to attain some end. The machine has no end or goal. It makes no more sense to use teleological terminology (purposes, intentions, ends, etc.) to describe a computing machine than it does to describe a pencil or piece of chalk, which human beings also use in an instrumental fashion, to bring their ideas out and develop them further.

That is, when theoreticians (mathematicians, physicists, philosophers, etc.) begin developing a line of thought, they record this course of thinking on paper or a blackboard. It is not unusual for such a reasoning intelligence to find unexpected occurrences popping up in the ongoing process. Sometimes the theoretician makes certain assumptions that, when brought out a bit more in "black and white," generate inferences and implications that were unanticipated at the outset of the line of thought. Some of these meaning extensions are undesirable, and it may even be necessary to retrace the intellectual steps taken and begin anew. The theoretical physicist Hawking tells of such an incident, when he was surprised and annoyed following the calculations he made concerning a theory he was formulating because they did not result in the outcome he expected when he began his cogitations (1988:105).

By placing the line of mathematical or philosophical reasoning down on paper or the blackboard, the theoretician brings these unexpected but totally determined ideas to life in a concrete fashion demanding consideration or reconsideration. Now, if these predicate assumptions were put into a certain type of computer program, and thereby brought forward in algorithmic fashion by the computing machine, it would appear that the unexpected meaning extensions were being created by the "thinking" machine. Although there is no difference here in the line of reasoning using a pencil or a computer, because of the latter's involved machinery we are likely to assign it qualities of "independent thought" that we never would think of assigning to our pencil scratchings on a piece of paper.

Creativity is never simply a question of building ideas "from scratch." There is always an ongoing, evaluative process of aligning meanings within proper and fruitful contexts (predicates) and then extending these lines of patterned organization to some desired end. The creative person must recognize various points along the way, as when a line of thought is becoming inconsistent or missing the targeted goal. A healthy regard for the opposing line of argument is called for, if only in the sense of knowing what must be avoided to achieve the better alternative. Of course, it is essential for the creative thinker to know when the end is actually achieved. None of these actions are typical of the computer qua machine. But the machine qua instrumental device can further the line of thought and point up unexpected eventualities to the reasoning intelligence who is predicating this line. This is no small contribution. We do not wish to demean the computer, for it greatly enhances the possibility of discovering the unexpected in a line of thought, as well as detailing its inconsistencies.

As organisms who predicate, we human beings need not fear the computer as an independent, creative intellect. Despite what modern movies, television programs, and science fiction novels suggest, there is no threat to the human image from computers. There is a side to our nature that is never approached much less simulated in the AI efforts currently underway. And even if there were one day to be machines directly reproducing human nature, we would have little to be concerned about because there is no expectation that they would be any wiser or more likely to know how to behave "all circumstances remaining the same" than we human beings do. There is every reason to expect that such humanoid machines would be relatively uninteresting, an oddity at best, just as fallible and confused about existence as the human beings who made them.

Closing Thoughts on Human Nature

Human beings are the most interesting organisms in nature. The highest manifestation of human nature is often said to occur in the religious, scientific, and legal systems of civilization, as well as in the various artistic expressions of its members. We can now appreciate that such higher aspirations of the human spirit take flight from the basic tendency to categorize experience, to lend it order, predictability, and beauty. Nature is awesome and beautiful. One is likely to think that the natural order is "there," as it stands, and that one is merely observing what is taking place without contributing to it by way of personal predication. Our analysis suggests that it is never quite this simple. We human beings are not only "in" the natural order, we help to create and sustain the natural order, as well as the (opposite) unnatural orders that are formulated from time to time.

We noted early in this volume how the Greeks sought to identify the ultimate categories of nature (Chapter 2). This abstract ordering is merely one of the many manifestations of the human tendency to pattern existence in terms of a reassuring certainty. People are ever drawn to the ultimate categorization, the "final" word, the "revealed" truth, the "proven" fact. This reaching for the ultimate certainty is readily understood if we see it as an extension of the basic need to predicate. We have said that predication makes learning possible. Predication also makes a higher knowledge possible—a knowledge we call the dream, the wish, the aspiration. Human teleology (introspectively understood) begins right here. People search for the ultimate categorical understanding through contact with a deity. They project ideal governments and inevitable classless states. Some merely seek the "perfect" relationship with the natural order (e.g., nirvana).

Of course, being oppositional or dialectical reasoners, people can also challenge the validity of such universal perfectability and certainty. Indeed, it would be possible to argue that in the present day we face a virtual crisis in the confidence to be placed in any grand, overarching scheme based on some presumed, immutable universal truth. We saw in chapter 2 how modern science no longer holds to the universal Newtonian view that the world is a machine (see especially Kuhn 1970, 1977). The occurrences taking place at the subatomic level have violated long-standing beliefs concerning the ultimate or "basic" nature of reality. In philosophy, the grand schemes of yesteryear have come tumbling down, so that today's philosophical efforts are in the main attacks on universal assertions (see Rorty 1979). The claims of religion regarding eternal truths seem almost daily to come under attack in this increasingly complex world, where even members of the same faith cannot agree on the unquestioned assumptions of their belief (see, e.g., Martin 1987). Teachers no longer agree on a standard curriculum that was once the hallmark of the educated person (Bloom 1987). Attacks such as these on universals do not, of course, herald the demise of predicational reasoning. The "new universals" in our time predicate "no universals." But this dialectically generated conundrum presents a difficult challenge to the human being, whose telic intelligence ever prompts a belief in the ultimate certainty and perfection of things.

Doubtless the strong identification of *telos* (end, reason, goal, etc.) with "higher" begins in this aspiration to know the most perfect order of all. Human teleological description has probably been hurt by this one-sided interpretation of final causation as working toward the "best" end. Psychologists and other cognitive scientists are suspicious when they hear talk of intentions, for in the teleological writings of history there has usually been an effort to bring in a moral, to suggest that the person "naturally" seeks the good, the higher, and the godly. Of course, the greater truth is that people seek for both positive advantages and for negative retributions. People can and do opt for "this (harmful) alternative, as opposed to that (helpful) alternative, all circumstances remaining the same." A proper recognition of dialectical reasoning in the cognitive sciences was also checkmated owing to the emphasis placed on the positive aspects of the telos in human reason.

It was probably the desire to find and the belief in a "perfect" scheme of categorization that led to the study of logic as strictly error-free. The assumption made here was that reasoning could be ironclad. Logic was not promulgated as a means for understanding both accuracy and error in human reason. Formal logic held out hope that *only* accuracy in human reason could be achieved. Soon, the admonition was that logic *must* result in perfect categorical understanding. If logical reasoning was not 100 percent accurate, it was said to be illogical. When we come to dialectical logic, to the processing of what are in formal logic erroneous assumptions and contradictory conclusions, there *is* a vast area of human reasoning to be considered that generates as much confusion as perfection. Principles of contradiction (*A* is not non-*A*) and strict disjunction (either x or y, but not both xy) are violated, rigorous perfection is lost, and yet there is something preciously human to be found in the resultant logical quagmire.

To the classical logician, opting for the negative or harmful alternative seems prima facie evidence that the reasoner is functioning illogically. If life were only so clear that the most positive or best alternative was readily known, we could then select this alternative through an initial deliberation and carry our lives forward to a better future with an assured certainty that things will always turn out right. This style of explanation, which suggests that people can *first* deliberate over alternatives and *then* select from among these the best of the lot, has also made it appear that people are logicians weighing alternatives before behavior gets underway. This gives agency a narrow interpretation, as if it occurs only *before* behavior takes place. Some theoreticians find it pointless to discuss freely willed behaviors *after* a course of events has been enacted. Yet, as we noted in chapter 6, every human being has had the experience of ruminating over a missed opportunity or of harboring resentment over some past frustration. We wonder why we did not get a better table at the restaurant, when we could see with our own eyes that better locations were unoccupied at the time of our seating and remained so until we left. And we do not accept the waiter's explanation of this unhappy incident. All circumstances remaining the same, the waiter *could have* redirected our evening's entertainment down a more positive path. We picture ourselves storming out of the restaurant, but lacking the courage to do so, or having no decent alternative for an evening's outing,

THE COMPUTER ANALOGUE AND HUMAN NATURE   173

we stay put and make the best of it. But no doubt about it, our evening is, if not ruined, then at least significantly diminished.

We do not usually view such instances as reflecting free will, but this is what is suggested if we think about people in terms of predication and opposition. As Penfield and Libet were to find (see Chapter 8), people can exert influence on biological promptings *after* they have arisen. Checkmating a biological demand is often referred to as willpower, and properly so. To harbor resentment over some perceived indignity such as being given improper service in a restaurant is the interpersonal counterpart to such biological checkmates. Logical processes begin in predicated assumptions that are affirmed or agreed to by the thinker—often in a tentative or ambivalent sense. Such assumptions can also be flatly opposed/rejected. So it is not in the actual *origination* of a line of thought or behavior that free will is to be exclusively identified (although it might be found here as well). Free will is to be seen in the oppositional efforts to change what is presently underway, to retrace steps to where the line of thought or action began, to revert to where the waiter "could have" assigned a different table, and so forth.

Another manifestation of free will that is frequently overlooked is simple boredom. Why is it that in time, an activity that was so pleasant becomes unpleasant, calling for an alternative activity—if only for a brief respite from the now "routine" activity? Biological explanations of this phenomenon pale to insignificance alongside the realization that as we are engaged in any activity we are also cognizant that we could be "doing otherwise," which in turn invites our attention to seek some even "better" diversion as a change in routine for long or short periods of time. Of course, it is also true that certain activities retain their interest and fail to manifest boredom. But, the human being's telic capacity for evaluating ongoing circumstances and realizing that an opposite direction is always "there" for selection (or not!) is readily understood as the source of boredom.

As scientists learned more about their personal contribution to their work as participating conceptualizers (see chapter 2) they were also to learn more about their free-will capacity to set the grounds for the sake of which their empirical findings would be determined. This recognition broadens our understanding of determinism in nature to include all four causal meanings, and most assuredly if there are such predicational contributions to be made in science there are comparable contributions to be made in other cultural institutions. The legal systems of humanity are therefore correct in presuming that the person is an agent, that free will is a proper basis for deciding responsibility before the bar of justice. Religions are rooted in teleology, and people are drawn to such formulations out of a fundamental recognition that personal responsibility is a legitimate aspect of the human experience. Guilt, remorse, a desire to set things right are all reflections of the human capacity to understand that, all things remaining the same, events could have gone differently in a life situation that is now past but not forgotten. And, of course, there is the idealized future, in which the "highest" form of experience will, it is hoped, be realized in the "hereafter" once this physical existence is terminated. The role of predication here is undeniable.

In art we find the highest expressions of the human spirit, the reaching for beauty, itself a presumed universal category. Of course, we know that the grounds for the judgment of beauty vary. But there are many reflections of opposition in art, as in the stark contrasts of thematic material, the contrapuntal musical expressions that convey opposite moods at the same time, and the twists and turns of literary story lines that mislead and surprise us with their unexpected outcomes. It is often said that beauty is in the eye of the beholder, and if this is true it is also true that the judgments "I like this" versus "I dislike that" are made within an oppositional frame, aligning thereby aesthetic judgments in the typical fashion of predication. Indeed, such personal judgments of like-dislike have been shown to predicate and thereby exert an important influence on cognitive processes, facilitating or inhibiting learning, memory, and various other psychological functions (see Rychlak 1988, ch. 9).

This matter of rendering affective preferences leads us to a consideration of emotions in human behavior. It is almost routine today to hear that since human beings are emotional organisms, and since computers cannot experience emotions, there can be no real hope that computers actually simulate what the human being is going through during cognitive processing. I have not employed this argument in the present volume, for two reasons. First of all, it does not strike me that this is a strong argument. It would seem to hold out hope that if one day a technology were developed so that machines could indeed have "feelings" through some kind of unpredictable short circuitry or the automatic heating of elements at difficult decision points in the processing of information, a rapprochement would be effected and machines would then be said to completely encompass the human experience. In other words, the problem is framed as strictly a technical difficulty in the present state of the engineering process. Actually, attempts have already been made to write programs that can guess at the emotion that would be experienced, given certain descriptions of events (see Frijda and Swagerman 1987).

Second, and more to the point: It is my belief that emotional behavior is itself dependent on predication and reflects oppositionality in many ways. Ambivalence is a common emotional feeling. As in the aesthetic experience of listening to opposing melodic moods at the same time, it is also possible to "feel" both love and hate for the same individual in highly charged emotional circumstances. There is ample evidence that people must predicate their emotional experience, they must frame it in some way in order to lend it meaning, relying on what they believe to be the case rather than on what may actually be the case (Schachter and Singer 1962; Valins 1970). We cannot dismiss the basic physiological facts. Physiological correlates of emotions have been demonstrated (see, e.g., Ekman, Levenson, and Friesen 1983). But there are also individual predications brought to bear in identifying emotions, both in ourselves and in the experience of others. And the social context within which an emotion is experienced is always crucial in this identification process. The more complex the emotional mood, the more complex the predicated circumstance is to the emoting individual. It is in this sense that the computer analogue falls short of capturing the emoting organism.

A final point I should like to make concerning human nature relates to a comment made in my Introduction, where it was noted that people are not slaves to their social environments. We can understand now that the point being made had to do with the fact that human beings can predicate their lives in consonance with social norms of various sorts, or they can reason to the opposite of such norms and behave quite differently from the generally accepted norms. I have called this human agency. Sometimes people conform to a subgroup norm, such as a gang, racial/ethnic identity, or a religious group that affirms values in opposition to the broader or shared culture. In light of such obvious influences, how can we state that people are not under great normative influence, and is this not a form of slavish compliance?

The concept of the "norm" is an interesting one. There are significant theories of human behavior advanced today, such as social constructionism (Gergen 1985; Sampson 1988), which contend that people are mere mediators of a supraindividual influence rather than individual creators of the normative influence "for the sake of which" they will behave. Actually, the early social psychologists who introduced normative theory tended to view social norms introspectively, from the vantage point of the individual who sought to conform to them, move beyond them to a higher social-class value system, rejected them in favor of a downward mobility, and so forth (see Krech and Crutchfield 1948; Scheerer 1954). But under the firming grasp of behaviorism and its claims to be "observing" behavior in extraspective fashion, psychological explanation has turned the norm from a "premise held in common" by people to a "grand manipulator in the social skies," bringing to bear a directedness on the individuals under its yoke in an efficient-cause fashion. The move from predicational to mediational theorizing here has been dramatic.

As we have seen, often the vehicle for such theories of social "forces" acting on individuals is that of language. It is not that people are sharing meanings, expressed through language, but that their language per se acts as a shaping influence to direct what will be said, believed in, and expressed. The concept of "society" as a collective body, observable in many instances as in political groups, ethnic identities, and so forth, seems to assure that a social theory will be framed extraspectively. It is possible to think of the "point of view" of the "group mind," but obviously we cannot literally observe such a collective mentality actually functioning ("thinking"). When we look "at" the collective, therefore, it is a simple matter to construe people within this identifiable group as being moved along by supraindividual normative forces—in other words, as mediators of social influence. We are back to the Jones and Nisbett (1971) findings (see chapter 1).

The point I wish to make is that although people do indeed receive significant influences from their social milieu, from the groups with whom they identify, the nature of this *learning process* is *not* what social theorists make it out to be, if indeed they comment on this aspect of human behavior at all (see chapter 5). Cultural shaping is no longer tenable as a form of associative conditioning. As predicating organisms, what people take from their social group is the "wider compass," the grounding assumptions that everyone needs to lend stability and a sense of certainty to life. The person is not manipulated into taking on such normative influences. One *needs* a grounding "that" for the sake of which one can know and thereby use to enlarge a sense of meaningfulness. Here is where life's most basic values spring from—a need to grasp a worthwhile context in which to target what is to be experienced. Children are, by and large, credulous and accepting of parental beliefs simply because they require a basis, a grounds, on which to frame their growing experience. This is not a "shaping" process from parent to child but rather a "sharing" effort that can go awry but in most cases is decisively influential.

The normative influence here is predicational, which demands a formal/final-cause explanation. And when this mutual sharing of beliefs, attitudes, and values fails, this is not *always* because the parents and related social influencers have failed to provide the correct "inputs" to the shaping process. At least some of the time, the child's deviation from the accepted norm is due strictly to an opposite affirmation of the proper meanings that have been properly "input." Viewing the person this way is not as simple as the mediational model permits one to suggest, but it is surely more accurate in capturing the human situation. Of course, we are not at this point out to "simulate" anything. When it comes to framing human nature we hope to be as literal and accurate as possible, even if this means that we must complicate our scientific efforts to capture this human image in a research context.

It would seem that there is a side to the human being that is going unconsidered in today's social and cognitive sciences. We require a broadened base—a richer predication!—of the human image. The teleologist has a most important place in the study of human nature today, not because of some human vanity or religious necessity to believe in personal responsibility and free will. No, the requirement is more objective and empirically based than this. We have a continuing line of research evidence to support the view that human beings are telic animals. Such research evidence has accrued in the face of a concerted effort since the seventeenth century to keep agential considerations out of the scientific account. Surely, the science of psychology and related disciplines are mature enough today to repredicate the human image, to retrace steps taken since the seventeenth century, and to pursue an alternative course of human description in the future even as "all things remain the same" in the empirical record.

References

Adler, M. J. 1978. *Aristotle for Everybody: Difficult Thought Made Easy.* New York: Bantam Books.
Anderson, J. R. 1983. *The Architecture of Cognition.* Cambridge: Harvard University Press.
Anderson, J. R. 1985. *Cognitive Psychology and Its Implications.* 2d ed. New York: W. H. Freeman.
Aristotle. 1952. In R. M. Hutchins, ed. *Great Books of the Western World*, vol. 8. Chicago: Encyclopedia Britannica.
  [a] *Categories* (pp. 5–21)
  [b] *On Interpretation* (pp. 25–36)
  [c] *Prior Analytics* (pp. 39–93)
  [d] *Posterior Analytics* (pp. 95–137)
  [e] *Topics* (pp. 143–223)
  [f] *Physics* (pp. 257–355)
  [g] *Metaphysics* (pp. 499–626)
  [h] *On the Soul* (pp. 631–668)
  [i] *On Memory and Reminiscence* (pp. 690–695)
Aristotle. 1952. In R. M. Hutchins, ed., *Great Books of the Western World*, vol. 9. Chicago: Encyclopedia Britannica.
  [j] *On the Parts of Animals* (pp. 161–229)
  [k] *On the Generation of Animals* (pp. 255–331)
  [l] *Nicomachean Ethics* (pp. 339–436)
  [m] *Rhetoric* (pp. 593–675)
Bacon, F. 1952. In R. M. Hutchins, ed. *Great Books of the Western World*, vol. 30. Chicago: Encyclopedia Britannica.
  [a] *Advancement of Learning* (pp. 1–101)
  [b] *Novum Organum* (pp. 105–195)
Bartlett, F. C. 1958. *Thinking: An Experimental and Social Study.* London: George Allen & Unwin.
Bastian, J. 1961. Associative factors in verbal transfer. *Journal of Experimental Psychology* 62:70–79.

Beck, E. C. and R. W. Dorty. 1957. Conditioned flexion reflexes acquired during combined catalepsy and de-efferentation. *Journal of Comparative and Physiological Psychology* 50:211–216.

Bennett, J. 1976. *Linguistic Behavior.* London: Cambridge University Press.

Berlin, B. and P. Kay. 1969. *Basic Color Terms: Their Universality and Evolution.* Berkeley and Los Angeles: University of California Press.

Block, J. D. 1962. Awareness of stimulus relationships and physiological generality of response in autonomic discrimination. *Recent Advances in Biological Psychiatry* 4:43–53.

Bloom, A. 1987. *The Closing of the American Mind.* New York: Simon and Schuster.

Bloom, L. 1973. *One Word at a Time: The Use of Single Word Utterances Before Syntax.* The Hague: Mouton.

Boden, M. A. 1977. *Artificial Intelligence and Natural Man.* New York: Basic Books.

Boden, M. A. 1981. *Minds and Mechanisms: Philosophical Psychology and Computational Models.* Ithaca, N.Y.: Cornell University Press.

Bohm, D. 1957. *Causality and Chance in Modern Physics.* Philadelphia: University of Pennsylvania Press.

Bohm, D. 1980. *Wholeness and the Implicate Order.* London: Routledge and Kegan Paul.

Bohm, D. 1987. *Unfolding Meaning: A Weekend of Dialogue.* New York: Routledge, Chapman, and Hall.

Bohr, N. 1934. *Atomic Theory and the Description of Nature.* Cambridge, England: Cambridge University Press.

Boole, G. 1854/1958. *The Laws of Thought.* New York: Dover Publications, Inc.

Boring, E. G. 1950. *A History of Experimental Psychology.* New York: Appleton-Century-Crofts.

Bower, T. G. R. 1974. *Development in Infancy.* San Francisco: Freeman.

Bradley, J. 1971. *Mach's Philosophy of Science.* London: Athlone Press.

Braine, M. D. S. 1976. Children's first word combinations. *Monographs of the Society for Research in Child Development* 41 (serial no. 164).

Bransford, J. D. and J. J. Franks. 1975. The abstraction of linguistic ideas. *Cognitive Psychology* 2:331–350.

Brewer, W. F. 1974. There is no convincing evidence for operant or classical conditioning in adult humans. In W. B. Weimer and D. S. Palermo, eds., *Cognition and the Symbolic Processes,* pp. 1–42. Hillsdale, N.J.: Lawrence Erlbaum Associates.

Brewer, W. F. and E. H. Lichtenstein. 1974. Memory for marked semantic features versus memory for meaning. *Journal of Verbal Learning and Verbal Behavior* 13:172–180.

Brogden, W. J. 1951. Some theoretical considerations of learning. *Psychological Review* 58:224–229.

Broglie, L. A. de. 1949. A general survey of the scientific work of Albert

Einstein. In P. Schlipp, ed. *Albert Einstein, Philosopher Scientist*, vol. 1:38–51. New York: Harper and Row.

Brown, P. L. and H. M. Jenkins. 1968. Auto-shaping of the pigeon's key peck. *Journal of Experimental Analysis of Behavior* 11:109.

Brown, R. 1973. *A First Language: The Early Stages*. Cambridge: Harvard University Press.

Browne, M. P. 1976. The role of primary reinforcement and overt movements in auto-shaping in the pigeon. *Animal Learning and Behavior* 4:287–292.

Bullock, M., R. Gelman, and R. Baillargeon. 1982. The development of causal reasoning. In W. J. Friedman, ed., *The Development of Psychology of Time*, pp. 112–136. New York: Academic Press.

Bunge, M. 1980. *The Mind-Body Problem: A Psychobiological Approach*. New York: Pergamon Press.

Burtt, E. A. 1955. *The Metaphysical Foundations of Modern Physical Science*, rev. ed. Garden City, N.Y.: Doubleday.

Campbell, D. T. 1974. "Downward causation" in hierarchically organized biological systems. In F. J. Ayala and T. Dobshansky, eds. *Studies in the Philosophy of Biology*, pp. 179–186. London: Macmillan.

Carey, S. 1978. The child as word learner. In M. Halle, J. Bresnan, and G. A. Miller, eds. *Linguistic Theory and Psychological Reality*. Cambridge: MIT Press.

Carey, S. 1985. *Conceptual Change in Childhood*. Cambridge: MIT Press.

Carlson, J. G. and R. M. Wielkiewicz. 1976. Mediators of the effects of magnitude of reinforcement. *Learning and Motivation* 7:184–196.

Cassirer, E. 1950. *The Problem of Knowledge*. New Haven, Conn.: Yale University Press.

Cerella, J. 1979. Visual classes and natural categories in the pigeon. *Journal of Experimental Psychology: Human Perceptual Performance* 5:68–77.

Cermak, L. S. 1976. *Improving Your Memory*. New York: McGraw-Hill.

Chatterjee, B. B. and C. W. Eriksen. 1960. Conditioning and generalization of GSR as a function of awareness. *Journal of Abnormal and Social Psychology* 60:396–403.

Chomsky, N. 1972. *Language and Mind*, enlarged ed. New York: Harcourt Brace Jovanovich.

Chomsky, N. 1983. Views on the psychology of language and thought. In R. Rieber, ed. *Dialogues on the Psychology of Language and Thought*, pp. 33–63. New York: Plenum.

Clark, H. C. and E. V. Clark. 1977. *Psychology and Language: An Introduction to Psycholinguistics*. New York: Harcourt Brace Jovanovich.

Cohen, L. B. and E. Salapatek, eds. 1975. *Infant Perception: From Perception to Cognition*, 2 vols. New York: Academic Press.

Cornwell, D., S. Hobbs, and R. Prytula. 1980. Little Albert rides again. *American Psychologist* 35:216, 217.

Coulter, J. 1983. *Rethinking Cognitive Theory*. New York: St. Martin's Press.

Cousins, N., ed. 1985. *Nobel Prize Conversations with Sir John Eccles, Roger Sperry, Ilya Prigogine, and Brian Josephson.* San Francisco: Saybrook.

Craik, F. I. M. and E. Tulving. 1975. Depth of processing and the retention of words in episodic memory. *Journal of Experimental Psychology: General* 104:268–294.

Cranston, M. 1957. *John Locke: A Biography.* New York: Longmans, Green.

Davies, P. C. W. and J. R. Brown, eds. 1986. Interview with John Bell. *The Ghost in the Atom,* pp. 45–57. Cambridge, England: Cambridge University Press.

Dawson, M. E. 1970. Cognition and conditioning: Effects of masking the CS-UCS contingency on human GSR classical conditioning. *Journal of Experimental Psychology* 85:389–396.

DeNike, L. D. 1964. The temporal relationship between awareness and performance in verbal conditioning. *Journal of Experimental Psychology* 68:521–529.

Dennett, D. C. 1984. *Elbow Room: The Varieties of Free Will Worth Wanting.* Cambridge: Bradford Book of the MIT Press.

Dickinson, A. 1980. *Contemporary Animal Learning Theory.* Cambridge, England: Cambridge University Press.

Dollard, J. and N. E. Miller. 1950. *Personality and Psychotherapy: An Analysis in Terms of Learning, Thinking, and Culture.* New York: McGraw-Hill.

Dooley, P. K. 1975. *Pragmatism as Humanism: The Philosophy of William James.* Totowa, N.J.: Littlefield, Adams.

Dorf, R. C. 1974. *Computers and Man.* San Francisco: Boyd and Frazer.

Dreyfus, H. L. 1979. *What Computers Can't Do: The Limits of Artificial Intelligence,* rev. ed. New York: Harper and Row.

Dreyfus, H. L. and S. E. Dreyfus. 1986. *Mind Over Machine.* New York: The Free Press.

Dulany, D. E., Jr. 1961. Hypotheses and habits in verbal "operant conditioning." *Journal of Abnormal and Social Psychology* 63:241–263.

Eccles, J. C. 1977. In K. R. Popper and J. C. Eccles. *The Self and Its Brain,* part 2, pp. 225–421. London: Springer International.

Ekman, P., R. W. Levenson, and W. V. Friesen. 1983. Autonomic nervous system activity distinguishes among emotions. *Science* 221:1208–1210.

Elmer-DeWitt, P. 1988, November. The kid put us out of action. *Time,* p. 76.

Ettlinger, G. A. 1982. A comparative evaluation of the cognitive skills of the chimpanzee and the monkey. Paper presented at the Harry Frank Guggenheim Conference, June 2–4, Columbia University, New York.

Eves, H. 1953. *An Introduction to the History of Mathematics,* 3d ed. New York: Holt, Rinehart and Winston.

Farrington, B. 1949. *Francis Bacon: Philosopher of Industrial Science.* New York: Henry Schuman.

Festinger, L. 1957. *A Theory of Cognitive Dissonance.* Stanford, Calif. Stanford University Press.

Feuer, L. S. 1974. *Einstein and the Generations of Science.* New York: Basic Books.
Finch, G. 1938. Salivary conditioning in atropinized dogs. *American Journal of Physiology* 124:136–142.
Fish, S. 1980. *Is There a Text in This Class? The Authority of Interpretive Communities.* Cambridge: Harvard University Press.
Fodor, J. A 1975. *The Language of Thought.* New York: Thomas Y. Crowell.
Fodor, J. A. and Z. W. Pylyshyn. 1981. How direct is visual perception? Some reflections on Gibson's "Ecological Approach." *Cognition* 9:139–196.
Fouts, R. S. 1972. The use of guidance in teaching sign language to a chimpanzee. *Journal of Comparative and Physiological Psychology* 80:515–522.
Frijda, N. H. and J. Swagerman. 1987. Can computers feel? *Cognition and Emotion* 1:235–258.
Frisch, K. von. 1974. Decoding the language of the bee. *Science* 185:663–668.
Gamzu, E. R. and D. R. Williams. 1973. Associative factors underlying the pigeon's key pecking in auto-shaping procedures. *Journal of the Experimental Analysis of Behavior* 19:225–232.
Gardner, H. 1985. *The Mind's New Science: A History of the Cognitive Revolution.* New York: Basic Books.
Gardner, R. A. and B. T. Gardner. 1969. Teaching sign language to a chimpanzee. *Science* 165:664–672.
Gazzaniga, M. S. 1985. *The Social Brain: Discovering the Networks of the Mind.* New York: Basic Books.
Gellert, E. 1962. Children's conceptions of the content and functions of the human body. *Genetic Psychology Monographs* 65:291–411.
Gergen, K. J. 1985. The social constructionist movement in modern psychology. *American Psychologist* 40:266–275.
Gibson, J. J. 1950. *The Perception of the Visual World.* Boston: Houghton Mifflin.
Gibson, J. J. 1979. *The Ecological Approach to Visual Perception.* Boston: Houghton Mifflin.
Gleick, J. 1988. *Chaos: Making a New Science.* New York: Penguin Books.
Granit, R. 1977. *The Purposive Brain.* Cambridge: MIT Press.
Greenfield, P. M. and J. H. Smith. 1976. *The Structure of Communication in Early Language Development.* New York: Academic Press.
Greenspoon, J. 1955. The reinforcing effect of two spoken sounds on the frequency of two responses. *American Journal of Psychology* 68:409–416.
Grene, M. 1965. *Approaches to a Philosophical Biology.* New York: Basic Books.
Griffin, D. R. 1981. *The Question of Animal Awareness: Evolutionary Continuity of Mental Experience.* New York: The Rockefeller University Press.
Grossman, L. and M. Eagle. 1970. Synonymity, antonymity, and associa-

tion in false recognition response. *Journal of Experimental Psychology* 83:244–248.

Haber, R. N. 1983. Stimulus information and processing mechanisms in visual space perception. In J. Beck, B. Hope, and A. Rosenfeld, eds. *Human and Machine Vision*, pp. 341–346. New York: Academic Press.

Haber, R. N. 1985. Perception: A one-hundred-year perspective. In S. Koch and D. E. Leary, eds. *A Century of Psychology as Science*, pp. 250–281. New York: McGraw-Hill.

Haith, M. M. 1981. *Rules That Infants Look by*. Hillsdale, N.J.: Lawrence Erlbaum Associates.

Haith, M. M., T. Bergman, and M. J. Moore. 1977. Eye contact and face scanning in early infancy. *Science* 198:853–855.

Hampton, J. A. and P. J. Taylor. 1985. Effects of semantic relatedness on same-different decisions in a good-bad categorization task. *Journal of Experimental Psychology: Learning, Memory, and Cognition* 11:85–93.

Harlow, H. F. 1949. The formation of learning sets. *Psychological Review* 56:51–65.

Hawking, S. W. 1988. *A Brief History of Time: From the Big Bang to Black Holes*. New York: Bantam Books.

Hayes, K. J. and C. Hayes. 1961. The intellectual development of a home-raised chimpanzee. *Proceedings of the American Philosophical Society* 95:105.

Hebb, D. O. 1949. *The Organization of Behavior*. New York: John Wiley.

Heil, J. 1983. *Perception and Cognition*. Berkeley: University of California Press.

Helmholtz, H. von. 1979. Selections on the empirical theory of space perception. In R. I. Watson, ed. *Basic Writings in the History of Psychology*, pp. 125–127. New York: Oxford University Press.

Herbert, J. J. and C. M. Harsh. 1944. Observational learning by cats. *Journal of Comparative Psychology* 37:81–95.

Hernstein, R. J., D. H. Loveland, and C. Cable. 1976. Natural concepts in pigeons. *Journal of Experimental Psychology: Animal Behavioral Processes* 2:285–302.

Hochberg, J. E. 1968. In the mind's eye. In R. N. Haber, ed. *Contemporary Research and Theory in Visual Perception*, pp. 53–82. New York: Holt, Rinehart and Winston.

Hochberg, J. E. 1981. Levels of perceptual organization. In M. Kubovy and J. R. Pomerantz, eds. *Perceptual Organization*, pp. 93–114. Hillsdale, N.J.: Lawrence Erlbaum Associates.

Hofstadter, D. R. 1980. *Gödel, Escher, Bach: An Eternal Golden Braid*. New York: Vintage Books.

Holton, G. 1973. *Thematic Origins of Scientific Thought: Kepler to Einstein*. Cambridge: Harvard University Press.

Honeck, R. P., P. Riechmann, and R. R. Hoffman. 1975. Semantic memory for metaphor: The conceptual base hypothesis. *Memory and Cognition* 3:409–415.

Howard, D. V. 1983. *Cognitive Psychology: Memory, Language, and Thought.* New York: Macmillan.
Hull, C. L. 1937. Mind, mechanism, and adaptive behavior. *Psychological Review* 44:1–32.
Jacob, F. 1976. *The Logic of Life,* transl. by B. Stillman. New York: Vintage Books.
Johnson-Laird, P. N. 1983. *Mental Models: Towards a Cognitive Science of Language, Inference, and Consciousness.* Cambridge: Harvard University Press.
Jonas, H. 1966. *The Phenomenon of Life.* New York: Dell Books.
Jones, E. E. and R. E. Nisbett. 1971. *The Actor and the Observer: Divergent Perceptions of the Causes of Behavior.* Morristown, N.J.: General Learning Press.
Kagan, J. 1981. *The Second Year: The Emergence of Self-Awareness.* Cambridge: Harvard University Press.
Kagan, J. 1984. *The Nature of the Child.* New York: Basic Books.
Kahnemann, D., P. Slovic, and A. Tversky, eds. 1982. *Judgement Under Uncertainty: Heuristics and Biases.* New York: Cambridge University Press.
Kant, I. 1952. In R. M. Hutchins, ed. *Great Books of the Western World,* vol. 42. Chicago: Encyclopedia Britannica.
  [a] *Critique of Pure Reason* (pp. 14–250)
  [b] *The Critique of Judgement* (pp. 461–613)
Karwoski, T. F. and J. Schachter. 1948. Psychological studies in semantics: III. Reaction times for similarity and differences. *Journal of Social Psychology* 28:103–120.
Katz, A. 1982. Metaphoric relationships: The role of feature saliency. *Journal of Psycholinguistic Research* 11:283–295.
Kelly, G. A. 1955. *The Psychology of Personal Constructs,* vol. 1: *A Theory of Personality.* New York: W. W. Norton.
Kennedy, T. D. 1971. Reinforcement frequency, task characteristics, and interval of awareness assessment as factors in verbal conditioning without awareness. *Journal of Experimental Psychology* 88:103–112.
Kjeldergaard, P. M. 1962. Commonality scores under instructions to give opposites. *Psychological Reports* 11:219–220.
Koffka, K. 1935. *Principles of Gestalt Psychology.* New York: Harcourt, Brace.
Kornhuber, H. H. and L. Deecke. 1965. Hirnpotential-anderungen bei willkurbewegungen und passiven bewegungen des menschen: Bereitschaftpotential und reafferente potentiale. *Pflugers Archive fur die gesamte Physiologie des Menschen und der Tiere* 284:1–17.
Krasner, L. 1958. Studies of the conditioning of verbal behavior. *Psychological Bulletin* 55:148–170.
Krech, D. and R. S. Crutchfield. 1948. *Theory and Problems of Social Psychology.* New York: McGraw-Hill.
Kreutzer, M. A., C. Leonard, and J. H. Flavell. 1975. An interview study of

children's knowledge about memory. *Monographs of the Society for Research in Child Development* 40:159.
Kuhn, T. S. 1970. *The Structure of Scientific Revolutions*, 2d ed. Chicago: University of Chicago Press.
Kuhn, T. S. 1977. *The Essential Tension: Selected Studies in Scientific Tradition and Change.* Chicago: University of Chicago Press.
Kukla, A. 1989. Nonempirical issues in psychology. *American Psychologist* 44:785–794.
Lakoff, G. 1980. Whatever happened to deep structure? *The Behavioral and Brain Sciences* 3:22–23.
Lakoff, G. 1987. *Women, Fire, and Dangerous Things: What Categories Reveal About the Mind.* Chicago: The University of Chicago Press.
Lamiell, J. T. 1987. *The Psychology of Personality: An Epistemological Inquiry.* New York: Columbia University Press.
Levin, S. M. 1961. The effects of awareness on verbal conditioning. *Journal of Experimental Psychology* 61:67–75.
Libet, B. 1973. Electrical stimulation of cortex in human subjects, and conscious memory aspects. In A. Iggo, ed. *Handbook of Sensory Physiology*, vol. 2:743–790. New York: Springer-Verlag.
Libet, B. 1985. Unconscious cerebral initiative and the role of conscious will in voluntary action. *The Behavioral and Brain Sciences* 8:529–566.
Libet, B., C. A. Gleason, E. W. Wright, and D. K. Pearl. 1983. Time of conscious intention to act in relation to onset of cerebral activities (readiness-potential); the unconscious initiation of a freely voluntary act. *Brain* 106:623–642.
Lipsitt, L. P., H. Kaye, and T. N. Bosack. 1966. Enhancement of neonatal sucking through reinforcement. *Journal of Experimental Child Psychology* 4:163–168.
Locke, J. 1952. *An Essay Concerning Human Understanding.* In R. M. Hutchins, ed. *Great Books of the Western World*, vol. 35:85–395. Chicago: Encyclopedia Britannica.
Lorayne, H. and J. Lucas. 1974. *The Memory Book.* New York: Ballantine.
Lucas, J. R. 1961. Minds, machines, and Gödel. *Philosophy* 36:112–127.
Lumsden, C. J. and E. O. Wilson. 1983. *Promethean Fire: Reflections on the Origin of Mind.* Cambridge: Harvard University Press.
Lyons, J. 1977. *Semantics*, vol. 1. London: Cambridge University Press.
MacCorquodale, K. and P. E. Meehl. 1948. On a distinction between hypothetical constructs and intervening variables. *Psychological Review* 55:95–107.
MacKay, D. M. 1967. *Freedom of Action in a Mechanistic Universe: The Eddington Lecture.* Cambridge, England: Cambridge University Press.
Mackintosh, N. J. 1983. *Conditioning and Associative Learning.* New York: Oxford University Press.
Mandler, R. 1967. Organization and memory. In K. W. Spence and J. Taylor Spence, eds., *The Psychology of Learning and Motivation: Advances in Research and Theory*, vol. 1:327–372. New York: Academic Press.

Mandler, G. 1985. *Cognitive Psychology: An Essay in Cognitive Science.* Hillsdale, N.J.; Lawrence Erlbaum Associates.

Mandler, J. M. and N. S. Johnson. 1977. Remembrance of things parsed: Story structure and recall. *Cognitive Psychology* 9:111–151.

Martin, M. 1987. *The Jesuits: The Society of Jesus and the Betrayal of the Roman Catholic Church.* New York: The Linden Press of Simon and Schuster.

Martin, R. B. and S. J. Dean. 1971. Instrumental modification of the GSR. *Psychophysiology* 7:178–185.

Massaro, D. W. 1986. The computer as a metaphor for psychological inquiry: Considerations and recommendations. *Behavioral Research Methods, Instruments, and Computers,* 18:73–92.

McCabe, A. 1982. Conceptual similarity and the quality of metaphor in isolated sentences versus extended contexts. *Journal of Psycholinguistic Research* 12:41–63.

McCulloch, W. and W. Pitts. 1943. A logical calculus of the ideas immanent in nervous activity. *Bulletin of Mathematical Biophysics* 5:115–133.

McNeil, D. 1968. On theories of language acquisition. In T. R. Dixon and D. L. Horton, eds. *Verbal Behavior and General Behavior Theory,* pp. 406–420. Englewood Cliffs, N.J.: Prentice-Hall.

Menzel, E. W., Jr. and S. Halpern. 1975. Purposive behavior as a basis for objective communication between chimpanzees. *Science* 189:652–654.

Meyers, R. E. and R. W. Sperry. 1953. Interocular transfer of a visual form discrimination habit in cats after section of the optic chiasm and corpus callosum. *Anatomical Record* 115:351–352.

Miller, G. A. 1956. The magical number seven, plus or minus two: Some limits on our capacity for processing information. *Psychological Review* 63:81–97.

Miller, G. A., E. Galanter, and K. H. Pribram. 1960. *Plans and the Structure of Behavior.* New York: Holt, Rinehart and Winston.

Mink, W. D. 1963. Semantic generalization as related to word association. *Psychological Reports* 12:59–67.

Minsky, M. 1967. Why programming is a good medium for expressing poorly understood and sloppily formulated ideas. In M. Krampen and P. Seeitz, ed. *Design and Planning II,* pp. 116–137. New York: Hastings House.

Minsky, M. 1986. *The Society of Mind.* New York: Simon and Schuster.

Mountcastle, V. B. 1975. Modality and topographic properties of single neurones of cat's somatic sensory cortex. *Journal of Neurophysiology* 20:408–434.

Nagel, E. and J. R. Newman. 1958. *Gödel's Proof.* New York: New York University Press.

Neisser, U. 1967. *Cognitive Psychology.* New York: Appleton-Century-Crofts.

Nelson, K. E. 1974. Concept, word, and sentence: Interrelations in acquisition and development. *Psychological Review* 81:267–285.

Nelson, K. E. and J. D. Bonvillian. 1973. Concepts and words in the eighteen-month-old. *Cognition* 2:435–450.

Newell, A. and H. A. Simon. 1972. *Human Problem Solving.* Englewood Cliffs, N.J.: Prentice-Hall.

O'Brien, E. J. and C. R. Wolford. 1982. Effect of delay in testing on retention of plausible versus bizarre mental images. *Journal of Experimental Psychology: Learning, Memory, and Cognition* 8:148–152.

O'Connor, D. J. 1971. *Free Will.* Garden City, N.Y.: Doubleday.

Ogden, C. K. 1967. *Opposition: A Linguistic and Psychological Analysis.* Bloomington: Indiana University Press.

Orne, M. T. 1962. On the social psychology of the psychological experiment: With particular reference to demand characteristics and their implications. *American Psychologist* 17:776–783.

Osgood, C. E. 1952. The nature and measurement of meaning. *Psychological Bulletin* 49:197–237.

Ozier, M. 1978. Access to the memory trace through orthographic and categoric information. *Journal of Experimental Psychology: Human Learning and Memory* 4:469–485.

Page, M. M. 1969. Social psychology of a classical conditioning of attitudes experiment. *Journal of Personality and Social Psychology* 11:177–186.

Page, M. M. 1972. Demand characteristics and the verbal operant conditioning experiment. *Journal of Personality and Social Psychology* 23:372–378.

Papousek, H. 1967a. Conditioning during early postnatal development. In Y. Brackbill and G. G. Thompson, eds. *Behavior in Infancy and Early Childhood*, pp. 11–41. New York: Free Press.

Papousek, H. 1967b. Experimental studies of appetitional behavior in newborns and infants. In H. W. Stevenson, E. H. Hess, and H. L. Rheingold, eds. *Early Behavior*, pp. 26–49. New York: John Wiley & Sons.

Patterson, F. C. 1978a. The gestures of a gorilla: Language acquisition in another pongid. *Brain and Language* 5:72–97.

Patterson, F. C. 1978b. Conversations with a gorilla. *National Geographic* 154:438–465.

Penfield, W. 1975. *The Mystery of the Mind: A Critical Study of Consciousness and the Human Brain.* Princeton, N.J.: Princeton University Press.

Pepper, S. C. 1970. *World Hypotheses.* Berkeley: University of California Press.

Perkins, D. N. 1976. How good a bet is good form? *Perception* 5:393–406.

Perkins, D. N. 1983. Why the human perceiver is a bad machine. In J. Beck, B. Hope, and A. Rosenfeld, eds. *Human and Machine Vision*, pp. 341–364. New York: Academic Press.

Piaget, J. 1929. *The Child's Perception of the World.* London: Routledge and Kegan Paul.

Plato. 1952. In R. M. Hutchins, ed. *Great Books of the Western World*, vol. 7. Chicago: Encyclopedia Britannica.

[a] *Philebus* (pp. 609–639)
[b] *Sophist* (pp. 551–579)
Polanyi, M. 1964. *Personal Knowledge: Towards a Post-Critical Philosophy.* New York: Harper and Row.
Premack, D. 1976. *Intelligence in Ape and Man.* Hillsdale, N.J.: Lawrence Erlbaum Associates.
Premack, D. 1986. *Gavagai! or the Future History of the Animal Language Controversy.* Cambridge: MIT Press.
Pribram, K. H. 1986. The cognitive revolution and mind/brain issues. *American Psychologist* 41:507–520.
Pribram, K. H. In Press. *Brain and Perception: Holonomy and Structure in Figural Processing.* Hillsdale, N.J.: Lawrence Erlbaum Associates.
Pribram, K. H. and E. H. Carlton. 1986. Holonomic brain theory in imaging and object perception. *Acta Psychologica* 63:175–210.
Prigogine, I. and I. Stengers. 1984. *Order out of Chaos: Man's New Dialogue with Nature.* New York: Bantam Books.
Pylyshyn, Z. W. 1981. Imagery and artificial intelligence. In N. Block, ed. *Readings in Philosophy of Psychology*, vol. 2:170–194. Cambridge: Harvard University Press.
Quine, W. V. 1981. *Theories and Things.* Cambridge: Harvard University Press.
Reed, E. S. and R. K. Jones. 1978. Gibson's theory of perception: A case of hasty epistemologizing. *Philosophy of Science* 45:519–530.
Reese, W. L. 1980. *Dictionary of Philosophy and Religion: Eastern and Western Thought.* Atlantic Highlands, N.J.: Humanities Press.
Richards, I. A. 1967. Introduction. In C. K. Ogden. *Opposition: A Linguistic and Psychological Analysis*, pp. 7–13. Bloomington: Indiana University Press.
Rickaby, J. 1906. *Free Will and Four English Philosophers.* London: Burns and Oates.
Robinson, D. N. 1989. *Aristotle's Psychology.* New York: Columbia University Press.
Rock, I. 1957. The role of repetition in associative learning. *American Journal of Psychology* 70:186–193.
Rock, I. 1973. *Orientation and Form.* New York: Academic Press.
Rock, I. and W. Heimer. 1959. Further evidence of one-trial associative learning. *American Journal of Psychology* 72:1–16.
Rogers, C. R. 1963. Learning to be free. In S. M. Farber and R. H. L. Wilson, eds. *Control of the Mind: Conflict and Creativity*, vol. 2:268–288. New York: McGraw-Hill.
Rorty, R. 1979. *Philosophy and the Mirror of Nature.* Princeton, N.J.: Princeton University Press.
Rosch, E. H. 1975. Cognitive representations of semantic categories. *Journal of Experimental Psychology: General* 104:192–233.
Rosenblueth, A., N. Wiener, and J. Bigelow. 1943. Behavior, teleology, and purpose. *Philosophy of Science* 10:18–24.

Rubin, E. 1921. *Visuell wahrgenomenne Figuren*. Copenhagen: Gyldendalske.

Rumbaugh, D. M., ed. 1977. *Language Learning by a Chimpanzee: The LANA Project*. New York: Academic Press.

Rundus, D. 1971. An analysis of rehearsal processes in free recall. *Journal of Experimental Psychology* 89:63–77.

Ryan, J. J., III. 1960. Comparison of verbal response transfer mediated by meaningfully similar and associated stimuli. *Journal of Experimental Psychology* 60:408–415.

Rychlak, J. F. 1979. *Discovering Free Will and Personal Responsibility*. New York: Oxford University Press.

Rychlak, J. F. 1981a. *A Philosophy of Science for Personality Theory*, 2d ed. Malabar, Fla.: Robert E. Krieger.

Rychlak, J. F. 1981b. *Introduction to Personality and Psychotherapy: A Theory-Construction Approach*, 2d ed. Boston: Houghton Mifflin.

Rychlak, J. F. 1986. Logical learning theory: A teleological alternative in the field of personality. *Journal of Personality* 54:218–246.

Rychlak, J. F. 1988. *The Psychology of Rigorous Humanism*, 2d ed. New York: New York University Press.

Sameroff, A. J. and P. J. Cavanagh. 1979. Learning in infancy: A developmental perspective. In J. D. Osofsky, ed. *The Handbook of Infant Development*, pp. 344–392. New York: John Wiley and Sons.

Sampson, E. E. 1988. The debate on individualism: Indigenous psychologies of the individual and their role in personal and societal functioning. *American Psychologist* 43:15–22.

Savage-Rumbaugh, S. 1986. *Ape Language: From Conditioned Response to Symbol*. New York: Columbia University Press.

Schachter, S. and J. Singer. 1962. Cognitive, social, and physiological determinants of emotional states. *Psychological Review* 69:379–399.

Schank, R. C. and R. P. Abelson. 1977. *Scripts, Plans, Goals, and Understanding*. Hillsdale, N.J.: Lawrence Erlbaum Associates.

Scheerer, M. 1954. Cognitive theory. In G. Lindzey, ed. *Handbook of Social Psychology*, pp. 91–142. Cambridge, Mass.: Addison-Wesley.

Schrödinger, E. 1935. Discussions of probability relations between separated systems. *Proceedings of the Cambridge Philosophical Society*, vol. 31. Cambridge, England.

Schvaneveldt, R. W., F. R. Durso and B. R. Mukherji. 1982. Semantic distance effects in categorization tasks. *Journal of Experimental Psychology: Learning, Memory and Cognition* 8:1–15.

Searle, J. R. 1969. *Speech Acts*. Cambridge, England: Cambridge University Press.

Searle, J. R. 1980. Minds, brains and programs. *The Behavioral and Brain Sciences* 3:417–457.

Seidenberg, M. S. and L. A. Pettito. 1979. Signing behavior in apes: A critical review. *Cognition* 1:177–215.

Seligman, M. E. P. 1970. On the generality of the laws of learning. *Psychological Review* 77:406–418.

Shannon, C. E. 1938. A symbolic analysis of relay and switching circuits. Master's thesis, Massachusetts Institute of Technology; published in *Transactions of the American Institute of Electrical Engineers* 57:1–11.

Shannon, C. E. and W. Weaver, eds. 1962. *The Mathematical Theory of Communication.* Urbana: University of Illinois Press.

Shean, G. D. 1970. Instrumental modification of the galvanic skin-response: Conditioning or control? *Journal of Psychosomatic Research* 14:155–160.

Sheldrake, R. 1989. *The Presence of the Past: Morphic Resonance and Habits of Nature.* New York: Viking Books.

Shimp, C. P. 1984. Self reports by rats of the temporal patterning of their behavior: A dissociation between tacit knowledge and knowledge. In H. L. Roitblat, R. G. Bever, and H. S. Terrace, eds. *Animal Cognition,* pp. 215–229. Hillsdale, N.J.: Lawrence Erlbaum Associates

Siipola, E., W. N. Walker, and D. Kolb. 1955. Task attitude in word association, projective and nonprojective. *Journal of Personality* 23:441–459.

Simon, H. A. 1985. *The Science of the Artificial,* 2d ed. Cambridge: MIT Press.

Skinner, B. F. 1963. Operant behavior. *American Psychologist* 18:503–515.

Sperry, R. W. 1961. Cerebral organization and behavior. *Science* 133:1749–1757.

Sperry, R. W. 1985. *Science & Moral Priority: Merging Mind, Brain, and Human Values.* New York: Praeger.

Spielberger, C. D. and S. M. Levin. 1962. What is learned in verbal conditioning? *Journal of Verbal Learning and Verbal Behavior* 1:125–132.

Stapp, H. 1975. Bell's theorem and world process. *Nuovo Cimento* 29:270–278.

Stein, B. S. 1977. The effects of cue-target uniqueness on cued recall performance. *Memory and Cognition* 5:319–322.

Stevens, S. S. 1935. The operational definition of psychological concepts. *Psychological Review* 42:517–527.

Stich, S. P. 1986. *From Folk Psychology to Cognitive Science: The Case Against Belief.* Cambridge: MIT Press.

Sugarman, S. 1983. Why talk? Comments on Savage-Rumbaugh et al. *Journal of Experimental Psychology: General,* 112:493–497.

Terrace, H. S. 1979. *NIM.* New York: Alfred A. Knopf.

Terrace, H. S. 1984. Animal cognition. In H. L. Roitblat, T. G. Veber, and H. S. Terrace, eds. *Animal Cognition,* pp. 7–28. Hillsdale, N.J.: Lawrence Erlbaum Associates.

Tolman, E. C. 1932/1967. *Purposive Behavior in Animals and Men.* New York: Appleton-Century-Crofts.

Tolman, E. C. 1938. The determinants of behavior at a choice point. *Psychological Review* 45:1–41.

Trapold, M. A. 1970. Are expectancies based upon different positive reinforcing events discriminably different? *Learning and Motivation* 1:129–140.

Trier, J. 1931. *Der deutsche wortschatz im sinnbezirk des verstandes*. Heidelberg: Winter.

Tulving, E. 1983. *Elements of Episodic Memory*. New York: Oxford University Press.

Tulving, E. and Z. Pearlstone. 1966. Availability versus accessibility of information in memory for words. *Journal of Verbal Learning and Verbal Behavior* 5:381–391.

Tulving, E. and D. M. Thomson. 1973. Encoding specificity and retrieval processes in episodic memory. *Psychological Review* 80:352–373.

Turing, A. M. 1964. Computing machinery and intelligence. In A. R. Anderson, ed. *Minds and Machines*, pp. 8–14. Englewood Cliffs, N.J.: Prentice-Hall.

Ullman, S. 1980. Against direct perception. *Behavioral and Brain Sciences* 3:373–415.

Ultan, R. 1969. Some general characteristics of interrogative systems. *Working Papers in Language Universals* (Stanford University) 1:41–63.

Umemoto, T. 1959. Japanese studies in verbal learning and memory. *Psychologia* 2:1–19.

Umiker-Sebeok, J. and T. Sebeok. 1981. Clever Hans and smart simians: The self-fulfilling prophecy and methodological pitfalls. *Anthropos* 76:89–165.

Valins, S. 1970. The perception and labeling of bodily changes as determinants of emotional behavior. In P. Black, ed. *Physiological Correlates of Emotion*, pp. 123–136. New York: Academic Press.

Vygotsky, L. 1986. *Thought and Language*, transl. by A. Kozulin. Cambridge: MIT Press.

Warren, R. M. and R. P. Warren. 1970. Auditory illusions and confusions. *Scientific American* 223:30–36.

Watson, J. B. 1924. *Behaviorism*. New York: W. W. Norton & Co.

Watson, J. B. and R. Rayner. 1920. Conditioned emotional reactions. *Journal of Experimental Psychology* 3:1–14.

Weiss-Shed, E. 1973. Synonyms, antonyms and retroactive inhibition with meaningful materials. *Psychological Reports* 33:459–465.

Weizenbaum, J. 1976. *Computer Power and Human Reason: From Judgment to Calculation*. San Francisco: W. H. Freeman.

Whitehead, A. N. and B. Russell. 1963. *Principia mathematica*, 3 vols, 2d ed. Cambridge: Cambridge University Press.

Wickens, D. D. and L. S. Cermak. 1967. Transfer effects of synonyms and antonyms in a mixed and unmixed list design. *Journal of Verbal Learning and Verbal Behavior* 6:832–839.

Wickens, D. D. and C. Wickens. 1940. A study of conditioning in the neonate. *Journal of Experimental Psychology* 26:94–102.

Wieman, L. A. 1976. Stress patterns of early child language. *Journal of Child Language* 3:283–286.

Wiener, N. 1954. *The Human Use of Human Beings.* New York: Doubleday Anchor Books.
Williams, B. A. 1986. Reinforcement, choice, and response strength. In R. C. Atkinson, R. J. Hernstein, G. Lindzey, and R. D. Luce, eds. *Stevens Handbook of Experimental Psychology*, 2d ed., pp. 232–269. New York: John Wiley & Sons.
Wilson, G. D. 1968. Reversal of differential GSR conditioning by instructions. *Journal of Experimental Psychology* 76:491–493.
Winograd, T. 1980. What does it mean to understand language? *Cognitive Science* 4:209–241.
Witkin, A. P. and J. M. Tenenbaum. 1983. On the role of structure in vision. In J. Beck, B. Hope, and A. Rosenfeld, eds. *Human and Machine Vision*, pp. 76–92. New York: Academic Press.
Wittgenstein, L. 1922. *Tractatus Logico-Philosophicus.* London: Routledge and Kegan Paul.
Wittgenstein, L. 1968. *Philosophical Investigations*, 3d ed., transl. by G. E. M. Anscomb. New York: Macmillan.
Yartz, F. J. 1984. *Ancient Greek Philosophy: Sourcebook and Perspective.* Jefferson, N.C.: MacFarland & Co.
Yonas, A. and M. A. Hagen. 1973. Effects of static and kinetic depth information on the perception of size by children and adults. *Journal of Experimental Child Psychology* 15:254–265.
Zener, K. 1937. The significance of behavior accompanying conditioned salivary secretion for theories of the conditioned reflex. *American Journal of Psychology* 50:384–403.
Zukav, G. 1979. *The Dancing Wu Li Masters: An Overview of the New Physics.* New York: Bantam Books.

Author Index

Abelson, R. P., 69, 190
Adler, M. J., 20, 179
Anaximander, 21
Anderson, A. R., 192
Anderson, J. R., 44, 47, 48, 58, 81, 179
Anscomb, G. E. M., 193
Anselm, 26
Aquinas, T., 26
Aristotle, 16, 18-26, 29, 31, 33, 41, 45, 55, 56, 68, 102, 103, 106, 108, 125, 179, 189
Atkinson, R. C., 193
Ayala, F. J., 181

Babbage, C., 46
Bach, J. S., 184
Bacon, F., 24-26, 41, 125, 166, 179, 182
Baillargeon, R., 73, 181
Bartlett, F. C., 69, 179
Bastian, J., 77, 179
Beck, E. C., 130, 180
Beck, J., 184, 188, 193
Bell, J., 36, 182, 191
Bennett, J., 72, 77, 106, 180
Bergman, T., 141, 184
Berlin, B., 99, 180
Bever, R. G., 190
Bigelow, J., 104, 105, 124, 189
Black, P., 192
Block, J. D., 95, 180
Block, N., 189
Bloom, A., 171, 180
Bloom, L., 75, 180

Boden, M. A., 63, 105, 114, 180
Bohm, D., 35, 36, 39, 180
Bohr, N., 34, 35, 37, 180
Bonvillian, J. D., 75, 188
Boole, G., 12, 54, 55, 180
Boring, E. G., 138, 180
Bosack, T. N., 89, 186
Bower, T. G. R., 141, 180
Brackbill, Y., 188
Bradley, J., 32, 180
Braine, M. D. S., 72, 180
Bransford, J. D., 99, 180
Bresnan, J., 181
Brewer, W. F., 76, 92, 95, 180
Brogden, W. J., 127, 180
Broglie, L. A. de, 32, 180
Brown, J. R., 36, 182
Brown, P. L., 130, 181
Brown, R., 72, 181
Browne, M. P., 130, 181
Bulloch, M., 73, 181
Bunge, M., 53, 145, 146, 149, 181
Burtt, E. A., 26, 181

Cable, C., 133, 184
Campbell, D. T., 149, 181
Carey, S., 73, 76, 181
Carlson, J. G., 132, 181
Carlton, E. H., 143, 189
Cassirer, E., 35, 181
Cattell, J. M., 29
Cavanagh, P. J., 89, 190
Cerella, J., 133, 181
Cermak, L. S., 77, 99, 181, 192
Chatterjee, B. B., 95, 181

AUTHOR INDEX

Chauvin, N., 78
Chomsky, N., 78, 79, 181
Clark, E. V., 72, 181
Clark, H. C., 72, 181
Cohen, L. B., 141, 181
Cornwell, D., 88, 181
Coulter, J., 7, 44, 70, 72, 181
Cousins, N., 149, 155, 182
Craik, F. I. M., 97, 98, 182
Cranston, M., 67, 68, 182
Crutchfield, R. S., 176, 185

Davies, P. C. W., 36, 182
Dawson, M. E., 95, 182
Dean, S. J., 94, 187
Deecke, L., 146, 185
DeNike, L. D., 93, 182
Dennett, D. C., 36, 105, 107, 111, 112, 115, 124, 182
Dickinson, A., 131, 182
Diogenes, 18
Dixon, T. R., 187
Dobshansky, T., 181
Dollard, J., 90, 91, 182
Dooley, P. K., 29, 182
Dorf, R. C., 46, 182
Dorty, R. W., 130
Dreyfus, H. L., 7, 43, 44, 47, 50, 53, 61, 64, 86, 182
Dreyfus, S. E., 61, 182
Dulany, D. E., Jr., 91, 92, 182
Durso, F. R., 77, 190

Eagle, M., 76, 183
Eccles, J. C., 146, 147, 149-52, 156, 157, 159, 182
Einstein, A., 34, 36, 37, 55, 71, 181, 184
Ekman, P., 175, 182
Elmer-DeWitt, P., 59, 182
Empedocles, 21
Eriksen, C. W., 95, 181
Escher, M. C., 116-18, 140, 184
Ettlinger, G. A., 135, 182
Euler, L., 16
Eves, H., 54, 182

Farber, S. M., 189
Farrington, B., 26, 182
Festinger, L., 156, 182

Feuer, L. S., 35, 37, 183
Finch, G., 130, 183
Fish, S., 78, 183
Flavell, J. H., 76, 185
Fodor, J. A., 63, 79, 141, 183
Fouts, R. S., 133, 183
Franks, J. J., 99, 180
Frege, F. L. G., 124
Friedman, W. J., 181
Friesen, W. V., 175, 182
Frijda, N. H., 175, 183
Frisch, K. von, 131, 183

Galanter, E., 44, 52, 62, 69, 87, 143, 187
Galileo, G., 26, 27, 44
Gamzu, E. R., 130, 183
Gardner, B. T., 133, 183
Gardner, H., 4, 43, 54, 63, 183
Gardner, R. A., 133, 183
Gazzaniga, M. S., 152-59, 183
Gellert, E., 73, 183
Gelman, R., 73, 181
Gergen, K. J., 175, 183
Gibson, J. J., 138-41, 150, 183, 189
Gleason, C. A., 158, 186
Gleick, J., 38, 183
Gödel, K., 71, 120, 121, 184, 186, 187
Granit, R., 47, 146, 148, 151, 156, 157, 183
Greenfield, P. M., 72, 183
Greenspoon, J., 90, 91, 93, 183
Grene, M., 39, 183
Griffin, D. R., 131-33, 183
Grossman, L., 76, 183

Haber, R. N., 142, 143, 184
Hagen, M. A., 142, 193
Haith, M. M., 141, 142, 184
Hall, G. S., 29
Halle, M., 181
Halpern, S., 132, 187
Hampton, J. A., 76, 184
Harlow, H. F., 132, 184
Harsh, C. M., 133, 184
Hawking, S. W., 169, 184
Hayes, C., 135, 184
Hayes, K. J., 135, 184
Hebb, D. O., 145, 184
Hegel, G. W. F., 40

AUTHOR INDEX

Heil, J., 141, 184
Heimer, W., 96, 189
Heisenberg, W., 32, 71
Helmholtz, H. von, 139, 184
Heraclitus, 21, 55, 140
Herbert, J. J., 133, 184
Hering, E., 139
Hernstein, R. J., 133, 184, 193
Hess, E. H., 188
Hobbes, T., 28
Hobbs, S., 88, 181
Hochberg, J. E., 142, 184
Hoffman, R. R., 99, 184
Hofstadter, D. R., 47, 59, 114-16, 118-24, 140, 184
Holton, G., 34, 37, 38, 184
Honeck, R. P., 99, 184
Hope, B., 184, 188, 193
Horton, D. L., 187
Howard, D. V., 58, 97, 185
Hull, C. L., 30, 185
Hume, D., 28, 68
Hutchins, R. M., 179, 185, 186, 188

Iggo, A., 186

Jacobs, F., 39, 185
James, W., 29, 182
Jenkins, H. M., 130, 181
Johnson, N. S., 73, 187
Johnson-Laird, P. N., 63, 64, 185
Jonas, H., 39, 185
Jones, E. E., 3, 22, 176, 185
Jones, R. K., 141, 189
Josephson, B., 182

Kagan, J., 74-76, 185
Kahnemann, D., 53, 185
Kant, I., 28, 29, 34, 40, 63, 67, 78, 84, 103, 120, 123, 139, 185
Karwoski, T. F., 76, 185
Katz, A., 98, 185
Kay, P., 99, 180
Kaye, H., 89, 186
Kelly, G. A., 85, 90, 132, 185
Kennedy, T. D., 93, 185
Kepler, J., 184
Kjeldergaard, P. M., 76, 185
Koch, S., 184
Koffka, K., 116, 118, 185

Kolb, D., 76, 191
Kornhuber, H. H., 146, 185
Kozulin, A., 192
Krampen, M., 187
Krasner, L., 91, 185
Krech, D., 176, 185
Kreutzer, M. A., 76, 185
Kubovy, M., 184
Kuhn, T. S., 36, 38, 171, 186
Kukla, A., 83, 186

Lakoff, G., 77, 79, 90, 186
Lamiell, J. T., 11, 53, 186
LaPlace, P. S. de, 28
Leary, D. E., 184
Leonard, C., 76, 185
Levenson, R. W., 175, 182
Levin, S. M., 92, 93, 186, 191
Libet, B., 149, 158, 159, 173, 186
Lichtenstein, E. H., 76, 180
Lindzey, G., 190, 193
Lipsitt, L. P., 89, 186
Locke, J., 28, 67, 68, 84, 109, 110, 112, 115, 124, 182, 186
Lorayne, H., 99, 186
Loveland, D. H., 133, 184
Lucas, J., 99, 186
Lucas, J. R., 120, 122
Luce, R. D., 186, 193
Lumsden, C. J., 136, 186
Lyons, J., 72, 75, 77, 186

McCabe, A., 98, 187
McCarthy, J., 43
MacCorquodale, K., 66, 186
McCulloch, W., 6, 54, 187
Mach, E., 32, 33, 180
MacKay, D. M., 157, 186
Mackintosh, N. J., 131, 186
McNeil, D., 72, 187
Mandler, G., 44, 45, 56, 63, 85, 187
Mandler, J. M., 73, 187
Mandler, R., 100, 186
Martin, M., 171, 187
Martin, R. B., 94, 187
Marx, K., 40
Massaro, D. W., 44-46, 48, 187
Meehl, P. E., 66, 186
Menzel, E. W. Jr., 132, 187
Meyers, R. E., 152, 153, 187

Mill, J., 28
Mill, J. S., 28
Miller, G. A., 44, 52, 62, 69, 87, 100, 143, 181, 187
Miller, N. E., 90, 91, 182
Mink, W. D., 77, 187
Minsky, M., 43, 44, 49, 59, 69, 75, 105, 106, 110, 111, 114, 187
Moore, M. J., 142, 184
Mountcastle, V. B., 149, 152, 187
Mukherji, B. R., 77, 190

Nagel, E., 71, 120, 187
Napoleon, 78
Neisser, U., 44, 85, 86, 187
Nelson, K. E., 73, 75, 187, 188
Neumann, von., J., 46
Newell, A., 43, 62, 68, 69, 86, 188
Newman, J. R., 71, 120, 187
Newton, I., 27, 34, 71
Nietzsche, F. W., 112
Nisbett, R. E., 3, 22, 176, 185

O'Brien, E. J., 99, 188
O'Connor, D. J., 104, 188
Ogden, C. K., 21, 188, 189
Orne, M. T., 92, 188
Osgood, C. E., 76, 188
Osofsky, J. D., 190
Ozier, M., 87, 188

Page, M. M., 93, 94, 188
Palermo, D. S., 180
Papousek, H., 89, 90, 188
Patterson, F. C., 133, 135, 188
Pearl, D. K., 158, 186
Pearlstone, Z., 97, 192
Penfield, W., 147-50, 158, 173, 188
Pepper, S. C., 38, 188
Perkins, D. N., 142, 188
Pettito, L. A., 133, 190
Piaget, J., 73, 188
Pitts, W., 6, 54, 187
Plato, 15, 18, 22, 188
Polanyi, M., 74, 113, 123, 189
Pomerantz, J. R., 184
Popper, K. R., 182
Portmann, A., 39
Premack, D., 133, 189

Pribram, K. H., 44, 52, 62, 69, 87, 143, 144, 187, 189
Prigogine, I., 34, 38, 39, 182, 189
Prytula, R., 88, 181
Pylyshyn, Z. W., 63, 141, 183, 189
Pythagoras, 21

Quine, W. V., 55, 189

Rayner, R., 88, 192
Reed, E. S., 141, 189
Reese, W. L., 12, 16, 55, 124, 189
Rheingold, H. L., 188
Richards, I. A., 75, 189
Rickaby, J., 110, 189
Rieber, R., 181
Riechmann, P., 99, 184
Robinson, D. N., 20, 189
Rock, I., 96, 97, 142, 189
Rogers, C. R., 30, 31, 189
Roitblat, H. L., 190, 191
Rorty, R., 171, 189
Rosch, E. H., 99, 119, 189
Rosenblueth, A., 104, 105, 124, 189
Rosenfeld, A., 184, 188, 193
Rubin, E., 116, 140, 190
Rumbaugh, D. M., 133, 190
Rundus, D., 97, 190
Russell, B., 54, 124, 192
Ryan, J. J., III, 77, 180
Rychlak, J. F., 2, 15, 21, 40, 53, 76, 104, 113, 174, 190

Salapatek, E., 141, 181
Sameroff, A. J., 89, 190
Sampson, E. E., 175, 190
Savage-Rumbaugh, S., 134, 190
Schachter, J., 76, 185
Schachter, S., 175, 190
Schank, R. C., 69, 190
Scheerer, M., 176, 190
Schlipp, P., 181
Schrödinger, E., 35, 190
Schvaneveldt, R. W., 77, 190
Searle, J. R., 1-6, 10, 12, 13, 72, 112, 190
Seeitz, P., 187
Seidenberg, M. S., 133, 190
Seligman, M. E. P., 89, 191

Sebeok, T., 133, 192
Shannon, C. E., 5, 6, 43, 50, 54, 60, 191
Shean, G. D., 94, 191
Sheldrake, R., 39, 191
Shimp, C. P., 132, 191
Siipola, E., 76, 191
Simon, H. A., 43-45, 48, 49, 56, 62, 68, 69, 86, 100, 188, 191
Singer, J., 175, 190
Skinner, B. F., 30, 31, 91, 129, 191
Slovic, P., 53, 185
Smith, J. H., 72, 183
Socrates, 21
Spence, K. W., 186
Sperry, R. W., 152-55, 157, 187, 191
Spielberger, C. D., 93, 191
Stapp, H., 36, 191
Stein, B. S., 98, 191
Stengers, I., 34, 38, 39, 189
Stevens, S. S., 31, 191
Stevenson, H. W., 188
Stich, S. P., 51, 191
Stillman, B., 185
Sugarman, S., 133, 191
Swagerman, J., 175, 183

Taylor, P. J., 77, 184
Taylor-Spence, J., 186
Tenenbaum, J. M., 142, 193
Terrace, H. S., 133, 190, 191
Thales, 18
Thompson, G. G., 188
Thomson, D. M., 98, 192
Thorndike, E. L., 29
Tolman, E. C., 29, 30, 106, 127, 128, 191
Trapold, M. A., 132, 191
Trier, J., 75, 192
Tulving, E., 5, 45, 84-86, 97, 98, 182, 192
Turing, A., 4, 46, 192
Tversky, A., 53, 185

Ullman, S., 141, 192
Ultan, R., 81, 192
Umemoto, T., 77, 192
Umiker-Sebeok, J., 133, 192

Valins, S., 175, 192
Veber, T. G., 191
Vygotsky, L., 75, 79, 90, 192

Walker, W. N., 76, 191
Warren, R. M., 98, 192
Warren, R. P., 98, 192
Watson, J. B., 29, 88, 89, 192
Watson, R. I., 184
Weaver, W., 5, 50, 191
Weimer, W. B., 180
Weiss-Shed, E., 77, 192
Weizenbaum, J., 51, 59, 61, 62, 192
Whitehead, A. N., 54, 192
Wickens, C., 88, 192
Wickens, D. D., 77, 88, 192
Wielkiewicz, R. M., 132, 181
Wieman, L. A., 73, 192
Wiener, N., 50, 51, 104, 105, 124, 189, 193
Williams, B. A., 131, 193
Williams, D. R., 130, 183
Wilson, E. O., 136, 186
Wilson, G. D., 95, 193
Wilson, R. H. L., 189
Winograd, T., 7, 61, 64, 70, 72, 193
Witkin, A. P., 142, 193
Wittgenstein, L., 78, 99, 119, 193
Wolford, C. R., 99, 188
Wright, E. W., 158, 186

Yartz, F. J., 15, 193
Yonas, A., 142, 193

Zener, K., 132, 193
Zukav, G., 34, 36, 193

Subject Index

Activation, spreading, as *Bios* concept, 47
Affirm the consequent, logical error, in science, 33; *see also* Euler circles; Logic
Affordance(s): definition of, Gibson, 138; as predications, 141; subjective aspects of, 141
Agency: definition of, 102; capacity to alter reality, or not, 103; as controlled goal attainment, 104-8; after goal attainment, 107; as delay in processing of mediators, 108-12; via recursive self-reflexivity, 113-24; in higher apes, 136; complete, versus distorted, 161; as fundamental assumption of legal systems, 174; role of social norms in, 175, 176; *see also* Free will
Aitiá, Greek word for "cause," 19
Algorithm: definition of, 46; as effective procedure, 50
Anthropomorphization: quasi-homunculus in, 1; in Hull's quote, 30; computer programs and, 60, 62; children's preference in causation, 73; in telic description of lower animals, 127, 128; *see also* Reverse Turing test
Apposition: side by side, 13, 58, 160; *see also* Opposition
A priori: mind as, Kant, 28, 74; in Kantian construing, 32; Machian usage, 32; Kantian representation, 63; *see also* Model(s)

Artificial intelligence: coined by John McCarthy, 43; 1955–1960 beginning, 43; programs in, 44
Association: role of frequency and contiguity in, 10, 110; versus recollection, Aristotle, 24; as predication, Aristotle, 24, 162; contrariety in, 24; *see also* Learning; Memory

Baconian criticism: leveled against Aristotle, 24; what does final cause add to an account?, 25, 106; religious motives in, 26, 27; as inappropriate criticism, 28, 41, 103, 136, 167; as appropriate criticism, 28, 166; leveled at Hull and Tolman, 30; leveled at AI theory, 45, 166; leveled at extraspective teleology, 106; and animal behavior, 128
Bell's theorem, 36
Binary logic: underwritten by Boolean algebra, 12, 56; as non-dialectical, 56; *see also* Logic
Bios: definition of, 46; not all AI scientists reduce to, 47; process, does not produce the *Logos*, 49; sets limits on the organism, 49; important in animal study, 126; permits organism to participate in *Logos*, 168; *see also* Logos
Bit: halving of information, 5; and binary logic, 12; *see also* Binary logic

Brain research: rise of teleology in, 144; interneurons, and alternative viewpoints, 146; readiness potential, and volition, 146, 158, 159; cortex stimulation, 147, 148; dualism vs. monism, 148; opposition in, 149; holism in, 149; supplementary motor area, and volition, 149, 150; role of meaning in, 150; two kinds of neurons, 151; half of brain's neurons lack axons, 151; dendritic cellular network, as inhibitory, 151; modules, in conflict, 152; split-brain, 152-57; different hemisphere predications, 155; interpreter module, Gazzaniga, 156, 158; "emergent" theoretical conceptions, 157; negating physical urges to act, Libet, 158, 159

Categories: as predicates, 16; of understanding, Kant, 67; process or content?, 67; in children's developmental learning, 75, 76; category error, children, 76; best exemplars of, 119; in pigeons, 133; framed by chimps, 135; *see also* Predicate(s); Predication

Cause(s): aitiá, 19; Aristotelian terms for, 19, 20; formative, 39; all four required for human science, 41; in children's language learning, 73; downward, brain research, 149; *see also* Efficient cause; Final cause; Formal Cause; Material cause

Chinese room: Searle's example, 1, 2; lacks oppositionality, 11; limitation of example, 12

Choice: non-existent, in behaviorism, 31; in scientific theories, 32, 33; opposition, as rationale for, 109, 164, 165; can be for an evil alternative, 171; *see also* Agency; Final cause; Free will; Teleology

Cognitive revolution: modern origins, 43; *see also* Artificial intelligence

Communication: as control, Wiener, 51; true, as empathic, 87, 88; purpose essential to, Winograd, 70

Computer: "acting" sans meaning, 5; as a matching device, 7, 168; does not predicate, 12, 168; and Boolean disjunction, 12; reasons appositionally, 13; lacks episodic memory, 45; supposedly teleological, 45; metaphor, as solving mind-body problem, 45; hardware as the physical side of, 46; analogue versus digital, 47; simulating or duplicating things?, 48; digital, never in dialectical mode, 55; future generations of, 164; as predicational (phantasy), 164-66; as instrumental, 168; no threat to the human image, 170; *see also* Mechanism; Mediation

Conditioning: decline of a tradition, 88-96; Little Albert, Watson, 88, 89; classical, 88, 128-30; operant, 89, 129; shaping, 89; oppositionality and, 90; human awareness in, 91-95; subject cooperation required, 93; precedent-sequacious factors in, 95; previous importance of observation in, 129, 130; animal awareness in, 131, 132; *see also* Learning

Consciousness, doubling of, Penfield, 148

Construction, Construing: Kantian view of, 28, 29, 145; alternatives in, Mach, 32; as Kantian a priori, 32; versus Newtonian realism, 32; as phenomenological, 32, 85; as predication, 83; introspective versus extraspective, 85; dialectically defined, Kelly, 85, 132; confusion regarding, 85, 145; as Lockean "bottom-up," 145; *see also* Model(s); Predication

Content(s): universals as, 49; vs. process, 49, 67; Lockean ideas as, 67; *see also* Process

Context: in predication, 7, 70; problem of, for AI, 69, 70, 86; definition of, as broader range, 70; tied to purpose, 70; Lockean vs. Kantian view of, 84; and hearing what is said, 98, 99; in animal condi-

tioning, 132; and the *Logos*, 168; see also Predication
Contradiction: law of, definition, 22; vs. contrary, 22, 23; via organization of brain neurons, 150; law of, frequently violated, 172
Control, vs. meaning expression, 52, 113
Creativity: machine versus human, 169; in natural order, 179
Culture, as a predicational process, 176, 177
Cybernetics: definition of, Wiener, 51; communication as control in, 51

Demonstrative reasoning: definition of, Aristotle, 22; favors extraspective explanation, 40; Boolean algebra as, 55; is all the computer simulates, 65; see also Dialectical reasoning
Determinism: as solely efficiently causal, 28; four types of, 107, 108; social, via language, 111; as setting limits on alternatives, 113; psychic, nature of, 162; all four types should be used in science, 173
Dialectical method, of Socrates, 21
Dialectical reasoning: definition of, Aristotle, 22; many in one, 22; transcendentalism, Kant, 29; Bohr's attraction to, 37; and Einstein, 37; never occurs in computer, 55; contradiction in, 55; in children's learning of language, 75, 76; as source of free will, 104; dangers of, 112; is not present in Lockean model, 114, 115; as arising via evolution, 128; as source of illogic, 172; see also Demonstrative Reasoning; Opposition
Difference engine, definition of, Minsky, 105
Disjunction: Boolean, 12, 54, 57, 68, 164; Boolean, is demonstrative in mode, 55; Lockean model and, 68; Penfield versus Boole, 148; Boolean, often violated, 148, 172

Efficient cause: definition of, 19; time's passage necessary in, 19; ether as, 35; collapse of, in subatomic physics, 35; collapse of, in chemistry, 38; as fundamental to both S-R and AI, 44; as the only determinism in science, 108; delay during sequence of, as agency, 109, 110; limitation, in free will theory, 110; underwrites lawfulness concept, 127; no longer basic to brain processes, 149; see also Cause; Final cause; Formal cause; Material cause
Emotion(s): a weak argument against computer metaphor, 174; rely on predication and opposition, 175
Euler circles: as depicting logical relations, 16, 17; "outside" larger, as oppositional, 23; and affirmation of the consequent, 33; see also Logic
Extraspective theory: definition of, 2; as "objective," 3; typifies British philosophy, 28; of Skinner's behavior, 30, 31; in Stevens' approach to psychology, 31; trends to demonstrative views, 40; machines exclusively so, 120, 121; of self-reflexivity, Hofstadter, 121; see also Introspective theory

Family-resemblance phenomenon: as predication, Wittgenstein, 99; difficult to define, 119; games as, 119
Feedback: in cybernetics, 51; positive, 104; negative, 105; as source of purpose, 105; negative, as teleological, 105; as a simple tangled hierarchy, 115
Figure-ground relations: gestalt, Rubin, 116; can be unstable, 116-18; contour shapes figure, 118
Final cause: definition of, 20; necessary tie to formal cause, 20; underlying teleologies, 20; both human and natural types of, Aristotle, 24; introspective form of, Aristotle, 24; as a reason for action, 25; extraspective form of,

Final cause (*Continued*)
Aristotle, 25; as allied to human nature, Bacon, 26; Bacon accepted in metaphysics, 26; extraspective form, in computer metaphor, 45; repressed by Newtonians, 102; Locke's interpretation of, 109; as selecting "this" over "that," 109, 110; determinism, 164, 165; as best framed introspectively, 166, 167; *see also* Cause; Efficient cause; Formal cause; Material cause

Formal cause: definition of, 19; as used by author, 20; as "that" in final cause definition, 20, 40, 41; rise of, in modern science, 31, 35, 36, 40; time as, 32; steady states as, 35; within chaos, 38; and morphic fields, 39; laws and rules as, 52; basic to brain functioning, 149; patternings, in computer, 166; *see also* Cause; Efficient cause; Final cause; Material cause

Free will, Freedom of the will: via negation, Aristotle, 24; introspectively framed definition of, 102; Kant's view of, 103; via dialectical reasoning, 104; central problem of: doing otherwise, 104, 112; as delay in efficient-cause series, Locke, 109; as unpredictability, 111; as adding to cause and chance, 110, 111; as degrees of freedom within determination, Dennett, 111; as interaction of self-symbol with others, 123; as an illusion, Gazzaniga, 156, 157; as consistent with brain research, 159; as behaving for this, opposed to that, 167; as occurring after an event has happened, 172, 173; as boredom, 173; in behavior of scientist, 173, 174; *see also* Agency; Intention; Purpose; Teleology

Goal: need not exist in reality, 106; as a predicated meaning, 107; -attainment, in relation to agency, 107

Hand-signing: American Sign Language, 133; use with higher apes, 133, 135

Hardware: definition of, 46; as simulating the *Bios*, 46; not important to all AI workers, 47, 48; as law-following, 53; speed of processing relevant to, 59; exclusively Boolean in disjunction, 164; *see also* Software

Hardwiring: based on Boolean assumptions, 12; *see also* Disjunction

Holonomic theory, of brain functioning, Pribram, 143; *see also* Brain research

Homunculus: as informal predicator in mechanistic theory, 110; why we seek for one, 167; *see also* Anthropomorphization

Idea(s): a priori, Mach, 32; simple versus complex, Locke, 67; innate, 67; Kant versus Locke, 67, 68; as mediators, 108, 109

Information: vs. meaning in computers, 5; unrelated to machine action, 6, 50; as representation, 62; "chunks" of, 100; as processed in the CNS, 138; *see also* Representation

Information processing: has nothing to do with meaning, 5; as halving electrical impulses, 5, 6, 50; as AI theory, 45; *see also* Artificial Intelligence

Input: in Chinese room, 2; definition of, 104; *see also* Output

Intention(s): role of empathy in, 12, 13; in disobeying rules, 13; person versus machine, 47; as non-scientific, Stich, 51; mechanistic interpretation of, 52; as basic to language acquisition, 72, 80; in lower animals, 129-33, 136; *see also* Purpose

Interpretive cortex: of brain, Penfield, 147; *see also* Brain research

Introspective theory: definition of, 3; as "subjective," 3; role of empa-

SUBJECT INDEX   205

thy in, 3, 12, 87; Einsteinian, 34; principle of complementarity and, 34; and Gödel's proofs, 120; inapplicable to machines, 120, 121; *see also* Extraspective theory

Iteration: definition of, 50; and recursivity, 114, 118; *see also* Algorithm; Recursion

Kategorein, from Greek "to predicate," 7, 15; *see also* Categories; Predication(s)

Knowledge, tacit, as predicational, 74

Language: as mediating signals, 51, 110, 111; process or content?, 51, 66; role of context in speech act, Winograd, 64; intentional basis of, 72; children's two-word sentences, 72, 73; role of culture in, 73; based on assumption, Polanyi, 74; as thought, 75; oppositionality in learning of, 76, 77; predicational nature of, 77; iconic gesture in, 77; must "know" to express language, 78; syntax versus semantics in, 78, 79; definition of, Simon, 86; as vehicle of social determinism, 111, 176; as biologically based, 111, 112; *see also* Representation

Law(s): non-arbitrary action, 6; as formal-cause concept, 52; extraspectively framed, 53, 127; efficient-cause meaning in, 127; of thought, as physical, 145; *see also* Rule(s)

Learning: as predicational process, 23; of cognitive representations, 69; of scripts, 69; of language, as predicational, 74; principles of frequency/contiguity in AI, 86, 87, 98, 110; of "stupidity," 87; Kantian explanation of, 87; one-trial, 96, 97; of categories, 97; initial predication and, 98; theory, unclear status today, 100; of affordances, 139; as forming neural connections, 145; *see also* Conditioning

Liberation, Escher lithograph, 117

Logic: as both demonstrative and dialectical, 22, 53, 151; fallacy of "affirming the consequent," 33; as duplicated in computer "simulation," 53, 54; inference and implication in, 55; based on validity of predication, 55; as exclusively demonstrative in AI, 56; binary, 56; time's passage irrelevant to, 78; of predication, 80; and iron-clad truth versus error, 172; *see also* Logos

Logos: definition of, 47; not under simulation but duplication in AI, 48, 49; not a content of the *Bios* process, 49, 160; as rationale, Heraclitus, 55; dialectical and demonstrative meanings in, 103, 151; relevance to lower animals, 126; study of, as vitalism, mentalism, 129; as invariant pattern, 140; neural interpretation of, 145; in organization of physical items, 150; formal-cause basis of, 151; relies on *Bios* as instrumentality, 168; *see also Bios*

Many in (and) one principle: underwrites dialectical reasoning, 22; in distinguishing from the complement, 56

Matching, of computer: vs. predicating, 12, 14, 50, 65, 77, 168; results in literalness, 64; *see also* Predication

Material cause: definition of, 19; *see also* Cause; Efficient cause; Formal cause; Final cause

Meaning(s): vs. information in computers, 5; as introspective, 6; -extension, in predication, 7, 8; as a relational process, 8; in dialectical reasoning, 37; of major importance to people, 65; of context, 70; as intention, 72; precedent-sequa-

Meaning(s): vs. information (*Cont.*) cious nature of, 77; families of, 99; organization in, 100; framed extraspectively, Dennett, 112; loss of in computer analogue, as threatening, 112, 113; opposite, forces predication, 124; within physical brain patterning, 150; *see also* Opposition; Predication

Mechanism: as embodying lawfulness, 6; in Galileo's universe, 27; Newtonian, 27, 28; Watsonian, 29; vs. a stochastic process, 38; simulations of, 48; as law-following, 53; vs. anthropomorphism in language, 73; cannot select goals, 107; looping in, 120; machines are never introspective, 120, 121; no self-reflexivity in, 122; humans make poor machines, 142; of brain functioning, 144, 156; *see also* Computer

Mediation: definition of, 9; as used in this book—a mechanism, 9; in Tolmanian theory, 29; in Hullian theory, 30; via language signals, 51; via idea "mediators," 108, 109; in Tolman's "cognitive maps," 128; of scripts, rats, 132; in perception, 138

Memory: episodic, absent in computer, 5, 45; as recollection, Aristotle, 23; contrariety in recollecting, 24; of a computer, as storage, 46, 68, 69; working vs. declarative, Anderson, 69; long-term, as learning in AI, 86; importance of organization to, 97; retrieval cues and, 97; facilitated by patterned organization, 99, 100; *see also* Learning

Mind: as a priori, Kant, 28; as a posteriori, British philosophy, 28; nativistic explanation of, 79; as contributing to knowledge, 84; as a plastic neural system, Bunge, 145; self-conscious, Eccles, 146; as executive in cognition, Penfield, 148; as an emergent pattern, Sperry, 155; as a confederation of mental systems, Gazzaniga, 156; *see also* Construction; Tabula rasa

Mind-body problem: and the computer metaphor, 45; and *Logos* versus *Bios*, 47, 151; *see also Bios; Logos*

Model(s): Lockean, no oppositionality, 68; pseudo-Kantian formulations, 84, 85; Lockean versus Kantian, on representation, 86; Kantian, as intentional, 103; Lockean, in animal research, 126; Kantian, in brain research, 149

Nativism: in explanation of the mind, 79; and explanation of language learning, 80, 81

Natural selection, as non-teleological, 27

Norm(s): social, changing interpretation of, 175-77; as predicate assumptions, held in common, 176, 177

Opposition, Oppositionality: definition of, 10, 11; in implication, 10, 11; intrinsic bipolarity of, 11; vs. apposition, 13; necessarily tied to predication, 20, 124; central to Aristotle, 21; in transcendence, Kant, 29; in nature, 36; in Einsteinian theory, 37; in verbal learning, 76, 77; in operant conditioning, 93, 94; in classical conditioning, 94, 95; and "taking a position on," 103; as rationale for choice, 109, 164, 165; and strange loops, 121; and evolution, 128; in chimps, 132, 134; in a gorilla, 135, 136; in perception, 140; in brain research, 149; in *Logos*, 150; of physical urges to act, 159; in free will, 164, 165, 167; *see also* Dialectical reasoning; Predication

Output: in Chinese room, 2; definition of, 104; *see also* Input

Perception: vs. sensation, 138; as picking up information, Gibson, 138, 139; local signs and, 139; inference in, 139, 143; Kantian views on, 139, 140; predication and opposition in, 140, 142, 143; innate capacities vs. learning in, 142

Plan: intention in, 52; mechanistic definition of, 52

Precedent, in meaning extension: as initial, wider realm of meaning, 7; encompasses oppositionality, 11; -sequacious forces of deduction, induction, 53; in program psychologic, 62; role of, in language usage, 78; as innate organization, Chomsky, 78, 79; *see also* Sequacious, in meaning extension

Predicate(s): as categories, 16; universals as, 18; causal meanings as, 19; paradigms as, 38; root metaphors as, 38; themata as, 38; as context meaning, 70, 168; complete, 80; goals as, 107; as solely food, for chimps, 135; *see also* Categories

Predication: immediacy of, 7; definition of, 7, 10, 18; vs. matching, 7, 14, 77, 168; implication as, 10; Plato's usage, 15; demands that we take meaning seriously, 18; necessarily tied to oppositionality, 20; in association, 24; influence on "reality," 41; and indeterminacy, 71; and time, 71; as tacit knowing, 74; and iconic gestures, 77; as cause not effect of learning, 82, 100; Lockean vs. Kantian interpretations of, 84-86; in conditioning, 91-95; as defining a learning trial, 97; in learning and recall, 98; as family-resemblance phenomenon, 99; as "taking a position," 102-4, 108, 148, 149; contour as a variant form of, via ground, 118; Gödel's proof as, 121; in animals, 131; of chimps, 135; in perception, 140, 142, 143; expectancy as a form of, 142, 143; via endogenous neuronal patterning of brain, 150; in split-brain experiment, 155; lends order and control, 157; summary of, ten points, 161-64; as an innate process, 163; no theoretical ceiling to this process, 163; as a cultural process, 176, 177; *see also* Meaning; Opposition

Premise(s): definition of, Aristotle, 18; syllogistic usage, 18; includes a predication, 18, 82; demonstrative vs. dialectical formation of, 21, 22; as symbolized by Euler circles, 17, 23; belief as encompassed by, 157; *see also* Predication

Process: definition of, 8; vs. content, 49, 67; cognitive representations as, 66; Kantian ideas as, 67, 68; *see also* Content(s)

Program(s): sans meaning, 2; vs. human reasoners, 44; intention/anticipation, in the writing of, 52, 59-61; bug, virus in, 59; DOCTOR, Weizenbaum, 61

Purpose: based on formal and final causation, 20; Hull's view of, 30; role of, in modern science, 35; context tied to, 70; attributed by subjects in research, 92; as self-control of machine, 105; explained extraspectively, Tolman, 106; as mediating intervening variable, 128; as a pattern of neural activity, Bunge, 145; as a "point of view," Granit, 146; *see also* Final cause; Formal cause; Intention

Readiness potential: definition of, 146; as measure of volitional acts, 146, 158, 159; *see also* Brain research

Reason, Reasoning: human, as a logical process, 8; oppositional vs. appositional, 13; Aristotelian syllogism as, 16; demonstrative vs. dialectical, Aristotle, 21, 22; introspective vs. extraspective view of, 22; Kantian definition of, 29; dialectical, in science, 37; logical, as dialectical, 53; missing aspect of

SUBJECT INDEX

Reason, Reasoning (*Continued*)
thought in AI, 56; machine, a fait accompli, 168; *see also* Mind; Opposition; Predication

Recursion, Recursivity: definition of, 113, 114; as self-reflexivity, 114; and iteration, 114, 118; vs. Kantian transcendence, 114; in figure-ground relations, 116; tied to nesting, 118; as looping in a machine, 119, 120; as always "within" the system, 121; *see also* Algorithm; Iteration

Reductionism, as limitation of causal usage, 27

Representation(s): definition of, 62, 63; various forms of, 62, 63; source of their formation, internal or external, 63, 64; AI versus Kantian formulations of, 63, 84, 85; role of context in, Dreyfus, 64; cognitive, as intervening variable, 66; as process or content?, 66-71; frame, 69; script, 69; scheme, 69, 87; as learned, but no learning theory given by AI, 86; as due to internal mechanisms, 86; Kantian versus Lockean views of, 86; internal, in animals, 131; in vision, 141; *see also* Categories; Language; Predicates; Predication

Reverse Turing test: as anthropomorphization, 60; definition of, 60; *see also* Anthropomorphization; Turing test

Rule(s): as changeable, 6, 7; predication in, 7; as formal-cause concept, 52; introspectively framed, 53; *see also* Law(s)

Science: Newtonian approach to, 24; natural, as non-telic, 27; and deity teleology, 28; modern, rise of formal causation in, 31, 35; modern scientist, as participator, 32, 39, 40; Einsteinian, as "humanized," 34; principle of complementarity in, 34; of psychology, as AI, 44

Self: -reflexivity, via Kantian transcendence, 29, 114; -reflexivity, as recursion, 114, 121, 122; as "predicator," 115; -referring, Gödel's proof as, Lucas, 120; -reflexivity, as introspective, 122; -reflexivity, and "taking a position," 122, 123; -symbol, Hofstadter, 123; -conscious mind, Eccles, 146

Semantics, in language learning, 78, 79

Sequacious, in meaning extension: immediacy of, 7, 8; as logical necessity, 8; as deduction, inference, 53; extension in word usage, 77, 78; *see also* Precedent, in meaning extension

Simulation: of oppositional reasoning, 13; definition of, 43, 44; simulator versus simulated, 45; versus duplication, 48; does not extend to the *Logos*, 48, 49; computer, limited to demonstrative reasoning, 65

Software: as quasi-opposition in reason, 13; as the programming level, 46; based on formal and final causation, 47; as rule following, 53; as "one" with the hardware, 164; *see also* Hardware

Split-Brain: corpus callosum sectioning in, 153; introspective versus extraspective view of, 154, 155; Sperry's telic views on, 155, 156; Gazzaniga's mechanistic views on, 156, 157; *see also* Brain research

Strange loop(s): definition of, 115; as tangled hierarchy, 115; as at core of intelligence, 116; as machine recursion, 119; as extraspective action, 120, 121; as jumping out of the system, 121; oppositionality and, 121; *see also* Recursion

Syllogism: steps of, 16-18; via Euler circles, 17; role of predication in, 18

Syntax: in language learning, 78, 79; *see also* Meaning, Semantics

Tabula rasa, 23

Teleology: study of ends, reasons, purposes, 20; Aristotle's two forms of, 24, 25; natural versus deity, 26; theology as deity form of, 27, 174; explained away, by behaviorism, 30; in computer science, 45; in language learning, 73; via negative feedback, 105; four aspects of, 106; as unpredictability, 111; in brain research, 146; in art, 174; in law, 174; *see also* Final cause; Intention; Purpose

Telos: Greek word for "end," purpose, reason, 20; as equated with "higher," 171; *see also* Final cause; Intention; Purpose; Teleology

Time: as required in mediation, 9; passage of, versus order, 9; as fundamental to efficient causation, 19; as formal-cause mosaic, 32; irrelevant, in steady state changes, 35; speed of, in simulations, 59; as relative in predication, 71; irrelevant, in logical progression, 78

Transcendence: via dialectical reasoning, Kant, 29; Kantian, vs. recursivity, 114, 120

Turing test: broader interpretation of, 4; extraspective in formulation, 4; as imitation game, 4; program writer's skill in, 59, 60; *see also* Reverse Turing test

Universal(s): as grand predicates, 16; deity, as one, 18; search for, in ancient Greece, 18; causal meanings as, 19; modern crisis in belief of, 171; *see also* Categories; Predicate(s)

Variable(s), intervening, as purposive, Tolman, 29, 128

Will: causality of, Kant, 103; -power, 108, 113; as personal affirmation, Polanyi, 113; *see also* Agency; Free will